NATURAL CORPORATE MANAGEMENT

FROM THE BIG BANG TO WALL STREET

William C. Frederick

Greenleaf
PUBLISHING

M6man

WISSER MEMORIAL LIBRARY

HD31

·F7515

2012

c·1

© 2012 Greenleaf Publishing Limited

Published by Greenleaf Publishing Limited
Aizlewood's Mill
Nursery Street
Sheffield S3 8GG
UK
www.greenleaf-publishing.com

Cover by LaliAbril.com

Printed in the UK on environmentally friendly, acid-free paper
from managed forests by CPI Group (UK) Ltd, Croydon

All rights reserved. No part of this publication may be reproduced,
stored in a retrieval system, or transmitted, in any form or by any
means, electronic, mechanical, photocopying, recording or otherwise,
without the prior permission in writing of the publishers.

British Library Cataloguing in Publication Data:
A catalogue record for this book is available from the British Library.

ISBN-13: 978-1-906093-80-8 [paperback]
ISBN-13: 978-1-907643-51-4 [PDF eBook]

Dedicated
to
my father
Duke Frederick
1877–1941

and
my mother
Rebecca Crittenden Frederick
1877–1983

For their parental care and my genetic heritage

and
my wife
Mildred Sochatoff Myers
For our love, always and forever

Contents

Introduction
What you will find in this book
and why you should read it

Two short sentences tell what this book is about.

- Business and nature are intertwined
- Business managers need to understand this linkage of business and nature if they are to do their job well

That's it!—the main idea of the entire book. Telling the whole story takes much more than two sentences—ten chapters in all—but keep these two openers in mind as you read along because they are a key that unlocks all the rest.

The business and nature connection runs much deeper than current concerns about global warming, climate change, and environmental disruptions, important as they are. All of nature's activities have both positive and negative impacts on the way companies do business, including life-supporting ecosystems that sustain a firm's long-term existence and the most destructive forces nature can unleash, such as flooding, tornadoes, tsunamis, earthquakes. In much the same way, all business activities—from profit seeking to technological productivity—depend on nature in the form of energy resources and an inborn natural drive in business leaders to succeed in the marketplace. Business and nature are truly locked into a lifelong partnership.

Nature also plays a central and highly influential role inside the business firm. You may be intrigued—even surprised—to discover that natural forces generate the profit motive, regulate market exchanges, create a firm's capital investments, set the organizational command-and-control shape of the corporation, spawn technological innovations (think iPhone, BlackBerry, YouTube, Facebook, GPS), and devise the brainy strategies that drive business corporations forward. Learning how to make practical use of these natural forces is the purpose of **Natural Corporate Management**.

To guide your reading, two key analytic concepts appear over and over again in all chapters: **Natural Corporate Management** and an **Evolutionary Cascade**. The core meaning of each idea is introduced next, followed by a brief summary of the book's chapters.

Natural Corporate Management is an expression, a manifestation, a consequence of a long—very long and ancient—evolutionary process. What managers do—their behavior, the goals they pursue for their firms, their competitive strategies, the ways they organize people and resources for production—all of these are natural phenomena in the most literal sense. Nature here means the basic, organic, bodily, physical, chemical, biological makeup of people and the natural environments they live in—a vast and highly variable, diverse, and constantly changing pageantry of natural forces. It also is literally true that managerial decisions made today reflect not just current natural forces but traces of the most primordial, time-distant aspects of the natural universe. It is a bit like astrophysicists observing the phantom-like background radiation left over from the universe's Big Bang origins. Business practices today are bathed in a similar cosmic glow stemming from the moment of our own human beginnings. As odd as it may seem, the Big Bang continues to light up actions and decisions taken in today's corporate boardrooms and executive suites.

But none of this happened overnight. Humans (and business firms) are where we are now after eons of prior development. To grasp the central message here, pretend you have accidentally hit the Delete button on all you ever knew about business. Better still, assume your computer has had a total crash, wiping out all of your files, back-ups, and memory about how and why business is done. Then you curb your momentary panic and frustration by installing a new version of what you had before, this time with a much improved and expanded perspective that, rather magically, can actually restore your old files while updating them. This new program is called an **Evolutionary Cascade** which is explained next. Once you get the hang of it, you will begin to see business in a new light—a light powered, believe it or not, by that primordial flame called the Big Bang. Here is the story in brief.

An **Evolutionary Cascade** begins with energy, its evolution, and the way energy has shaped business from the beginning of time. Think of the cascade as a waterfall of tumbling, flowing stages of energy's evolution, each successive plume partially formed by the preceding flows. The flows are cumulative, building on one another, each sending a part of itself along to join and reinforce all the others that appear later. This **Evolutionary Cascade** constitutes a thunderous, magnificently impressive, even fearfully tumultuous and powerful display of nature's (and energy's) ability to shape anything in its path, including the practice and management of business. The key here is to grasp the cumulative continuity and functional interdependence of all parts of the cascade—an entire, holistic, nested linkage of overlapping phases, leading eventually and opportunistically to nothing less than the center of corporate decision-making, labeled **Natural Corporate Management**.

The **Evolutionary Cascade** begins at the beginning of the Universe—the Big Bang that ushered in what was to become the entire panoply of existence, life, time, and whatever meanings were to be associated with this primal event. The Big Bang was *nothing but energy*, by definition of course—after all, it was an explosive outburst of immense force. This primordial blow-out and subsequent rapid expansion were to lead toward all presently known meanings and forms of energy, including those used in business. Its primal energy driving force shaped all that was to follow the initial outburst. The Big Bang created not just a universe but, equally important, set in motion a process of change and evolution that has never stopped. As someone once humorously said of oxtail soup, "That seems like going pretty far back for soup." The same might be said of the Big Bang and modern business. But the primal past is not as "far back" as you might imagine. It is right here in our midst. It's called the modern business corporation.

An accompanying illustration depicts the cascade's phases.

AN EVOLUTIONARY CASCADE

Once **Energy** evolution began, it took various forms that emerged ever so slowly. We'll skip over the earlier ones about elementary particles, the emergence of light, the formation of stars and galaxies, and other astrophysical exotica, and go directly to the emergence on Earth of **Life** itself along with the biospheres and ecosystems that sustain it. Then in successive steps on to a **Darwin** portrait of life's evolution, to the **Gene** as evolution's steering mechanism, to the appearance of **Homo** and that fertile bundle of neurons we call a **Brain** which spawned **Symbol** behavior, continuing on to **Organization** as a mode of work, to economic exchange in the **Market**, and finally arriving at the **Corporation's** doorstep. The stepped-down descriptor for each cascade phase is a signal of its proportional reach and influence—basically, the footprints of varying depth left in the sands of time by these natural forces. Keep in mind this critically important principle: *the mark of each preceding phase is present in each and all of the following phases.* An evolutionary thread—a cumulative penetration, a continuity of function, a saturation of prior effects—runs through the entire cascade.

Standing at the end of this cascade of evolutionary phenomena, the **Corporation** might be expected to become the inheritor and carrier of each of the cascading phases. Indeed it is, and that is why managers need to grasp the meaning of **Natural Corporate Management**. They are literally the "managers" of a system embedded deeply in, and evolved from, the natural world.

So, why should you read this book?

- **Managers.** Because you need to learn what these natural forces are, how they influence your decisions at work, and what you might do about it

- **Investors, creditors.** Because you provide important forms of natural capital that make possible, or can limit, the continued existence of business firms

- **Supply chain entities.** Because the production-to-consumer functions you perform are negotiated forms of natural social contracts

- **Government officials.** Because the laws you make, the regulations you apply, and the public policies you adopt toward business have the potential of promoting or negating the natural environment in which business operates

- **Business school deans and faculty scholars.** Because a torrent of new research in the natural sciences sheds new light on old questions about the business firm, its motives, its organization, its functions, its managerial cadre, and its social and environmental impacts

- **Students.** Because you need to understand the natural forces that will shape your career choices in business and other professions

- **Public citizens.** Because your material well-being and the quality of your life depend largely on the ability and willingness of business firms to heed the role of nature in societies everywhere

A brief guide for student readers

Learning about business is the way to discover new ideas that will help you build a professional career. You will find such perspectives in this book. But, at times, you may find it a tough read, and I want you to know that I realize that and—believe it or not—I sympathize with you. To lighten your load, I have used a few examples of actual companies that illustrate a complicated concept or theory. Other times, I'll try for a puny pun or lighter moment (lol) to brighten your day and relieve the boredom—but you don't have to laugh. Best of all, the end of each chapter has a bullet-point list of key ideas found in that chapter, so if you were up late the night before class, give these pivotal points a quick look, which might fool your instructor into believing you have read the whole chapter. More help is on the way in the chapter summaries below. Most of all, keep on chugging through the assigned chapters to the end because later on you will discover these ideas to be of practical use on the job and as you develop your professional career. You have my good wishes as you travel that path to success.

Chapter summaries

Chapter 1   The Big E ≈ ENERGY

The Big Bang initiated a process of energy evolution that influences and shapes Earthly life, ecosystems, economies, and business firms.

Chapter 2   The Big L ≈ LIFE

The cell is the basic unit of all organic life. All life forms exist only within ecosystems, which are networks of interconnected, interdependent organisms. Business corporations operate within ecosystems, exerting significant influence both positive and negative on the diverse life forms there.

Chapter 3   The Big D ≈ DARWIN

Darwin's theory of evolution by natural selection says that all forms of organic life, including humans, evolve from earlier ancestors. Business behavior is a blend of natural selection's influence on the behavior of individuals and groups.

Chapter 4   The Big G ≈ GENE

Genes are the cellular components that create, activate, and direct the form and life functions of all organisms, including humans. Business behavior is shaped by genetic influences.

Chapter 5   The Big H ≈ HOMO

The *Homo* genus—human beings—first appeared on Earth around 2.5 million years ago. The decisions of today's business managers are influenced by *Homo* evolution.

Chapter 6   The Big B ≈ BRAIN

The human brain regulates neural signals as humans interact with ecosystem environments. The actions and decisions of business managers are shaped by brain-centered impulses and motivations.

Chapter 7   The Big S ≈ SYMBOL

Symbolic human culture is a blend of tools, symbols, and group-living patterns. A business firm's culture helps the firm adapt to the social and ecosystem environment.

Chapter 8   The Big O ≈ ORGANIZATION

A business firm is organized in three ways—as a hierarchy, by technological teamwork, and as a nonlinear, complex system. Each organizational design supports the firm's profit-making operations.

Chapter 9   The Big M ≈ MARKET

Markets perform two functions: reciprocal balanced exchange without gain (social reciprocity) and economic exchange for gain. Through market transactions, business firms adapt to their environments by economizing and ecologizing strategies.

Chapter 10   The Big C ≈ CORPORATION

An analysis of how each cascade phase affects managerial behavior and the shaping of corporate policy and strategy. A natural theory of the firm then summarizes the book's major themes.

That's the book's introduction. Getting the rest of the story is up to you, the reader—a journey I hope you will find informative and professionally valuable.

As the evolutionary story unfolds, I wish to pose a question of special importance for one group of readers: 'Wall Street—and corporate managers everywhere—are you listening?' I hope your answer will be, "Yes."

1

The **Big E ≈ Energy**

Everything in the observable universe can be seen, analyzed, and
explained in energy terms.
Vaclav Smil

Energy is the ultimate agent of causation in the universe.
Alexis Mari Pietak

Energy is where it all began—at the Big Bang beginning of our Universe
13.75 billion years ago. Today's energy is a remnant of that initial, primordial explosive outburst—an energy constant that pervades everything that
presently exists. Energy is literally the *original* substance or essence of the
world we know. Energy generates, even creates, the biosphere and ecosystems that shelter and sustain organic life, including our own human lives.
Energy takes myriad forms, both living and non-living: menacing destructive storms; earthquakes; volcanic eruptions; subtle genetic organic drivers; neural modules of stunning complexity; unique symbolic patterns;
behavioral networks; life-sustaining economic systems; and the diverse
ways the organic world copes with the Big Bang's energy legacy.

One of the most important forms that energy takes in today's world is the modern business corporation. In all corporations, from top-level corporate executive suites to cramped computer cubicles, energy is the major player, the ultimate driver, the motivator, the organizer, the evaluator, the strategizer, the policy maker, the decision-maker, the goal-setter, the profit-and-loss calculator, the competitive network, the capital sources, the productive output, the polluting wastes, the technological dynamic, the longevity determinant, the workforce driver, the consumer choice, the supply-chain diversity, the regulatory controls, the global expansion of trade, and the current energy crisis and questions of sustainability. All of these aspects of corporate life reflect—literally—the leftover glow of nature's Big Bang. Business is all about energy and how and what to do with it.

Just how energy became so central to the business corporation is best understood by starting at the Big Bang's initial moments and tracking its pathway through the ages to the present. In doing so, we draw on a dramatically unique, new concept of evolution developed by physicists—not the more familiar evolution advocated by biologists and fathered by Charles Darwin. Darwin will get his moment later in the story but not yet. For now, a physics perspective on evolution adds a new dimension that tells about the forceful drive to change that is built into nature. In fact, as we shall see, energy evolution is all-encompassing and provides a broad platform from which to understand not only business but many other life features that we take for granted. You will be amazed by what it reveals.

The Big Bang

"Somewhere between 10 and 15 billion years ago, a flash of radiation marked the beginning of the Universe. This radiation filled the cosmos with energy, part of which soon transformed itself into the matter we see today ... The cosmic radiation ... grew ever weaker but continued to permeate all of space, a relic of the fierce brilliance of the big bang" (Goldsmith 1997: 126-27).[1]

---

1 In "Who Saw the Face of God?", Goldsmith reviews *The Very First Light: The True Inside Story of the Scientific Journey Back to the Dawn of the Universe* by John C. Mather and John Boslough (New York: Basic Books, 1996).

Energy is the most basal, primal component of the Universe. *There was nothing but energy in the form of radiation as everything began.* The Big Bang concept (widely accepted by scientific experts) captures that central idea—an explosive force of truly unimaginable size and proportions. More remarkably—but not always grasped by most of us—is that the initial energy outburst almost immediately began to assume various forms and shapes—which kick-started *an evolutionary process that has never ceased.* The most basic ingredients—space itself, matter, time—had their beginning here at this moment. "Initially, it was pure radiant energy, but as it expanded it congealed into a gas cloud of particles [the basic atomic constituents, protons, neutrons, electrons]. And as it continued to expand, tiny ripples developed, which over billions of years condensed into galaxies, stars, and planets" (Parker 1993: 1; Greene 2005: 285).

Take note of that last sentence, and remember that Earth is one of those planets revolving around one of those stars, our Sun, located in one of those galaxies, our Milky Way. This says it as clearly as anything can: *Earth is a direct descendent of the initial Big Bang.* It is literally one of the many forms taken by the energy radiation flowing out from the Big Bang. Matter, space, time—in all of their varied forms—are a potent energy cocktail spewed out to become in time our familiar Earthly world. We experience a continuity of time, a thread of matter, a spatial link, and a chain of energy stretching, as one author has said, "from eternity to here" (Carroll 2010).

Thermodynamic (energy) evolution

Thermodynamics is the physicist's way of talking about energy and its movement.[2] Literally, "thermo" means "heat" which is a form of energy, while "dynamics" simply means the "movement" or "flow" of energy. The thermodynamics (the heat flow) of a cup of Starbucks cappuccino

---

2 Energy evolution here will take the meaning given to it by a remarkably creative thinker: Arto J. Annila, a physicist, biotechnologist, and bioscientist at the University of Helsinki, Finland. Because the language and mathematical formalism of physics are sometimes intimidating, I shall be finding easier, though still correct, ways of explaining his ideas. A list of Annila's articles is included in the Bibliography.

occurs when it begins to cool off. As you sip it and talk to a companion, the hot coffee and its toppings lose heat to the coffee house and warm your mouth and throat as you swallow it. The coffee's heat moves, is "dynamic." That's the basic idea of thermodynamics: heat (as a form of energy) flowing and cooling off as it goes somewhere else. Physicists have a formal name for this kind of energy movement: the Second Law of Thermodynamics, which says that energy (in all forms) has a tendency to do just what your Starbucks cappuccino does—cool off. In this book, the more user-friendly "heat flow" will substitute for the physicists' technical term "thermodynamics," and "energy evolution" will replace the more cumbersome-sounding "thermodynamic evolution." So, how can so simple an idea explain much of anything? Here's how.

Energy from its very first moments of existence in the Big Bang was unevenly distributed in the emerging Universe, thus causing energy to expand, move, flow, and to evolve ever since. The Big Bang's initial burst of energy encountered no resistance because there was nothing there to push back against it, so it moved outward. From that moment onward, all subsequent forms of radiation and matter emerging from the Big Bang became different forms of energy. In interacting with one another, these energy components did not possess energy in equal amounts or of equivalent content. Those energy differences—called energy gradients—set up the essential conditions for the subsequent flow or movement of energy from one point to another: *the flow was then, and is now, always from higher-energy levels to lower-energy levels.* That is the essential meaning of what physicists call the Second Law of Thermodynamics.

Physicists speak of this high-to-low flow as a difference of energy "gradients," which means simply that some forms and types of energy represent or contain a higher grade or amount of energy than others. So when energy flows from one place to another, the energy gradients that initially separated them are reduced or lessened, moving toward an equal balance. *This is the core meaning of energy evolution: the reduction of energy gradients through flows from one place, or in one direction, to another, and from higher-energy levels/amounts toward lower-energy conditions.* If in your coffee house conversation, you talked too much and forgot to sip your cappuccino, you would find it had evolved while you weren't looking or listening—from warm and tasty to cold and unpleasant. Its higher energy flowed out of the (hot) cup into the lower-energy (cooler) coffee house atmosphere. The lesson: Heat flow = energy evolution.

This book will try to convince you that energy evolution *is the focal, core, master concept underlying and driving all phases of the **Evolutionary Cascade** leading to **Natural Corporate Management***. Energy evolution is an active force appearing over and over again that shapes and molds ecosystems, the appearance and evolution of organic life, genes, *Homo sapiens*, neural modules, symbolic/cultural systems, organized networks, economies, and business firms. Energy evolution should be understood as a basal natural force that generates, accumulates, multiplies, aggregates, replicates, and maximizes—but also degrades, reorganizes, and drives—all aspects of the natural world, including business.[3]

How energy evolves

Knowing how—as well as why—energy evolves is the key that unlocks many doors in the modern corporation, revealing the firm's basic functions, goals, strategies, and decision-making apparatus—and even telling a bit about a company's chances of having a long (or short) life. The reason is straightforward: the modern corporation is one of nature's principal promoters, carriers, and facilitators of energy evolution. In carrying out this natural function, the firm has lots of company and help from other parts of the natural world: ecosystems, organic life, the Sun, even volcanoes, earthquakes, floods, hurricanes, and monsoons. All such natural systems, including business firms, help move energy from one place to another, sometimes supporting life in its many forms, other times diminishing its quality and longevity.

These energy-flow facilitators are called "energy transduction mechanisms" in the technical language of physics. Fortunately, their activity is much simpler than the arcane-sounding term itself. They make possible, promote, and speed up energy flows from the Sun to Earth, from the top

---

3 The concept of an evolutionary process coexistent with the early Universe was also proposed by the Lund University molecular cytologist, Antonio Lima-de-Faria, in *Evolution without Selection: Form and Function by Autoevolution* (Amsterdam: Elsevier, 1988). His work was a pioneering forerunner of subsequent research by scholars in other fields, such as physics and molecular phylogenetics.

of an ecosystem's food chain to the bottom (and vice versa), from coal, oil, and gas to factory-produced goods, from store shelves to consumer purchases, from spring-time green leaves to autumn's riot of colors, from El Niño's fluctuations to tropical storms. Wherever nature displays energy gradients, those differing stores of restless and unstoppable energy move toward a lower level or a less energy-dense gradient.

Listen to a principal author of these ideas, Arto Annila, and one of his colleagues, who point out how this process works. "Evolution as an energy transfer process aims at an equilibrium where gradients and differences have vanished. Energy does flow from higher to lower potentials within the system in the quest for a stationary state with its surroundings. In general, all paths are explored to distribute energy flows through them [and these] excursions will sooner or later naturally converge on the most probable, the shortest paths that follow the steepest gradients in energy" (Kaila and Annila 2008: 3,058-67).

All parts of the natural world are potential candidates for carrying out this energy transfer activity. Consider the energy differences between Sun and Earth: solar energy radiates constantly toward Earth, with some of it absorbed and other amounts reflected back into space. Ask yourself, how does Earth capture the Sun's radiant light? Some sinks into the oceans, some heats the landmass, some of that solar energy interacts with inert chemical compounds thus creating new combinations of basic elements. Tropical rainforests absorb immense amounts of solar radiation. A small portion is captured by manufactured solar energy panels. All such actions convert the Sun's powerful radiant energy to new Earthly forms that absorb only a tiny fraction of that solar influx. In other words, the disparate gradients are lessened and reduced, moving toward (but not actually achieving) an equal energy balance of Sun and Earth. Energy constantly seeks such an equilibrium. The general rule is this: Energy moves to eliminate all higher-to-lower energy gradients, regardless of where they are, what form they assume, or how long it may take. As Annila says, all such energy-flow "excursions" will "converge on the most probable, the shortest paths that follow the steepest gradients in energy." In doing so, the energy is indifferent to what or how long it takes to carry out this activity. All systems—inanimate (nonliving) and animate (living)—couple external (solar) energy sources to internal (Earthly) receptors capable of becoming energy-transfer mechanisms.

Energy fitness

Some of those energy packets that speed the flow of energy from higher to lower levels are better at it than others. We'll see many examples in the following chapters because these superior energy transfer agents appear in all guises and take highly diverse shapes. As the Gulf Stream's warmer waters flow toward Europe, it is transferring its built-up southern heat to the cooler northern waters (and keeping Europe warmer in the process), but it eventually cools off entirely (like your cup of cappuccino). A fierce tornado organizes atmospheric heat and spins it out destructively by reducing the different heat gradients found between the atmosphere and the Earth's surface. A tropical rainforest is an extremely efficient system for taking in the Sun's plentiful energy, converting it into multi-form plants while sheltering a diversity of animal life—in contrast to the relative barrenness of a desert's climate where much of the Sun's energy influx is bounced back into space.

The same principle—superior efficiency in promoting energy flows—applies to many human activities. Modern technology-driven economies gather, organize, and use energy in larger amounts and in more diverse ways than was true of earlier farm-based economies or even more ancient hunter-gatherer modes of economic life. Some organic species are obviously more successful than others at energy intake and its use, especially when one recalls that over 99 per cent of all Earthly species have disappeared—with many others facing extinction. Human and animal muscle power are no match for water- and wind-driven mills, gasoline-powered plows and reapers, productive machinery, electric grids, and the stupendous reach and power of modern electronic technology.

In other words, energy evolution comes with a built-in fitness criterion—a standard of survival and continuity. It's not quite like the one Darwin promoted but tends to work toward a similar result. Any device, mechanism, or entity found in nature that can support, push forward, and maximize the flow of energy is more "fit" to survive than others less efficient in doing so. Nature displays a plethora of such devices. There can even be, and often is, a competition between these energy transductors. Stronger, bigger, more powerful animals (of any species) oftentimes can and do dominate weaker, smaller, less aggressive members of the group. And as we shall see in a later chapter, it's not just physical strength that promotes fitness. Brain power (another form of energy) can outwit a competitor. In all cases, though, "The driving force [of energy evolution] favours all those that are dispersing energy more and more effectively" (Kaila and Annila 2008: 3,067-68). In short, that's the ultimate fitness (survival) test.

So, "survival of the fittest" acquires a new and much broader meaning: survival depends on an ability to quicken the flow of incoming energy; to move it from high levels to lower grades; to disperse energy outward into the surroundings; to push heat "into the cool" (Schneider and Sagan 2005). And it matters not one bit whether the entity doing the dispersing is a living organism or a bunch of inert chemicals in a pond or even a business corporation—survival fitness depends on energy push and flow. In this curious way, energy depends on energy for its existence and continuity.

The entropy puzzle

Energy evolution poses a profound dilemma for the modern business corporation. The problem is so challenging, so fundamental, that one finds no easy or quick answers. In fact, there may be no answers at all, or no acceptable ones, either for the business firm or its host communities. Just why this should be so depends, in another odd way, on the basic function of energy and particularly on its relentless, unstoppable, cascading flow.

The dilemma is this: Where are all of those energy flows going? And with what effects, both negative and positive? And how is business affected?

We know that energy flows are helped along by energy-transfer mechanisms. We also know that some of those energy pushers are more effective than others and more likely to survive. What we haven't explored yet, though, is the *destination* of all that energy. We know where most of it comes from: we bask constantly in today's radiant glow of our Sun and draw on ancient buried remnants (coal, gas, oil) of yesterday's solar energy influx. Is there any way to know, to find out, what happens to energy as it travels toward and then reaches its destination? Or is it possible there is no final station where all energy passengers disembark? As Marshall McLuhan once asked about television's social impact, "Is the medium the message?"[4] So, is energy itself the message, the destination? If so, does that hint at a possible downside to energy evolution? That is what "the entropy puzzle" is all about.

The modern business corporation is unavoidably, perhaps even tragically, caught up in this massive dilemma, as we shall see. By taking in and organizing energy (capital, technology, employees, resources), the business firm becomes an active participant in a society's energy-flow systems. It seems to play a key role in promoting and channeling energy flows. Does it help or hinder? Does it channel energy in ways helpful to itself or to others? Or to both? What is corporate energy's destination, its goal, its purpose, its mission? That depends on what one means by the idea of entropy.

The dual meanings of entropy

"Entropy" is a conceptual invention of physicists to help explain how, where, and why energy moves as it does. Adopted from an ancient Greek word meaning "transformation," entropy is what happens when energy is transformed or changed as it flows from one place to another. So entropy may just be the key that unlocks the mystery of energy-flow's destination—if there really is an end point—and what happens along the way.

The problem is that entropy has been given two contrasting—perhaps even contradictory or inconsistent—meanings by physicists.

Entropy as destination

Entropy in an older, classical sense refers to energy's destination or end state where all energy movement ceases; an equilibrium or balance is reached with all energy components scattered and spread out; the inert energy has lost its power to move, to accomplish work, or to remain warm.

---

4 Marshall McLuhan, professor at the University of Toronto, was recognized as "one of the major intellectual influences of our time" and "one of the most brilliant socio-cultural theorists writing today". His 1967 book, co-authored with Quentin Fiore with the ironic title *The Medium is the Message*, revealed television's impact on people, families, neighborhoods, jobs, government, and business.

(Your cappuccino is now stone cold.) What was once an orderly, active arrangement of energy has now become an entirely passive and disorderly scattering of energy; all form has disappeared; no further activity occurs. If that strikes you as a bit ominous, you are on to something important. This kind of entropic equilibrium is equivalent to the demise of any organism that relies on energy to support its life. "Entropy can no more be avoided than death, which is what happens when a nonlinear, nonequilibrium thermodynamic system loses the ability to direct energy from the environment, and instead comes into equilibrium with it" (Schneider and Sagan 2005: 85). That is equivalent to saying that energy does indeed have a destination, a stopping point, an end state where not much happens or can happen, a kind of disorder or lack of organization. In other words, avoiding entropy—staying as far away as possible from that fatal (and final) energy equilibrium destination—is, shall we say, highly desirable. The basic formula is: High entropy is bad; low entropy is good. Whether that is also true of business corporations is something yet to be explored.[5]

Entropy as process

But what if entropy is thought of as a *process* instead of a *condition*? Suppose entropy turned out to be not a negative stable state or a final condition, but instead a dynamic, changing, moving flow of energy that produces positive results for its users. Suppose further that the higher the flow rate, the greater the chance of an organism's (or possibly a corporation's) survival. In that case, *high entropy*—the faster flow rate—maximizes a system's (or a business firm's) life instead of threatening it, whereas *low entropy*—a slower flow rate—is to be avoided if at all possible. So the entropy formula is reversed: High entropy is good; low entropy is bad.

This seemingly contradictory conclusion emerges from the work of Finnish physicist Arto Annila. The key to the puzzle is this: there is an

---

5 Eric D. Schneider and Dorion Sagan offer another set of remarkable insights into energy evolution in *Into the Cool: Energy Flow, Thermodynamics, and Life*. The interplay of their views with those of Arto Annila constitutes much of the plot line of this and other chapters to follow. In general, Schneider and Sagan favor entropy as destination while Annila advocates entropy as process.

inherent evolutionary tendency built into the Universe for energy differences to be reduced from higher gradients to lower ones: ". . . evolution [is] a series of steps from one state to another to lower potential energy differences" (Annila and Annila 2008: 299). Evolution is entirely dependent on the availability of an in-flowing supply of external free energy plus effective transduction mechanisms to lower the energy's potential. The faster and more efficiently energy gradients can be reduced, the greater the subsequent energy flows and the likelihood that any such energy-transfer mechanism will survive.

Entropy is thus a dynamic *process*—an enhanced maximized flow of energy—*toward* but not necessarily *reaching* a stable, negative destination. ". . . the flow of external energy to the open system [e.g., to an organism] will *increase* entropy" (Sharma and Annila 2007: 126). "Increase in entropy means dispersal of energy [and] when all potential energy gradients were exhausted, the maximum entropy state . . . was reached" (Jaak-kola *et al.* 2008: 232, 235). Energy evolution favors "[a] flow of energy . . . that selects the fastest ways, i.e., the most voluminous steepest descents to level the free energy landscape . . . [E]ntropy [in this case] will not only be increasing but it will be increasing in least time" (Annila 2009: 1).

What is involved here is an exchange of energy between a system, for example, a tropical rainforest, and its environment. "A system [the rainforest] that is higher in energy density than its [environment] . . . will evolve from its current state to another more probable one by displacing [energy] quanta to its surroundings [i.e., to the plants and animals living there]. Likewise, a system [the rainforest's plants and animals] that is lower in energy density than its respective surroundings will evolve by acquiring [energy] quanta from the surroundings [i.e., from the rainforest ecosystem] . . . Systems evolve toward stationary states where their energy densities equal that of their surroundings. A system [a rainforest or its inhabitants] without net fluxes to or from its surroundings is in its entirety a stationary state" (Annila 2009: 2).

In other words, any system that can maximize these energy exchanges is highly entropic because the energy flows (a *process*) drive the energy toward a stationary state (a *condition* or *destination*). A high-energy environment *promotes and encourages entropy* in order to equal the balance between the entity and its environment. But the entropy is in the *process*, not the final destination. Another way of saying the same thing is that *going* there is more important than *getting* there. The higher the entropy flow rate, the better it is for the system that is driving the energy flows because it thereby keeps itself far away from a lifeless entropic condition.

Well . . . that puts an entirely different slant on things and systems generally, especially their function and future. Any high-rate entropy system—let's say a business firm that is good at efficiently organizing and using energy—thereby drives energy from higher to lower levels, and in doing so it maximizes its chances of survival. And this would be true even though its high-entropy actions might reduce the survival prospects of other organisms or systems with lower entropic capabilities. Seeing entropy as an energy *process* rather than as a final destination yields a more fluid, indeterminate situation for "all creatures (and business firms), large and small." Are they, then, driven by an overarching emergent evolution toward indeterminate, even intractable functions, goals, purposes, and strategies? Is corporate purpose thus beholden to nature's dominant forces and proclivities? Are such natural forces manageable—can they be intentionally directed—to achieve a business firm's goals? Or are those corporate goals and purposes already chosen, shaped, and channeled by nature itself—by an energy evolution that traces its origin to the Big Bang? These are the questions that are at the center of this book's search for the meaning of **Natural Corporate Management**.

The Big E's impact on the corporation

Even a casual observer of today's world events cannot fail to see that energy issues loom large in everyday affairs, sometimes positively, other times tragically. A fiercely powerful earthquake-generated tsunami wipes out tens of thousands of lives in and around Indonesia. Rising oceanic waters caused by climate warming pose present and long-term threats to island nations and to coastal regions. An Icelandic volcano spews out ash clouds that disrupt air travel and threaten airline safety across large regions of Europe. A catastrophic oil leak in the Gulf of Mexico wastes incredible amounts of needed energy while despoiling and destroying marine life and coastal fisheries. Methane gas explosions deep within coal mines erupt, taking the lives of miners in China, Russia, Chile, and the United States.

Beyond these spectacular episodes are other kinds of energy-generated problems that plague people in all parts of the world. Auto drivers in industrial nations fret over high and rising gasoline prices. Environmental authorities worry that those gasoline-generated pollutants pose threats to public health, along with alarming amounts of climate-warming pollutants coming from coal-burning factories in the United States and China.[6] And in areas where poverty is widespread, population increases outrun an ability to provide the basic energy sources of food and materials to support viable standards of living. Clearing of rainforest areas of Brazil to make room for farming raises alarms that irreplaceable energy-efficient forest ecosystems are being destroyed. In these many ways, nature's energy has indeed made its presence known by affecting countless human lives around the globe.

But the energy story is not entirely negative, either for humanity at large or business in particular. Enormously productive economic systems find, organize, process, and distribute energy in useful forms across the globe. Goods and services in astonishing amounts and qualities are themselves types of embodied energy derived from the production process. The raw materials, minerals, petroleum, natural gas, and chemical compounds that make production possible are direct forms of energy. All forms of capital—financial, human, social, organizational, technological, even information—that drive economies everywhere are a kind of human-invented energy capable of moving economic production, marketing, and distribution along channels devised and designed to enhance human welfare. Market-price systems—another energy device—link traders and consumers into networks that speed up the movement of goods and services through global markets. These economic and related political/governmental practices that vary from nation to nation and from one era to another have indeed made possible higher and increasing standards of living, thus supporting a constantly growing global population.

The central question to be explored in the following chapters is: What is the role of the contemporary business corporation as a direct and contributing participant in the movement/flow/evolution of energy through human economies and global ecosystems? The business firm is indeed

---

6 To improve its national energy efficiency, Chinese authorities in 2010 closed over 2,000 energy-guzzling steel mills, cement works, and other factories (Bradsher 2010: A-4).

a major player in finding, using, processing, transforming, and channeling energy in its many forms. The firm's owners, directors, managers, suppliers, employees, customers, and host communities are necessarily deeply and centrally involved as direct participants in a universal energy evolution.

So, **Big E** ≈ **Energy** obviously presents a fundamental challenge to today's corporate managers. To reorient managers' thinking and to assist them in meeting the energy challenge, this book proposes a new concept or model of management called **Natural Corporate Management (NCM)**. NCM is a way of taking into account the many natural forces, including energy, that influence the business firm's operations both internally and externally. The most obvious external concern for managers is a company's success in achieving its own long-term sustainability while reducing its negative impact on people and the natural environment. But as the following chapters show, nature also works inside the corporation, affecting goal-seeking, motives, work attitudes, organization design, decision-making, strategy, and corporate policy. **NCM** is a management approach based on knowing how these natural forces affect business and how business decisions might achieve long-term sustainability for business, society, and the Earth's ecosystems. Put another way, **Natural Corporate Management** involves learning enough about nature to improve the ways business managers do their work. Nature is thus in many fruitful and productive ways incorporated into the daily work of managers and their companies.

The Big E's pivotal points

It's time now for a summing up of this chapter's central message.

- Energy stemming from the Big Bang permeates and generates the shape, size, content, and dynamics of the Universe

- The Big Bang initiated a process of thermodynamic (energy) evolution that continues to the present day, influencing and shaping Earthly life, ecosystems, economies, and business firms

- The essential action of energy evolution is to drive all forms of energy from higher levels to lower levels

- The mechanisms for reducing energy levels are energy-transduction (transfer) systems that transform high-density energy into low-density energy. Both organic and non-organic entities perform these energy-transformation activities

- The energy-transfer systems that acquire and consume energy at high maximum rates are more fit (more likely) to survive than those less efficient in promoting energy flows

- Entropy has two contrasting meanings: one positive, a *process* that efficiently transforms energy in the shortest possible time; and one negative, a *condition* of minimum energy attained when a system's energy is changed into inactive forms. Contradictorily, the positive *process* produces the negative *condition*, thereby threatening the existence of an active or living system; hence, the entropy puzzle

- The business firm is an energy entity. It contains, carries, uses, and generates energy and is a major player in finding, using, processing, transforming, and channeling energy in its many forms. As such, the firm is an energy-transductor, with its actions influenced, shaped, and channeled by energy evolution

- **Natural Corporate Management** represents a new way of thinking about, understanding, and using the natural forces that influence a business firm's operations both internally and externally

- Because energy is an original, primordial, basal, dynamic force stemming from the Big Bang, energy evolution is the predominant change-making force in the Universe and in Earthly human affairs. For that reason, energy appears as an active agent in all phases of the **Evolutionary Cascade** as described in the following chapters.

The Big E's research base

Astrophysics

Carroll, S.M. (2010) *From Eternity to Here: The Quest for the Ultimate Theory of Time* (New York: Dutton).

Goldsmith, D. (1997) "Who Saw the Face of God?" *Scientific American*, March 1997: 126-27.

Greene, B. (2005) *The Fabric of the Cosmos: Space, Time, and the Texture of Reality* (New York: Vintage Books).

Hogan, C.J. (2002) "Observing the Beginning of Time," *American Scientist* 90 (September–October 2002): 420-427.

Parker, B. (1993) *The Vindication of the Big Bang* (New York: Plenum Press).

Thermodynamic evolution

Annila, A. (2009) "Space, Time, and Machines," *International Journal of Theoretical and Mathematical Physics* 2.3: 16-32 (arxiv.org/abs/0910.2629 arXiv:0910.2629v1).

Annila, A., and E. Annila (2008) "Why Did Life Emerge?" *International Journal of Astrobiology* 7: 293-300.

Jaakkola, S., S. El-Showk and A. Annila (2008) "The Driving Force behind Genomic Diversity," *Biophysical Chemistry* 134: 232-38.

Kaila, V.R.I., and A. Annila (2008) "Natural Selection for Least Action," *Proceedings of the Royal Society A* 464: 3,005-70.

Lima-de-Faria, A. (1988) *Evolution without Selection: Form and Function by Autoevolution* (Amsterdam: Elsevier).

Schneider, E.D., and D. Sagan (2005) *Into the Cool: Energy Flows, Thermodynamics, and Life* (Chicago: University of Chicago Press).

Sharma, V., and A. Annila (2007) "Natural Process—Natural Selection," *Biophysical Chemistry* 127: 123-28.

Energetics

Bradsher, K. (2010) "China to Close 2,000 Factories," *New York Times*, reprinted in *Pittsburgh Post-Gazette*, August 10, 2010: A-4.

Cheetham, N.W.H. (2011) *Introducing Biological Energetics: How Energy and Information Control the Living World* (Oxford, UK: Oxford University Press).

Pietak, A.M. (2011) *Life as Energy: Opening the Mind to a New Science of Life* (Edinburgh: Floris Books).

Smil, V. (2008) *Energy in Nature and Society: General Energetics of Complex Systems* (Cambridge, MA: MIT Press).

2

The **Big L ≈ Life**

The character and possibilities of life cannot be properly
appreciated without a working knowledge of the ways of energy.
Eric D. Schneider and Dorion Sagan

Omitting the concept of life-as-energy from our rational
reasoning limits our capacity to understand natural systems.
Alexis Mari Pietak

Life is one outcome of the energy evolution that followed the Big Bang.
Life was a latecomer, appearing on Earth around 3.75 billion years ago.
That's pretty young in the Universe's time span of 14 billion years. Earth
itself didn't take shape until about 4.5 billion years ago and then took a
billion more years to cool off enough for the earliest primitive forms of
life to emerge. Logically speaking, it could, and may, have happened in
other parts of the Universe as well. Even more mind-boggling is the possibility that non-Earthly life, whatever forms and functions it might take,
would be unrecognizable as life to Earthlings—and vice versa. Putting
aside the science-fiction imagination, it is true that Earthly life is complicated enough, not to say fascinating in its own right, to occupy the best of
scientific minds.

More to the point, life is one of the major components of **Natural Corporate Management**. Nothing business does is more important, more central, more fundamental than to serve and nurture life. The **Big L** ≈ **Life** looms as large in corporate operations as does the **Big E** ≈ **Energy**. Showing how that is so is the goal of this chapter.

Life as evolving energy

As sentient, consciously aware, self-centered, brainy creatures, we humans are inclined to assign prime importance to life's emergence on Earth. After all, it eventually led to us, so it is seen as a momentous event, a beginning that had a significance reaching beyond even the remarkable chain of other events emerging from the Big Bang: radiation, elementary particles, gravity, time itself, galaxies, stars, planets. In fact, many of the world's religions are based on just such a privileged human point of view. But in a larger, non-anthropocentric perspective, life's emergence may not have been so unusual an event after all. Before explaining why, let's review some basic facts about the phenomenon we call life.

- The best scientific estimate is that Earthly life first appeared 3.75 billion years ago, after the Earth had cooled enough to enable the required physical and chemical transitions to occur

- The physical-chemical constituents of both living and non-living matter are essentially the same, having been dispersed widely throughout the Universe by the explosive supernova collapse of stars. This stardust then becomes the basic ingredient or raw material of which life is composed. So the emergence of life required a rearrangement of these basic chemical compounds from an inert, passive, completely *inanimate* mixture or condition to an active, self-organized, *animated* unit or entity. A trigger, a catalyst, a biochemical process was needed that would distinguish living stardust from lifeless compounds

- Earthly locales most hospitable to life's trigger were warm bodies of water—oceans, ponds, lakes—rich with the basic organic compounds that are the building blocks of living matter. Other candidates include the biochemical possibilities found in very hot deep-ocean vents, or the biochemical makeup of clays, and/or rudimentary organic entities formed in deep space and deposited by cometary debris or meteorite impacts on Earth. It is possible that Earthly life emerged more than once and in more than one locale. No signs of life beyond Earth have been detected, although the search continues

- The most ancient known life forms—and they're still with us—include three lineages of microbes: archaebacteria, eubacteria, and eukaryotes, which probably evolved in that order. The three groups seem likely to share an even older common ancestor which is yet to be discovered. The first two bacterial groups are primitive one-cell organisms. The eukaryotes—all other organisms, including humans—have multiple cells containing a nucleus

- The cell is the basic unit of all organic life. It houses two critically important evolutionary activators: an organism's DNA—the cell's genetic hereditary material—and mitochondria— the cellular components that process energy. Their respective evolutionary roles deserve, and get, more attention in a later chapter

As evolutionary theory's most famous figure, Charles Darwin (featured in the following chapter), once said, "From so simple a beginning endless forms most beautiful and most wonderful have been, and are being, evolved." So, we are left to explain how it all came about—how that trigger or catalyst or biochemical process transformed inanimate, non-living, insensible matter into living, active, sensing organisms—into life itself.

The key that unlocks the seeming mystery is the process of thermodynamic (energy) evolution described in Chapter 1, "The Big E ≈ Energy." Arto Annila proposes that evolution is a thoroughly natural process consisting of a universal tendency to diminish energy gradients (different levels or amounts) found within physical entities which may be chemical compounds, molecular groupings, organisms, etc. This energy-reduction process is a form of entropy whereby a high level of "external energy" (e.g., from Sun to Earth) is "transducted" (i.e., flows) to or through an entity having lower energy content. It doesn't matter whether this energy converter is living or non-living. *All systems*, organic and inorganic, by coupling external energy sources to an entity's internal ingredients, are capable of becoming energy-transduction mechanisms. "The natural process that accumulated early functional chemical compounds is the one and the same that today involves complex entities, [organic] species. The scale is different and mechanisms are versatile and more effective but the principle is the same. All organisms assemble via numerous chemical reactions" (Annila and Annila 2008: 9).

Thus, Annila concludes that "life is a natural process. It is a consequence of increasing entropy, the quest to diminish free energy with no demarcation between inanimate and animate. According to thermodynamics there was no striking moment or single specific locus for life to originate but the natural process has been advancing by a long sequence of steps via numerous mechanisms reaching so far to acquire a specific meaning—life . . . Life is undoubtedly rare but not unnatural" (Annila and Annila 2008: 9).

Nor was life's emergence required or necessary but was "a likely sequence of events, not a miraculous singular event." It was simply another kind of "the coupling of external energy" much as also occurred in non-living primordial chemical soups and primitive compounds. More plainly, there is no life imperative: "There is no requirement for an autocatalytic self-replicating molecule being assembled by a fortuitous event and susceptible for natural selection to operate on it . . . [and] no incentive to discover a specific, vital mechanism" (Annila and Annila 2008: 14). In other words, reducing energy gradients could have gone merrily on without life's participation at all. However, "Earth, our home, is in between the huge potential energy difference due to the hot Sun and the cold space. Biota [organic life] has emerged . . . to diminish the difference by energy transduction" (Annila and Annila 2008: 14).

This sobering and rather deflating view of life's importance may be a comedown for some observers accustomed to finding human meaning and purpose in everything. They probably had the same kind of feeling and doubts when Charles Darwin proposed his evolutionary theory of natural selection, which nudged humankind away from a central place in the world, just as Annila's theory of energy evolution sends the same message about *all* Earthly life, not just the human version. In Chapter 3, we shall revisit these two major theories of life's evolution: Darwin's biology-based natural selection and Annila's physics-based energy evolution. Together, they contain management lessons of enormous importance for today's corporations.

For the moment, we are left with the idea that all life units are packets of energy. They absorb energy from their surroundings—oxygen, nutrients (minerals, vegetation, animals), light, and heat from the Sun—which they process internally, thus providing sustenance and growth, while casting off unusable waste products. In doing so, they are acting as simple energy-transduction mechanisms by reducing the incoming energy flows to lesser or lower forms of energy. Energy flows in; some remains inside; energy flows out. That is the entropic process described in Chapter 1. The higher the energy inflows and the faster the rate of energy use, the higher is the resulting entropy. High entropy is in fact a sign of a thriving organic life because incoming energy is dispersed away from the organism in a downward direction toward the lowest levels possible, thereby keeping the organism from sliding downhill into a lifeless, low-energy equilibrium. Like it or not, that is life at its most basic meaning—the fundamental process that defines, originates, and sustains life itself.

A complementary, parallel view of life as energy has been favored by two other experienced research scholars. Peter Corning believes that "living organisms feed upon available energy to create thermodynamic (energetic) order, physical order, and biological organization . . . Living systems harvest available energy in various forms. Some of it becomes embodied in biomass; some is utilized for work; and some becomes waste heat and is ultimately returned to the environment" (Corning 2005: 332). The same idea is promoted by Alexis Pietak: ". . . many of the organizations and processes of collective life forms (such as the life cycle and natural succession) can be understood in terms of similar thermodynamic laws that . . . hold for non-living material systems." She speaks of the "emergent energy states of living things" and "that collectives of living things . . . become directly analogous to a closed thermodynamic system which can reach thermodynamic equilibrium" (Pietak 2011: 145, 119). From both scholars, the central idea is clear: an equivalence of life and energy; an emergent flow of energy that sustains living things; and a movement of energy toward an entropic destination.

Pietak goes on to say that ignoring this thermodynamic view of life carries grave risks for humankind: ". . . omitting the concept of life-as-energy from our rational reasoning limits our capacity to understand natural systems. Consequently, we are limited in our capacity to develop actions capable of integrating human interests with the ways that nature ultimately functions" (Pietak 2011: 249). That cautionary note is a perfect segue to the ecosystem context of Earthly life.[1]

Life as ecosystem

Corporate managers whose decisions, policies, and strategies fail to comprehend, heed, and support these basic traits of life will find themselves and their companies in a confrontation, not just with human social customs and preferences but with powerful natural processes that have made life what it is and what it does—and has been doing for billions of years. The central message to business is simple: heed life. That sounds simple enough, but the puzzle of whose life should get the most attention, and what should or can corporate managers do about it, will continue through later chapters as a major challenge of **Natural Corporate Management**.

It would be difficult to find a clearer illustration of the need for **Natural Corporate Management** than the environmental catastrophe in the Gulf of Mexico in 2010 stemming from a malfunctioning deepwater oil platform operated by the corporate oil giant BP (British Petroleum). Heeding life—in any form—was clearly not the company's top priority: certainly not the lives of 11 oil-platform workers who died, not the countless forms of sea life choked by the oil, not the bird life whose oil-soaked feathers would not lift them into the air, not the oil-drenched shoreline vegetation along with the creatures nesting there, not the shellfish to be harvested by coastal enterprises, not the oil's impact on the livelihoods of coastal fisheries or the owners, employees, and customers in the entire coastline recreation industry, nor the magnified long-term effects of stagnant undersea oil pools and long-range oil plumes reaching far-distant shores. In short, BP operatives and managers failed to heed one of **Natural Corporate Management**'s central principles, namely that all life exists within ecosystems. More acutely put, life *is* ecosystem. To ignore and disregard these broad ecosystem effects is to act against the principal forces of nature.

---

1 Pietak's *Life as Energy* advocates an alternative view of scientific reductionism by emphasizing a holistic conceptual perspective on life and its evolution, which is proposed as a more secure basis for public policy.

But there is even more at stake. The BP deep-sea energy blowout goes far beyond ecosystem disruption and destruction. It engulfs, spans, and engages all phases of the entire Evolutionary Cascade: Energy → Life → Darwin → Gene → *Homo* → Brain → Symbol → Organization → Market → Corporation. This larger picture emerges in the chapters to follow—and its lessons apply equally to all business corporations, their employees, managers, and executives. The stakes for business, society, and nature are indeed central and massive, as we shall see. But now for a larger picture of ecosystem life.

No known form of life has ever existed apart from an ecosystem. While that is true in one sense by definition, the linkage is worth pondering. Even the very first tiny bacterial organisms that managed to animate a combination of basic periodic elements and inorganic compounds took those building blocks from their immediate surroundings. "By definition the first organisms could not have relied on other organisms for their energy. But the primitive ocean may have been rich in abiotically synthesized organic compounds and the source of energy in these compounds was sunlight. [Thus] reactions between organic compounds [was] the source of energy [and life] in the first cells" (Maynard Smith and Szathmary 1999: 55). Life literally became an inherent linkage of organism and environment, a combination of animating process and proximate chemical compounds, triggered by energy inflow from the surrounding environment. The probability is high (though unconfirmed thus far) that this kind of emergent linkage occurred not once but multiple times, thus simultaneously creating an intertwined life-and-ecosystem-network. Neither one preceded the other; each was essential to the other; simultaneity was the midwife. Thus has it ever been since that primal beginning of Earthly life some 3.75 billion years ago.[2]

So, what is an ecosystem and how does it support, extend, expand, and sustain life today? Ecologists define an ecosystem as an integrated, interdependent network of organisms—plants, animals, bacteria—living in association with each other and interacting with a physical (abiotic) environment. The key phrase here is "integrated, interdependent network"

---

2 An alternative, though not necessarily contradictory, interpretation of life's emergence is proposed by evolutionary psychologist Liane Gabora who hypothesizes a "communal exchange" process occurring between early life forms which preceded Darwinian generational evolution (Gabora 2012).

NEW YORK INSTITUTE OF TECHNOLOGY

which is another way of saying that the life of those individual organisms cannot exist apart from the ecosystem's network, reminiscent of John Donne's well-known 17th-century aphorism, "No man is an island, entire of itself."

An ecosystem is less comprehensive and less inclusive than the biosphere, which includes all areas of the Earth—land, water, and atmosphere—inhabited by living organisms (*Oxford Dictionary of Biology* 2000: 194, 74). In one sense, the broader biosphere is one vast ecosystem, although ecologists prefer to speak of multiple ecosystems which together add up to the biosphere. "On a larger and more complex scale than individual ecosystems is the global biosphere itself, arguably the integrated sum of all Earth-based ecosystems" (Chaisson 2001: 195). "The past billion years of evolution have caused our biosphere to become populated with a multitude of ecosystems, each exquisitely adapted to different environmental conditions and each having the means to sustain ongoing 'traffic patterns' of incoming resources, outgoing wastes, and distributed energy" (Chaisson 2001: 194).

To achieve this life-giving status did indeed consume several billion years as layer upon layer was built up. The key components emphasized by ecologists include an expanding diversity of life forms, the secure status of evolved species, food chains and nutrient cycles describing who-eats-whom, predator–prey links, intraspecies reproductive competition, interspecies competition for food and living space, the population dynamics of size, living space, density, increase and decline of the collective living entities—all of this occurring within a geological, climatological environment also subject to change and evolution.

Remarkably, each ecosystem component contributes in one way or another to the perpetuation of *collective* life inside the system. Even oil-giant BP, while devastating its own neighboring ecosystem, was searching for sources of human life-sustaining energy. Quite obviously, *individual* lives are less secure, given the prevalence of "food" chains, disease, alien invasion, fluctuating nutrient and water cycles, temperature fluxes, and natural upheavals caused by volcanic eruptions, asteroid impacts, earthquakes, tsunamis, landslides, floods, hurricanes, monsoons, etc. Though risky in the short term for an individual organism, ecosystems themselves are relatively stable over the long term. But as *systems of collective life*, ecosystems have become the ultimate sustainers of organic life in all of its forms. We need now to ferret out the specific whys and hows of ecosystems' role in sustaining life as a whole.

The energetics of ecosystems

In addition to being a collection of living organisms, ecosystems are a prime source and processor of energy. "Energy is the driving factor of ecosystems," says a leading ecologist (Jorgensen 2002: 84). Energy constantly animates and suffuses the entire ecosystem, providing the essential nutrients needed by organisms to maintain an active existence. "The difference between living and non-living systems is . . . the fact that living systems have many more and better embodied possibilities for utilization of the energy flow and are particularly adapted to maintaining high energy utilization in changed circumstances" (Jorgensen 2002: 343-44). Those "embodied possibilities" include the great diversity of organic life forms found in all corners of the Earth's biosphere, as well as other unique features we now describe . . .

Biodiversity throughout an ecosystem—a multiplicity and wide variety of plants, animals, and bacteria, all with highly varied strategies for capturing energy and converting it into useful forms—is perhaps the ecosystem's principal life-giver. Equally important is biodiversity's self-reinforcing quality. "In general, diversity has increased over evolutionary time, on sea and land. This increase of diversity reflected a series of evolutionary innovations: more efficient utilization of available energy; wider use of available nutrients; and a spread of organisms to a wider range of environments. These innovations all increased ecosystem productivity and diversity . . . higher productivity supports higher diversity. Diversity begets diversity . . ." (Leigh and Vermeij 2002: 711-16).

So, the much-acclaimed biodiversity of ecosystems is of central importance because it betokens more efficient energy processing. If that sounds like something you have heard earlier, say in Chapter 1, "The Big E ≈ Energy," you are spot on. Ecosystems and all of their many component parts are nothing but vast networks of energy transduction devices that drive incoming energy from higher to lower levels. "Ecosystems are open systems and are dependent on a throughflow of first-class energy. When the energy needs for maintenance . . . have been covered, there is a propensity to store the excess exergy.[3] The system thereby moves away from thermodynamic equilibrium" (Jorgensen 2002: 351). And what is true of the ecosystem is also true of individual members of its diverse population: "In a physical sense, the individual organism is a complex, open system that maintains itself far from thermodynamic equilibrium and reproduces itself by the continual throughput of energy that is degraded to perform work" (Brown 1995: 183).

Organism size is another positive life-multiplier within ecosystems. "Any self-sustaining ecosystem will contain a wide spectrum of organisms ranging in size from tiny microbes to large animals and plants. The small organisms account in most cases for the bulk of the respiration (energy turnover), whereas the larger organisms comprise most of the biomass [e.g., elephants, whales, humans, etc.]. It is therefore important for an ecosystem to maintain both small and large organisms, as it will mean that both the energy turnover rate and the energy storage in the form of biomass are maintained" (Jorgensen 2002: 82-83). A tropical rainforest consisting of large, closely compacted trees and vegetation of all types and sizes, along with the countless numbers of organisms both large and tiny, illustrates the point (Leigh 2002).

Species variety, another manifestation of biodiversity, further magnifies the flow of life-giving energy, partly by expanding the length and depth of the ecosystem's food chains (put more plainly, providing more to eat). A coral reef that attracts and shelters a large and varied population of aquatic creatures provides far more predator–prey encounters than a barren patch lacking such diversity. Likewise, the constant intra- and interspecies competitive struggles to find and defend a living niche and to reproduce offspring, not only consume enormous amounts of energy but also speed its journey toward an energy equilibrium for the entire ecosystem. It works this way: "The species of an ecosystem form a chain of energy transduction mechanisms that distribute solar energy acquired by photosynthesis. Since the mechanisms of energy transduction are also themselves repositories of energy, other mechanisms may, in turn, tap into and draw from them" (Kaila and Annila 2008: 3067). These competitive struggles are pure and simple fitness survival contests to establish the superiority of one species over another, or one dominant (usually

3 "Exergy" means energy available for work.

larger) member of a single species over weaker ones. "Species appear to be arrayed largely along a spectrum of dominance" (Brown 1995: 71). Think of the alpha male: the most powerful lion, chimp, or, oops, corporate CEO. Dominants, by commanding, controlling, and processing large amounts of energy, greatly increase ecosystem productivity (Leigh *et al.* 2009).

Pure numbers, or **population size**, of an ecosystem's organisms, however tiny they may be, count for much of the needed energy flow-through. Research reveals "evidence for a microbial world that contains the bulk of the planet's biodiversity . . . Most of Earth's microbes live in the open ocean, in soil, and in oceanic and terrestrial subsurfaces. Fertile soil contains billions of them" (Sapp 2009: 280). By processing chemical compounds (breathable oxygen being one such product), aiding digestion, breaking down detritus and other wastes, bacteria speed the flow of energy through the many life pathways found within ecosystems. In doing so, they promote ecosystem health and continuity. So much from so small a creature, though a populous one. Obviously, numbers count.

So the blooming of Earth's ecosystems—those life-nourishing complex communities of diverse organisms—is Earth's way of taking in the Sun's unrelenting radiant energy and turning it into what we recognize as life itself. From the most basic cellular level where mitochondria capture and process incoming energy, outward to the multicellular organisms of numerous kingdoms, domains, and species with their own respective energy-capture strategies, life builds up and accumulates in great variety. Ecosystem is the energy-constructed home; organisms are the home's energy-processing residents; life is the result.

Ecosystem productivity: The whole and the parts

Ecosystems generate, gestate, shelter, and promote life. As if that weren't enough, might one dare ask, "What else do they do?" That is not an idle inquiry but one that goes to the heart, not just of ecosystem function but also (and more importantly for the basic theme of this book) to the meaning of **Natural Corporate Management**. The central function of both ecosystem and business corporations (and their managers) is "production," presumably accomplished in the most efficient (profitable) way possible.

One doesn't normally think of an ecosystem as a "producer" but in fact that is exactly what it is and what it does. Equally important is an ecosystem's "productivity"—its overall *rate* of production and its net generation of product. So, what is this "product?"

The form taken by life is biomass: tissue, flesh, blood, nectar, blossom, hair, leaf, bone, root, organ, nerve, limb, etc.—and when gathered together these parts become plants, animals, bacteria—and bunched further they emerge as species, communities, and entire ecosystems nested within an even larger biosphere. Organic biomass, plus the energy flow to sustain it, is thus the principal "product" of ecosystem dynamics. The natural process that produces this outcome is evolutionary, chemically derivative, energy-driven, DNA-based, and dependent on an interweaving of the separate and elementary forms of organic life present in an ecosystem at any given time. "To ecologists, performance is measured as net productivity, the power beyond that needed for subsistence. The excess thus becomes available for growth, reproduction, or consumption" (Vermeij 2004: 23). Take special note: That is as true for a modern business corporation as for ecosystems: the performance of both "is measured as net productivity" that permits survival plus an extra amount "available for growth, reproduction, or consumption." The parallel of ecosystem and corporation is too obvious to miss.

Each life form captures inflowing energy as nutrients to sustain and build its biomass and to enable its reproduction generationally. "Every organism is, of course, a producer of sorts—growing, reproducing, and dying—potentially a resource for some other creature" (Vermeij 2004: 92). Typifying the gobble-gobble of ecosystem existence, we find that "In nature, primary producers—plants and other living things that make organic matter from inorganic sources—are the foundation of a food web in which consumers—herbivores, predators, parasites, and decomposers—eat other organisms and their products. Consumers are themselves producers in that other species may eat them or the things they make" (Vermeij 2004: 46). If this picture doesn't ruin your appetite (just assume you're not one of those being consumed), then it is possible to say that the aggregate of such individual activities is the entire ecosystem's "gross production." That includes the total biomass and all forms of energy inflow and outflow it takes to keep the entire process going. Tropical rainforests, by absorbing immense amounts of solar energy, "produce" enormous biodiversity and complex food webs, and are one of the best examples of a highly efficient productive ecosystem.

But rainforests are not alone: "The key to production lies in collecting and storing energy and raw materials, regulating and increasing the rate of supply, and distributing or allocating necessities require[d] to maintain and propagate the producer. These imperatives apply whether the producing entity is a cell, a redwood tree, an entire ecosystem, or an industrialized human economy" (Vermeij 2004: 93). Take note of that last candidate. We're talking about a natural production process at the very center of human economic enterprise, including the modern business corporation. Learning to manage such a process is the essence of **Natural Corporate Management**, as we shall see in subsequent chapters.

Parts and wholes

Remarkably, an ecosystem's overall production and productivity are of no concern whatsoever to the individual organisms whose interconnections cause it to become a system. How can this be? Principally because individual life units do not interact with the entire ecosystem but only with other nearby life units. With other members of their own species, they compete for food, mates, offspring, shelter, and favorable positioning or niche security. With some neighboring organisms, they are predators; with others, prey. With most, they do not interact at all, not just because of spatial distances but because there is no functional need to do so. The immediacy of life-support resources is what counts and what sustains their individual lives. For all life units, the larger "system" simply does not exist as they go about the daily grind of trying to survive. While an individual life unit's existence and continuity may be directly, or more likely indirectly, dependent on the presence of an ecosystem's food webs, nutrients, water, temperatures, stability, etc., any organism's most common interactions are with other individual life units without the slightest functional regard for system traits. Their principal interest and goal is in their own individual productivity, not the ecosystem's. That was pretty obvious, wasn't it, in the BP oil spill catastrophe: the company cared about "the part" (itself) but not the "whole" (the ecosystem).

For this reason, an ecosystem is entirely *supra*-individual—meaning it operates completely above and beyond the individuals in it. There is no *system* motivator or driver at the individual organism level, only an *individually oriented* survival function. Nor is there any immediate awareness, even for human organisms, of the overall system and its life-supportive productivity as a whole. Any ecosystem is simply an evolved network of organismic connections. As described earlier, an individual organism's strategy is to capture inflowing energy, appropriate some for its own interests, and export the used-up wastes, thereby reducing the energy gradients in its immediate vicinity. At a cellular level, this is done via energy-generating mitochondria and DNA-induced hereditary activities. All organisms are different types of energy-transduction mechanism, driving energy toward an entropic state. To perform these individual actions, the ecosystem is strategically incidental, merely providing opportunistic advantages and disadvantages to be incorporated into individual life strategies.

This partitioning of *system* and *individual* emphasizes that there is no apparent *biological* process that operates as a *system* generator—no functional, operational, organismic process—that reaches beyond the life perspective of an individual organism to embrace the whole of the ecosystem. And this functional gap prevails in spite of the presence of an ecosystem that supports the individuals who live in it. Neither does the ecosystem carry out its productive functions with any heed for its separate, though linked, parts. The *system* and its *productivity* are simply the consequential outcome of the member organisms' self-centered actions—and vice versa. As peculiar as this may be, even more peculiar is the dependence of each on the other, as next described.

Symbiosis, mutualism, and organic altruism

Although these ideas will appear in later chapters, it is worth taking note now of some kinds of organic behavior that seem to contradict the notion that all organisms are strictly self-centered.

- **Symbiosis** is a widespread feature of many, perhaps all, ecosystems, contributing to productivity of the individual symbionts as well as the ecosystem itself. Symbiosis occurs when members of *different species* interact in a supportive way that benefits both, such as a bee pollinating a flowering plant as it gathers the plant's nectar as food for itself while promoting continued production of fruit for the plant. Many such examples, plus several technical variations on the general process, make the point that individual organisms indeed seem to reach out beyond themselves to other organisms in a "helping" way

- **Mutualism** is a closely related form of organic collaboration. Mutualisms occur both inter-specially (between different species) and intra-specially (within a single species). For example, very basic to an ecosystem's productivity are the close ties between fungi and the roots of plants, where fungi benefit by obtaining nutrients from the root's cells which then are aided in absorbing needed ions by the presence of the fungus. This would seem to be a triple gain in productivity: for the roots, the fungi, and the surrounding ecosystem (Leigh 2010)

- **Organic altruism** would appear to be an even more hopeful sign that organic selfishness is not the sole behavioral trait of Earthly life. The biologist's version of altruism goes like this: when an animal takes risky action that threatens its own survival while simultaneously promoting the life of another creature (usually a close relative), it is said to be acting altruistically. For example, a rabbit upon seeing a predator fox may thump its tail on the ground as a warning to fellow rabbits and then scurry off waving its white tail, thereby making itself easily visible to the fox and risking its life to protect the other rabbits. Or a prairie ground squirrel may stand up straight from protective grass cover to spot any lurking predators in the vicinity and squeal an alarm to other squirrels, calling the predator's attention to itself. Altruistic acts such as these seem to reveal a built-in tendency to sacrifice one's survival chances for others. Another term for it is "kin selection," when the beneficial effects are spread among a group of close relatives. A more extended notion is captured in the phrase "reciprocal altruism," made famous by Robert Trivers who suggested that this kind of cooperative behavior can extend beyond immediate kin to distantly related members of an organic community (Trivers 1971).[4]

---

4 Altruism takes on a distinctly different meaning among evolutionarily advanced organisms with complex neurological systems where altruistic beneficence may be a deliberately intentional act. Research reporting such cooperative actions appears in later chapters of this book.

For now, though, let's look a little closer at this triad of seeming cooperativeness among neighboring organisms. Starkly put, each relationship simply exhibits the same-old, same-old self-centeredness encountered previously, in spite of appearances which, in these cases, are misleading. Each of the symbionts "helping" another is simply looking out for itself by "hooking up" with other organisms in a convenient way. For the bee, pollination of the flowering plant is entirely beside the point, which is to feed itself and its hive mates on the nutritious nectar. The plant is equally indifferent to what the bee is up to, as long as it does its sexual thing by stimulating production of the next round of fruit. Mutualistic support found among different organic species reveals the same kind of innocuous linkage: those tree roots are simply programmed by evolution to absorb needed ions in order to support the tree's life, which the fungi help them do as a way of supporting the fungi's own lives. What appears to be a triple gain for all is nothing but a singular gain for each: one of those random happy circumstances arising from the pursuit of separate life strategies.

At first glance, organic altruism seems a solid case for socially oriented behavior. After all, the primary actors—rabbit, ground squirrel, brother, sister, or cousin—do indeed risk their own lives in ways that support the lives of their species compatriots. Once again, though, each "altruist" is simultaneously promoting the generational continuity of its own genes or those of organisms possessing an identical or closely related genome. The rabbit, the ground squirrel, the near kin of the community are programmed by natural selection to act in survival ways. They do so as much, or more so, for the survival of their own genes as for those who benefit from their self-centered actions. Alas, an ecosystem and its inhabitants—long-term products of evolution, energy flow-and-capture, and energy-gradient leveling—operate as programmed by those forces. The ecosystem is a collectivity of diverse biomass, and the member organisms obey the natural evolutionary forces that impel them to survive, adapt, and reproduce. Appearances, to the contrary, can indeed be deceiving.

And if you are not convinced by the actions of bees, rabbits, squirrels, and fungi, think about this: every human being is host to thousands of bacterial species and millions of their genes, all living in your mouth and gut and organs (Zimmer 2012). They help you digest food, breathe, and function normally; doing so is *their* own bacterial way of getting along through life. Sure, you benefit but that's not why they do it—and of course, sometimes they do harm to you and your body. As a result, the human being you are is a living, walking, talking symbiont, mutualist, and organic altruist all rolled into one—and so are your in-house residential (but non-talking) bacteria. Now be honest: do you give a hang about all those "cooperative" bacteria? Only if they don't do their thing so you can keep on doing yours, right? "Me first" seems to hold it all together. That's life in an ecosystem, where paradoxically the Whole is a function of the Parts—and oddly enough, the Parts (individuals) are a function of the Whole (system).

The tendency to read good intentions into the self-centered actions of non-human organisms is a form of anthropophilia (love of humans) or anthropocentrism (humans at the center of everything), where human meanings and interpretations are overlaid on and used to describe animal and plant behavior. Examples are the use by biologists and ecologists of such terms as "cooperators," "competitors," "cheaters," "partners," "friends," "enemies," etc. (Pennisi 2003: 774-75; Bower 2004: 330-32). The same is true of Richard Dawkins' famous phrase, "selfish gene" to be discussed in a later chapter (Dawkins 1976). A strong implication frequently accompanying such language usages is that the described behavior is teleological or purposive, driven by explicit, unconscious or even deliberately conscious motives. From there, it is not far to the "anthropic principle" that the entirety of Earthly life, particularly the human part, exists for a purpose, though one not always (or ever?) clarified or identified. And one could then go on to the even farther-out notion of evolutionary creationism. All such belief systems, while sincerely held, attest to the presence of an understandable anthropophilia among Earth's human creatures. However, such ideas are of little help and often a hindrance in understanding organic, including human, behavior. A later chapter probes the source of such teleological beliefs.

The "togetherness" found in symbiosis, mutualism, and organic altruism can be more accurately described (and less philosophically compromised) as different types of integrated functional networks found in ecosystems. The organisms involved are "integrated" because they are parts of a whole set of associated organisms; they are "functional" in the different kinds of actions that result from their integration; and they are a "network" in the sense of interconnection and interdependence. There is nothing particularly special or privileged about such integrated functional networks inasmuch as they emerge across the organic world as manifestations of thermodynamic (energy) evolution; and, as such, they represent yet another form taken by a constantly evolving Earthly life. They simply "do their thing," perform their organismic functions as specified in their respective DNA maps, and are "rewarded" by their own survival. That's what it's all about—life in an ecosystem.

To sum up, the conditions most conducive to achieving and maintaining high levels and rates of ecosystem productivity—that is, life—are the following ones (Leigh and Vermeij 2002; Leigh *et al.* 2009):

- Large, diverse, and high-density organic populations living on long-established, large-scale landmasses and/or in sizable oceanic-riverine bodies of water

- Intense interspecies and intraspecies fitness competition for energy, reproduction, and secure life niches

- Extensive food webs dominated by large animals and plants

- Nutrient recycling promoted by bacterial processes

- Relatively stable long-run climatological and geological conditions

These conditions tend to maximize life-giving energy flows, DNA (genetic) reproduction, and homeostasis (stability) of the ecosystem as a whole, thus generating and sustaining the system's evolving biomass— and thereby overall ecosystem productivity.

The Big L's impact on corporate management

Modern business corporations are, shall we say, up to their necks in ecosystem life. Their actions, decisions, goals, policies, strategies, successes, and failures *in toto* directly impact all critical ecosystem components, both positively and negatively. Their highly effective energy capture-and-use techniques signal their superior status as energy transduction mechanisms—among the best in existence. Their economizing processes take that energy inflow—human labor, capital investment, organizational and social capital, technology, information, geological-chemical materials— and convert it into products and services offered in markets. As corporate giants, they stand at the top of most economic food chains, wielding great marketplace power over competitors and consumers. In competitive struggles for an enduring market niche, they often play the predator role, cannibalizing their foes, but in some cases falling prey to more powerful, clever, ruthless opponents. Market dominance is a primary goal, driven typically by an alpha-male CEO. Their collective corporate productivity is equated to the economic success of the ecosystems they occupy. The extent of corporate influence on ecosystems worldwide is limited only by the reach of their technology and the market ambitions of their executive cadre. Their typical lack of concern for the natural communities that host their operations replicates the long-standing self-centered evolutionary trends observed throughout the organic world.

However similar a corporation's operations may appear to be to the actions of organisms found in ecosystems, it is important to note that the corporation is not, itself, an organism. It is a *collectivity* of organisms—principally, an executive cadre and a specialized workforce—wielding technology to dominate markets. It becomes a coherent whole through agreed-upon behavioral standards that form the company's own unique corporate culture, although there is no guarantee of complete confor-mance by individual members of the collective enterprise (think of rogue CEOs, whistle-blowers, and defectors of various kinds who pursue their own evolutionary agendas). Though not an organism per se, this cor-porate collectivity—some have called it a complex adaptive system—is clearly a prime occupant of any ecosystem touched by its operations. It does indeed attempt to develop an adaptive lifestyle in the manner of bacteria, bees, rabbits, roses, corn, redwood trees, or the pack behavior of wolves, hyenas, and vultures.

Natural Corporate Management is a realization, an awareness, a con-sciousness of the corporation's central involvement in ecosystem life. It is more perception and acceptance of natural processes than specific managerial method and technique, although **NCM** moves a company in the direction of adapting corporate operations to those forces that first generated and then expanded life into its many forms. Easier said than done, of course, leaving much of that story and its possible realization to following chapters.

The Big L's pivotal points

- Life on Earth appeared approximately 3.75 billion years ago, taking the form of simple one-cell microbes that emerged from an integration of organic compounds subject to inflowing solar energy

- The cell is the basic unit of all organic life; it is the locale of an organism's DNA (genes) and mitochondria (energy source)

- Earthly life is an incidental (non-imperative) outcome of thermodynamic (energy) evolution by contributing to the reduction of inflowing solar energy gradients and driving life-supporting energy toward entropy

- All life forms exist only (or primarily) within ecosystems, which are networks or webs of interconnected, interdependent organisms

- An ecosystem's productivity is equivalent to the production and continued sustenance of the system's total biomass (organic life forms), enhanced by organic diversity, intense competition, population size, land/water mass, organism dominance, climate, heat flows, etc.

- Individual organisms are impelled by entropic energy-reduction and DNA (genetic) impulses to promote their own survival and sustenance, made possible and enhanced by the interconnected webs of life constituting the surrounding ecosystem

- Anthropophilia obscures an accurate interpretation of integrated functional networks of organisms responsible for the interdependencies of life forms within ecosystems

- Business corporations operate within ecosystems, exerting significant influence both positive and negative on the diverse life forms there. Its adaptive impacts can be mediated by adopting a style and approach called **Natural Corporate Management** that considers ecosystem-wide consequences of corporate operations

The Big L's research base

Origin of life

Annila, A., and E. Annila (2008) 'Why Did Life Emerge?' *International Journal of Astrobiology* 7: 293-300.

Cheetham, N.W.H. (2011) *Introducing Biological Energetics: How Energy and Information Control the Living World* (Oxford, UK: Oxford University Press).

Corning, P.A. (2005) *Holistic Darwinism: Synergy, Cybernetics, and the Bioeconomics of Evolution* (Chicago: University of Chicago Press).

Deamer, D. (2011) *First Life: Discovering the Connection between Stars, Cells, and How Life Began* (Berkeley, CA: University of California Press).

Eigen, M., with R. Winkler-Oswatitsch (1992) *Steps Towards Life: A Perspective on Evolution* (New York: Oxford University Press).

Kondratyev, K.Y., K.S. Losev, M.D. Ananicheva and I.V. Chesnokova (2004) *Stability of Life on Earth: Principal Subject of Scientific Research in the 21st Century* (Springer-Praxis Books in Environmental Science; Chichester, UK: Praxis Publishing).

Maynard Smith, J., and E. Szathmary (1999) *The Origins of Life: From the Birth of Life to the Origin of Language* (New York: Oxford University Press).

Pietak, A.M. (2011) *Life as Energy: Opening the Mind to a New Science of Life* (Edinburgh: Floris Books).

Popa, R. (2004) *Between Necessity and Probability: Searching for the Definition and Origin of Life* (Berlin: Springer).

Sapp, J. (2009) *The New Foundations of Evolution: On the Tree of Life* (New York: Oxford University Press).

Ecosystem dynamics

Bower, B. (2004) "One-celled Socialites," *Science News* 166 (November 20, 2004): 330-32.

Brown, J.H. (1995) *Macroecology* (Chicago: University of Chicago Press).

Chaisson, E.J. (2001) *Cosmic Evolution: The Rise of Complexity in Nature* (Cambridge, MA: Harvard University Press).

Dawkins, R. (1976) *The Selfish Gene* (Oxford, UK: Oxford University Press, 1989).

Dodds, W.K. (2009) *Laws, Theories, and Patterns in Ecology* (Berkeley, CA: University of California Press).

Gabora, L. (2012) "An Evolutionary Framework for Culture: Selectionism versus Communal Exchange," Cornell University Library; arXiv:1206.4386v1, accessed July 28, 2012.

Jorgensen, S.E. (2002) *Integration of Ecosystem Theories: A Pattern* (Dordrecht, Netherlands: Kluwer Academic Publishers, 3rd edn).

Jorgensen, S.E., and Y.M. Sverizhev (2004) *Towards a Thermodynamic Theory for Ecological Systems* (Amsterdam: Elsevier).

Kaila, V.R.I., and A. Annila (2008) "Natural Selection for Least Action," *Proceedings of the Royal Society A* 464: 3,055-70.

Kleinsmith, L.J., and V.M. Kish (1995) *Principles of Cell and Molecular Biology* (New York: HarperCollins, 2nd edn).

Leigh, E.G., Jr. (2002) *A Magic Web: The Tropical Forest of Barro Colorado Island* (New York: Oxford University Press).

Leigh, E.G., Jr. (2010) "The Evolution of Mutualism," *Journal of Evolutionary Biology* 23: 2,507-28.

Leigh, E.G., Jr., and G.J. Vermeij (2002) "Does Natural Selection Organize Ecosystems for the Maintenance of High Productivity and Diversity?" *Philosophical Transactions of the Royal Society, London B* 357: 709-18.

Leigh, E.G., Jr., G.J. Vermeij and M. Wikelski (2009) "What Do Human Economies, Large Islands and Forest Fragments Reveal about the Factors Limiting Ecosystem Evolution?" *Journal of Evolutionary Biology* 22: 1-12.

Oxford Dictionary of Biology (2000) *Dictionary of Biology* (New York: Oxford University Press, 4th edn).

Pennisi, E. (2003) "Fast Friends, Sworn Enemies," *Science* 302 (October 31, 2003): 774-75.

Raffaelli, D.G., and L.J.F. Christopher (eds.) (2010) *Ecosystem Ecology: A New Synthesis* (New York: Cambridge University Press).

Sapp, J. (2009) *The New Foundations of Evolution: On the Tree of Life* (New York: Oxford University Press).

Trivers, R.L. (1971) "The Evolution of Reciprocal Altruism," *Quarterly Review of Biology* 46: 35-57.

Vermeij, G.J. (2004) *Nature: An Economic History* (Princeton, NJ: Princeton University Press).

Wilson, E.O. (1992) *The Diversity of Life* (London: Allen Lane).

Winslow, R., and J.D. Rockoff (2012) "Gene Map of Body's Microbes Is New Health Tool," *Wall Street Journal*, June 14, 2012: A-1, 2.

Zimmer, C. (2012) "Tending the Body's Microbial Garden," *New York Times*, June 19, 2012.

3

The Big D ≈ Darwin

> Darwin's theory of biological evolution is one of the most
> revolutionary ideas in Western thought.
> **Douglas Futuyma**

> No biologist has been responsible for more—and for more
> drastic—modifications of the average person's worldview
> than Charles Darwin.
> **Ernst Mayr**

The editors of the *Wall Street Journal*, when they want to do a hatchet job on some public figure, will write an editorial with the title "Who Is So-and-So?" filling in the blank with the person's name and then proceeding to make their case against the current enemy-of-the-day. But for purposes of this chapter, perhaps that technique can be captured and turned around to call *favorable* attention to one of the world's most famous scientific figures. Why is he so famous, not to say highly controversial, long years after his death?

Who is Charles Darwin?

The basic facts: Charles Robert Darwin (1809–1882) was the son of a well-off English physician. He began studying medicine at Edinburgh University, then shifted to Cambridge University to prepare for the ministry, and, like so many of today's indecisive undergraduates, took yet another turn, this time to study the world of nature—and, as they say, the rest is (natural) history. That set him up in 1831 for a five-year, round-the-world sea voyage on a British navy ship named *H.M.S. Beagle*, where he collected mountains of data on geology and various forms of organic life. Upon returning to England, he eventually settled in at his home, Down House, where he and his wife raised their children—and where most importantly, he worked through his *Beagle* notes, did additional studies, and many years later (1859) published his most famous book, *On the Origin of Species by Means of Natural Selection*.

I once visited Down House and saw Darwin's decidedly modest study where, sitting by a large fireplace, he wrote his books and papers by hand on paper and in ink while occupying a large armchair with a writing board resting on the chair's arms. Imagine that! No typewriter, no PC, no Internet, no cellular device. See, it *can* be done, after all! A few bookcases, an ape skull fragment and other fossils, bottles of chemicals, family portraits on the walls—about the size of a small room in any English country home. And on the grounds outside, the famous winding Sand Walk where Darwin paced as he pondered the big puzzles that would make him so famous and worthy of the question, Who Is Charles Darwin?

This chapter describes the third "Big" phase of the **Evolutionary Cascade**, which began with the **Big E ≈ Energy** followed by the **Big L ≈ Life**. Remember that each phase of the Cascade overlaps with all of the following ones—a swelling, cumulative flow—so you can expect to see the **Big E** and the **Big L** pop up again as we discuss the **Big D ≈ Darwin** in this chapter. Just how all of these "Bigs" are related to the business firm and to corporate management will be explained after setting forth the fundamentals of Darwinian thought. But it is worth noting right away—and this chapter will demonstrate—that Darwin's ideas about evolution are directly and practically useful for anyone wanting to understand the decisions, policies, strategies, and goals of the modern corporation.

What Darwin said (originally)

Darwin's main ideas in *The Origin of Species* are simple, straightforward, and easy to grasp. Bear in mind that his principal biological focus was on the entire organic world (the **Big L**) and not just, or even mainly, on human behavior. In fact, it was over ten years later before he wrote a book about human evolution, *The Descent of Man*. The central points of *The Origin of Species* are these:

- All forms of organic life—plants and animals—emerge and change (evolve) over very long time periods. Evolution is slow and gradual

- Long-term evolution produces new, diverse forms of life—a new species—from an older common ancestor. Species originate from organic predecessors

- Small organic modifications occurring in a plant or animal population may promote species survivability by increasing the species' ability to adapt to its environment. Adaptation is the key to species survival and reproduction of offspring

- As small differences accumulate over long time periods, a new species—say a stronger lion or a fleet-footed deer—begins to outnumber the older predecessor species until eventually there are two distinct populations: the earlier one which may die out entirely, and the newer species which has a better chance of survival. Competition for life's necessities—food, mate, a secure niche—favors the most adaptable (the "fittest") members of a species, e.g., the stronger lion and the faster deer

- An organism's adaptive ability or behavior is inherited from its parents and ancestral kin through the reproductive process. For Darwin, individual adaptability is a function of parental inheritance (A later chapter discusses the role of learning in adaptation)

- Natural selection—the central and most significant Darwin idea—simply means that the most adaptable organisms are favored (or "selected") for survival. The less adaptable organisms or species are therefore eliminated by this process of natural selection

That's it—Darwin's theory in a nutshell. But what a firestorm it ignited! At the time, many people believed all species—plants and animals—were created whole in their present form and would not change in the future. Others recoiled at the notion of common ancestors, particularly those that little resembled the current forms. The idea that the stronger prevail over the weaker in life's competitive race ran against the grain of popular thought while others believed this rule justified the dominance of one race or social class over another. Some critics resisted what seemed to be a biological determinism that threatened free will and human reason. And the idea that nature—not God—"selects" who shall live and who shall die was total anathema to the religiously inclined. But the theory was hailed as a brilliant explanation of past and present life by many members of the scientific community who had sought an understanding of life's dynamics. For them, natural selection opened new frontiers that would continue to be explored to the present day. While Darwin, for all of his originality, may not have uttered the final word about evolution, he gave it the push needed to imprint its importance on all who followed in his footsteps.

Today, a century and a half after *The Origin of Species*, the core of Darwin's theory remains intact but only after many controversies and additions stemming from further advances in science. By the 1930s and 1940s, a new evolutionary synthesis emerged that is the modern version of Darwin's original theory of evolution by natural selection. For this book's purposes—and especially to explain evolution's impact on **Natural Corporate Management**—it is not necessary to describe all of the complex, intertwined scientific components of the evolutionary synthesis.[1] For now, just keep in mind that the mid-20th-century discovery of genes (DNA), which were totally unknown to Darwin, greatly extended and reinforced the core ideas of Darwinian thought. This genetic component of evolution is so overwhelmingly important that the following chapter is devoted entirely to the Gene phase of the **Evolutionary Cascade**.

---

1 For a concise summary of the evolutionary synthesis, see Futuyma 2005: 9-11. An entertaining account of the controversies associated with the evolutionary synthesis is Andrew Brown's (1999) *The Darwin Wars: The Scientific Battle for the Soul of Man*. A more comprehensive account is Michael Ruse's *The Evolution Wars* (Ruse 2009).

Does Darwin apply today?

The short answer is, Yes. It almost seems that competing theories have lost the battle because they were less fit or not well adapted to the prevailing scientific thought-system—perhaps an ironic confirmation of natural selection at work. But hold that possible interpretation until we take a closer look. The question is more complicated than you might think.

Does Darwin apply to humans?

Darwin, who studied for the ministry as a young man, was famously hesitant to publish his theory, fearing backlash from the religious community. Demolish the biblical Genesis story of God's creation? Extend the age of the Earth far beyond the generally accepted standard? Substitute natural selection for God as the world's primary change agent? Dare to imply that humans are related to apes? Replace free will and reason with impersonal biological determinism? Believe that children could not pass on through inheritance the admirable behaviors they had been taught by their parents? Imply that life itself was nothing but an improbable accident in a purposeless universe? And for Darwin personally, there was the added discomfort of facing his wife who was steadfastly religious. Well, little wonder that he held back for at least 15 years after formulating the idea of natural selection, and a full 23 years after his voyage on the *Beagle* which germinated his theory.

Darwin might never have revealed his ideas to the public had not a rival scientist prompted him to rush to publication before being scooped on the century's biggest idea. A naturalist, Alfred Russel Wallace, who for years had studied the flora and fauna of the Malay Archipelago, ". . . was an independent discoverer of natural selection. If it had not been for the mere chance that he chose to dispatch the account of his discovery to Darwin, we might today be acclaiming Wallace, rather than Darwin, as the founder of modern biology" (Eiseley 1959: 70). In the end, thanks to Darwin and his supporters, the original findings of both naturalists were announced simultaneously to members of the prestigious Linnaean Society of London. *The Origin of Species* was published the very next year, 1859.[2]

In that famous book, the author is chary of any mention of human beings, preferring to say "plants and animals" when referring to organic life. It was not until the book's third-to-last page that he was emboldened to say that "Much light would be thrown on the origin of man and his history [i.e., human evolution]." By contrast, ten years later when he wrote *The Descent of Man*, he proclaimed boldly, "The sole object of this work is to consider, firstly, whether man, like every other species, is descended from some pre-existing form" (Darwin 1871: 2). No surprise: he said, Yes.

So, does Darwin apply to humans? The multiple answer is, Yes.

- Yes, humans are a form of organic life, displaying the characteristic traits of all evolved organisms living in ecosystems, as described in Chapter 2, "The Big L ≈ Life"

- Yes, human beings and their ecosystems evolve gradually over long time periods

- Yes, humans adapt to their environment via small changes over many generations

- Yes, the modern human species, *Homo sapiens*, is descended from ancestral forms of hominid life. Chapter 5, "The Big H ≈ *Homo*," gives a fuller story of human evolution

- Yes, competition among humans for food, a mate for reproduction, and a secure life niche—perhaps easier to remember as sustenance, sex, and security—favors humans who are the most skilled (the most fit) in adapting to their physical, social, and economic environments

2 Anthropologists and students of technology call such simultaneous discoveries "independent inventions": the same result or outcome but reached without contact between the inventors. In this case, Darwin received most of the credit, while Wallace became "an attenuated shadow—a foil to the great Darwin," according to Loren Eiseley. A fuller account of this story and Wallace's many other scientific achievements are in Eiseley's article "Alfred Russel Wallace," in *Scientific American*, February 1959.

- Yes, natural selection acts on the organic variations in human populations, eliminating non-adaptive traits and sustaining those that aid adaptation

In spite of personal discomfort, popular disbelief, and philosophical opposition, Darwin's conclusion is inescapable: Humankind is yet another manifestation of Darwin-in-the-flesh, so to speak. Darwin had said as much in *The Descent of Man* in this bold declaration:

> . . . man is descended from some lower form . . . Man is liable to numerous, slight and diversified variations, which are induced by the same general causes, are governed and transmitted in accordance with the same general laws as in the lower animals. Man has multiplied so rapidly that he has necessarily been exposed to struggle for existence, and consequently to natural selection. He has given rise to many races, some of which differ so much from each other, that they have often been ranked by naturalists as distinct species. His body is constructed on the same homological plan [similarity of form and function] as that of other mammals. He passes through the same phases of embryological development. He retains many rudimentary and useless structures, which no doubt were once serviceable. Characters occasionally make their reappearance in him, which we have reason to believe were possessed by his early progenitors. If the origin of man had been wholly different from that of all other animals, these various appearances would be mere empty deceptions; but such an admission is incredible. These appearances, on the other hand, are intelligible, at least to a large extent, if man is the co-descendant with other mammals of some unknown and lower form (Darwin 1871: 166-67).

And in the book's final sentence: ". . . man still bears in his bodily frame the indelible stamp of his lowly [ancestral] origin" (Darwin 1871: 708). That's saying it as plainly as possible: humans are indeed one outcome of Darwinian evolution.

Does Darwin apply to business practitioners?

A good question, especially since this book seeks to explain the goals, decisions, and strategies of business firms and their managers. The answer once again is, Yes—and why not? The people who own and manage the firm, along with their employees, are: 1) organic forms of life subject to the disciplines and opportunities of the **Big L's** ecosystems; and 2) they are human organisms subject to the rigorous dynamics of the **Big D's** natural selection process.

Look at it this way: Each participant in any business firm—founder, owner, manager, employee—brings a lot of ancestral baggage to the workplace every day. Call it their inherited basic Darwin agenda: an innate urge or impulse to acquire the necessary means of livelihood (food), to support a family (a mate for reproduction), and to have shelter (a secure life niche). The firm's founder, by establishing a successful enterprise, gains a continuing source of income and accumulating wealth. Other owners (shareholders) gain quarterly dividends and share-price increases. Managers who direct the firm's day-to-day affairs receive handsome salaries and bonuses. Employees, especially if unionized, secure acceptable wage levels and associated benefits plus job-protective work rules. *Any business firm's population is a mixture, a blend, a roiling stewpot of competing Darwin agendas.* Some are more successful than others, thereby partitioning the firm's population into a hierarchy of achievement, acceptance, satisfaction, disappointment, resentment, and bitter rejection. Over the years, several ecosystem forests have been felled by the publishers of scholarly research to publish accounts of the internal dynamics of corporate workplaces, a scholarly field otherwise known as organizational behavior. Few of these accounts openly acknowledge—many are not even aware of—the Darwinian dynamics ever-present in the workplace.[3]

---

3   A notable exception to this lack of Darwinian insights is found in the work of Nigel Nicholson, professor of organizational behavior (OB) at the London Business School, who has taken the lead by introducing evolutionary psychology concepts into the OB field. Among his works are "Evolutionary Psychology and Organizational Behavior" (1997); "How Hardwired is Human Behavior?" (1998); his book *Executive Instinct: Managing the Human Animal in the Information Age* (2000); and, co-authored with Rod White, "Darwinism: A New Paradigm for Organizational Behavior?" (2006). Roderick White and Barbara Decker Pierce of Canada's Ivey Business School were other Darwinian

A later chapter explores the evolutionary dynamics of a business firm's organizational behavior.

Beyond the individual, personal Darwin agendas is the incessant competitive workplace pressure exerted by all parties: the founder competes with other founders for market success; the shareholder-owners keep a close market watch on the shares of competing firms; the managers compete with their counterparts inside and outside the firm to fight their way up the ladder of executive succession, reaching the top if possible; employees compete in schools and training institutes for admission, grades, skills, and job placements, then once hired, to surpass their workmates for higher wages, plum jobs, and further advancement. The preparation of candidates for future managerial ranks—the well-known MBA degree programs offered by business schools—is a prime example of Darwin-like competitive dynamics. Students compete for entry (and then for grades), schools compete for prestigious national and global ranking, corporate recruiters compete for the best graduates from the best schools, and the newly hired MBAs bring their competitively honed attitudes and skills into the Darwinian dynamo of their new employer (who may soon thin out the ranks of the new hires who prove inept or unable to handle the competitive stresses demanded by their competitive supervisors).

If all of this sounds a bit like natural selection at work, don't be too surprised. The competitive "winners" are those most adaptable to their organizational environment—not necessarily the smartest, the cleverest, the most far-sighted, the wisest, the most experienced, or the most cooperative—but only the ones who learn to play the organizational game in adaptive ways. Survival is the nature of the workplace game. The ultimate prize is the achievement of one's Darwin program—the three Ss: sustenance, sex, and security. And all of this is what one finds *inside* the firm, not to speak of the *external* competition lying just outside the corporate walls.

This is not to deny the simultaneous presence of other behavioral motives operative in the firm. Darwin-driven impulses may constitute the core of workplace behavior, but other behavioral layers are present and are powerful players. Foremost are the directives issuing from the human

---

OB pathfinders as co-authors of "The Evolution of Social Structure: Why Biology Matters" (1999). We revisit the views of this pioneering group in later chapters.

genome, the neural signals sent out by the human brain, the values and habits embedded in human symbolic culture, and the complex patterns and adaptive networks of human—and, especially, corporate—organization. All of these behavioral generators and motivators are brought into the dynamics of business corporations in later chapters of this book. But for now, in the search for an understanding of **Natural Corporate Management**, we need to explore yet another question—and a daring one—about yet other Darwinian possibilities and potentialities.

Does Darwin apply not just to business practitioners, but to the business firm itself, to the corporation as a whole?

You might believe that question has already been answered by the preceding discussion, but hold on. Maybe not. Here are some things to think about.

From all outward signs, business firms do indeed *appear* to act in Darwinian ways. They compete with each other in open markets, striving to out-perform their rivals, preferably driving them out of business altogether. They seek high ranking as a sign of survival and adaptation, measured by assets held, income earned, market share, and global reach. They are often directed by a CEO made in the image of a Darwinian alpha male, dominant over all others in the company, and who "personifies" the corporation's essence (think former General Electric Company CEO Jack Welch or, more recently, Bill Gates or Warren Buffett). New species of corporations appear from time to time (and slowly) as offshoots of earlier species or sometimes as radical departures (Facebook) from the older species (a process known to biologists as "punctuated equilibrium" or rapid evolutionary change). Leading corporations have learned the basic Darwin lessons of adapting to global, culturally diverse environments. Natural selection seems to have weeded out the weaker, slower, poorly managed competitors. The "fittest" firms seem to be the winners of the Darwinian marketplace wars.

Well, maybe—but not really. To qualify for Darwin standing, you have to be a biological organism: bacterium, fungus, plant, animal, human. So, let's see: the business firm, whether the local grocery store or a global corporation, is none of these. The corporation is not an organism but an invented legal entity—a symbolic, artificial, legal "person," a cultural artifact, nothing more. "[F]irms are temporary aggregations of people to help them do their producing in such a way as to help others do their consuming" (Ridley 2010: 115). The corporation has no DNA, the genetic building blocks of life. The corporation is not an ecosystem that sustains organic life, although it conducts business within ecosystems, sometimes damaging or destroying them in the process. The corporation has no common organic ancestor from which it can trace its origin. The corporation is not a species seeking the three prime Darwin goals: sustenance, sex, and security. Although fiercely competitive, the corporation as an invented legal entity does not answer the summons of natural selection but calculates its survival fitness by a different formula: mainly profits, capital accumulation, and market dominance. The conclusion is unavoidable: non-organic corporate operations cannot be explained by organic Darwinian principles.

But what about the inhabitants and stakeholders of the corporate entity: founders, shareholders, directors, managers, employees, suppliers, creditors, customers, and the citizens of host communities? Organisms all, do they not, manifest the Darwinian evolutionary imperative? The answer is a resounding, Yes. The corporation, though not itself an organism, is a *collectivity* of such Darwin-driven organisms. They, each and singly, harbor innate biological, evolutionary impulses that operate full bore in the corporate workplace. But not with equal force; the corporation's stereotypical pyramidal structure allocates power and influence hierarchically. Top-level executive organisms are better positioned, not just to pursue their own personal Darwin agendas but also to direct, channel, and "manage" the Darwin strivings of the organizationally subservient corporate citizenry. Indeed, there is frequently, perhaps typically, an attempt to create and impose an identity of CEO personality on the corporate collectivity, with the aim of driving company operations in ways that satisfice the combined Darwin aspirations that are alive throughout the corporate workplace. Seldom do these efforts succeed in dampening the basal Darwin urgencies felt by most corporate denizens and stakeholders who prefer their own agendas to those of the executive elite.

The concept of "corporate culture," which emerged in the 1980s, has been hailed as a new way to understand the collective behavior of business firms (Deal and Kennedy 1982; Martin 2002). Since then and presently, a corporation's culture implies the presence of behavioral rules and shared commitments within the workplace which shape and help achieve the firm's goals. Whatever collective behavioral influence corporate culture might exert, it is an instance of current, *learned* behavior that might well contribute to an employee's organizational acceptance, survival, security of place, and favorable income. Sounds a bit like the Darwin trio—sustenance, sex, and security—doesn't it?

But such sounds are misleading: Darwinian behavior is an *inherited* suite of traits, while conformity to a firm's cultural rules—its corporate culture—is nothing more than currently *learned* behavior, which is not inherited. The cultural learning may be supportive of one's inherited behavioral aims but learning need not represent a Darwin-like action; quite often, learned cultural behavior can contradict Darwinian adaptation. Learning's source lies elsewhere, which we shall explore in a subsequent chapter. The distinction is subtle but critically important. Corporate culture does not put the business firm into the Darwin column. Instead, it is an instance of learned, *symbolic* behavior, an offshoot of that cognitive contraption we call a brain. Both Brain and Symbol get full treatment in two subsequent chapters, "The Big B ≈ Brain" and "The Big S ≈ Symbol." While both are "natural," neither is entirely Darwinian. The puzzle's tantalizing answer will be revealed a bit later in the story.

Darwin and the arrow of time

Charles Darwin came late to the evolution party. And I am not speaking here of the line of pre-Darwin philosophers and scientists who hatched their own, sometimes peculiar, notions of life's evolution. Charles Lyell's uniformitarian idea laid the foundation of Darwin's theory by arguing that the change-making geological forces that operated in the long-distant past were still at work in the present. Darwin's own grandfather, Erasmus Darwin, anticipated several of his grandson's central ideas, a debt barely acknowledged by the younger Darwin. Then there was Jean-Baptiste Lamarck's goofy notion that "spontaneous generation" and a "nervous fluid" produced new species that could then pass their newly acquired traits along to future generations through inheritance. Then a trio of British natural historians repudiated Lamarck's theory but Darwin conveniently managed to ignore their work while clinging for a while to the idea that learned behavior could be inherited. Carl Linnaeus, who became famous for his scientific system of classifying plants and animals, did so partly to identify their place in God's creation plan. Much earlier, medieval Christian philosophers drew on the older thoughts of Aristotle and Plato to explain the "essence" of plants and animals, while justifying the idea of a Godly creation that started it all. Darwin did not so much stand on the shoulders of this motley crew of evolutionary speculators—he was influenced by both Lyell and Lamarck—as he simply rejected their views and created a new platform of his own making (Darlington 1959).

Darwin's evolutionary "tardiness" is due entirely to his concentration on the evolution of *organic life*, a big enough challenge for anyone. He and his many successors who later formed the evolutionary synthesis, plus others who produced competing theories of evolution's beginning and its mechanisms of change, focused exclusively on the emergence of *organic* life. They all sought to explain the factors that produce new organic species, the evolutionary processes at work throughout the entire world of organic creatures, and various observational manifestations of natural selection appearing in the organic world. That's all to the good and has produced mountains of scientifically confirmed knowledge of how Darwin's original ideas have worked well from the beginning of organic life to its present (perhaps imperiled) status.

However, it's time to put Darwin and his ideas in historical and theoretical context: *organic evolution is not the whole story*. Part of the story, yes, though possibly not even the main theme. Evolution embraces far more natural phenomena than just organic life. Evolution is much older, possibly more powerful, and more far-reaching even than Darwin's big stick of natural selection. So, it's not Darwin, the person, who is late. It's his subject: *organic* evolution. Evolution, in a more fundamental sense, far antedates the appearance and evolution of organic life.[4]

---

4 Details aside, scientists now identify four types of evolution: basic elements, minerals, chemical compounds, and organisms. Darwin deals only with organisms. Thermodynamic evolution, as described in the Big E chapter, encompasses all four. Lima-de-Faria's pioneering concept of the earlier phases of astrophysical evolution is found in his *Evolution without Selection: Form and Function by Autoevolution* (1988). Technical accounts of element evolution and mineral-chemical evolution are in Sterner and Elser (2002) *Ecological Stoichiometry: The Biology of Elements from Molecules to the Biosphere* and Williams and Frausto da Silva (2006) *The Chemistry of Evolution: The Development of Our Ecosystem*.

Recall from Chapter 1, "The Big E ≈ Energy," that thermodynamic (energy) evolution is as old (and as early) as one can get in this Universe. Thermodynamic evolution began simultaneously with the Big Bang, producing in turn the initial rush of radiation, the creation of rudimentary particles and elements, the eventual appearance of stars and galaxies, and from stellar furnaces came the formation of inorganic compounds spewed outward to seed other stars, planets, and chemical brews holding the possibility of life (Fox 1988: Chapter 1). It was only then—11 billion years after the Big Bang—that biological evolution appeared on Earth. In all that time, thermodynamic (energy) evolution was doing its thing— driving all forms of energy from high gradients to lower levels—doing its best to attain a state of energy equilibrium or entropy. In other words, thermodynamic evolution has been actively present throughout all time and is ubiquitous in today's Universe. You can't say that about organic life, which is an obvious youngster by comparison, and possibly rare.

Nor can it be claimed that life itself is essential for the operation and continuation of the more basic, more widespread thermodynamic (energy) evolution. From Chapter 2, "The Big L ≈ Life," recall Arto Annila's observation that organic life was a fortuitous "coupling of external energy . . . susceptible for natural selection to operate on it . . . to diminish the difference by energy transduction (flow)." "Life is a consequence of increasing entropy, the quest to diminish free energy with no demarcation between inanimate and animate" (Annila and Annila 2008: 299, 297). In other words, thermodynamic evolution was not dependent on the presence of organic life or Darwin's kind of evolution. The same is true for the interdependent, collective ecosystem networks that sustain organic life. Ecosystems are a consequential form of thermodynamic (energy) evolution—derivative and secondary, not primal.

As Eric Schneider and Dorion Sagan, authors of *Into the Cool*, say, "Natural selection is the centerpiece of Darwinian thought. When selection is put under the lens of thermodynamics . . . selection is framed in terms of increasing energy flow . . . Selective advantage will go to those . . . systems that best increase energy flow through their system, those that do so better than competitors . . . Natural selection favors systems adept at managing thermodynamic flows" (Schneider and Sagan 2005: 254, 256).

In these ways, Darwinian evolution takes on a new meaning, and Darwin steps back from center stage in the evolutionary drama. The conclusions are unavoidable:

- Darwin's concept of organic evolution is a function, an outcome, an expression of the much earlier and still active thermodynamic (energy) evolution

- Thermodynamic (energy) evolution initiates and generates Darwinian-evolution-by-natural-election, including the diverse forms and functions of organic life

- Darwin's evolution is an avatar—a literal organic incarnation—of thermodynamic (energy) evolution. Darwinian evolution serves thermodynamic evolution's constant search for energy transduction (flow) mechanisms. Darwin's evolution is just another "arrow of time" in thermodynamic evolution's quiver, aimed always in the direction of entropy

Darwin and Natural Corporate Management

No sooner do we have an answer, admittedly abbreviated, to this chapter's opening question—Who is Charles Darwin?—than another one, even more compelling, arises: Should corporate managers, those in charge of the business firm's goals, policies, decisions, and strategies, be on the lookout for Darwinian signals bubbling out of the minds and actions of the firm's workforce? If so, what should they do about them? Will, or can, Darwin be a help or a hindrance? Can Darwin impulses increase profits? Drive share prices up? Fend off competitors? In other words, how does knowledge of Darwin evolution help managers manage their company? Answering those questions is what **Natural Corporate Management** is about.

As noted earlier in this chapter, *everyone* in the firm's workforce—from top executives to the lowest employee rungs—is activated by inherited behavioral and attitudinal traits—and cannot do otherwise. They lie at the core of human (organic) nature. It matters not what culture, what race, what geographic locale, what age, what gender one is identified with, all act out the common heritage of humanity that bears a Darwin imprint. They can be expected to seek sustenance, sexual reproduction, and security first and foremost. They are prepared by evolution to be competitive, to seek personal advantage, and to be openly combative or slyly resistant to obstacles encountered. They will experience the victories or the defeats, the rewards or the penalties of a workplace open to natural selection pressures. The most adaptable ones survive to see another quarter. Some climb the corporate ladder, others find lower rungs, still others flee to more hospitable corporate climes. All of this is pure Darwinist behavioral legacy.

The history of management thought, and contemporary management research, are devoted to finding ways to corral, organize, and focus these Darwinian impulses to achieve the goals and purposes of the business firm. No single, and certainly no simple, answer has emerged, nor will one be found here. Darwin's major theoretical contribution was to put a label—natural selection—on the process that implants these basic impulses in organisms: slight variations accompanied by environmental interplay, giving a test of fitness or adaptability. The theory yields a set of behavioral constants and implanted motives that are essentially unchangeable during the life span of an organic (human) carrier, thereby placing severe limits on short-run alterations or modifications sometimes proposed by management theorists. As discussed earlier in this chapter, such changes are often sought in a corporation's culture in hopes of directing the company more rationally toward the goals it seeks. Derived largely from social science theories, few such management initiatives acknowledge the presence and influence of innate Darwinian workplace impulses, where the manager's hope is to override intractable innate behaviors deemed not favorable to corporate performance.

But Darwin's voice is increasingly being heard again, this time from scholars who draw their insights from the natural sciences: evolutionary biology, neuroscience, evolutionary psychology, molecular phylogenetics, and related fields. They represent the leading edge of what is called here **Natural Corporate Management**. Four such advances draw explicitly on Darwinian perspectives:

- Paul Lawrence and Nitin Nohria's *Driven: How Human Nature Shapes Our Choices* (2002) identifies four innate drives and skills that shape human choices, including decisions made in the workplace by both managers and employees—the drive to acquire, the drive to bond, the drive to learn, and the drive to defend—all four derived explicitly from Darwin's theory, as well as from neuroscience research. The authors propose that corporations can be better managed by greater awareness of the four drives' presence in the workplace

- Paul Lawrence's subsequent book, *Driven to Lead: Good, Bad, and Misguided Leadership* (2010), proposes that good corporate leadership seeks and finds a balance of all four innate drives, while bad or misguided leaders pick and choose among the four. Lawrence, one of the management field's long-time major scholars, demonstrates clearly that Darwin's ideas remain highly relevant for the work of today's corporate managers

- Taking a more expanded view of Darwinian evolution by incorporating neuroscience findings into his book, Paul Herr writes, in *Primal Management: Unraveling the Secrets of Human Nature to Drive High Performance* (2009), about the importance of emotions as motivators for all who work in the corporate world. The human brain houses five emotional appetites that must be satisfied if business managers and employees are to perform well in their jobs. These powerful Darwinian emotional impulses include a strong desire for cooperation, competence, skill-deployment, innovation, and self-protection. Feed these appetites, and the workplace hums with efficiency and effectiveness

- A still broader view that incorporates Darwin into an understanding of the entire market economy is *Nature: An Economic History* by Geerat J. Vermeij (2004), an ecology theorist. The author argues that human economic systems operate on the same principles and natural processes as ecosystems, including consumption, production, innovation, and organization. These key economic-ecosystem processes overlap significantly with the Darwin search for sustenance, reproduction, and shelter. As the book's title implies, studying nature is the way to understand modern economic systems that house business corporations. We explore the implications of Vermeij's insightful views in a later chapter

These four pace-setters represent the spearhead of natural science research and theory that reverses the more conventional outlook based on social science perspectives alone. Overriding or denying embedded Darwinian behavioral impulses is replaced by accepting their presence and using (or "managing") them to the corporation's advantage, an excellent illustration of **Natural Corporate Management** in action.[5]

However, in celebrating the growing recognition of Darwin-based behavioral impulses present within the corporation, management scholars should also be mindful that other, even more powerful evolutionary processes share that behavioral space in the business firm. In that way, Darwin evolution yields pride of place to energy evolution. The high-entropy-generating modern corporation, acting out its role as a prime energy transduction (flow) mechanism, is an awesome evolutionary phenomenon indeed. The fate of the corporation—its successful management—therefore rests as much with the physics of thermodynamic (energy) evolution as with the biology of Darwinian evolution. But keep your eye on both types of evolution as the **Evolutionary Cascade** flows onward. There is even more of the evolutionary story ahead.

. The Big D's pivotal points

- Charles Darwin's theory of evolution by natural selection says that: 1) all forms of organic life evolve from earlier ancestors; 2) evolutionary change occurs slowly over very long time periods as small modifications in organisms enable them to adapt more successfully to their environment; 3) new and more adaptable species replace older ones; and 4) natural selection is the process of winnowing out organisms least able, and favoring those most capable, to compete for sustenance, reproduction, and niche security

- By the mid-20th century, a Darwinian consensus, called the evolutionary synthesis, modified and extended the original theory of natural selection but did not change its basic tenets

---

5 An earlier example of **Natural Corporate Management** may be found in my book *Values, Nature, and Culture in the American Corporation* (Frederick 1995), and an extension of that book's major theme in my 2002 Ruffin Lecture, "The Evolutionary Firm and its Moral (Dis)Contents," in *Business, Science, and Ethics* (Frederick 2004). See also footnote 3, above, about the pioneering work of Nigel Nicholson, Roderick White, and Barbara Decker Pierce.

- Darwin's theory of natural selection explains the evolution of human organic behavior

- Darwin's theory also explains the behavior of business practitioners who, as individual human organisms, seek through their work to attain the Darwinian goals of sustenance, sexual reproduction, and niche security

- Darwin's theory cannot explain a *business firm's* behavior because the firm itself is not an organism but only a collectivity of human organisms who nevertheless respond individually to Darwinian impetus

- Organization theorists propose that learned behavior shaped by corporate culture can modify, focus, and direct workplace behavior toward desired corporate goals, thus modifying Darwinian inherited behavioral tendencies present in the workforce

- Darwin's theory of evolution is chronologically and functionally subservient to the older and more encompassing thermodynamic (energy) evolution

- Identifying and acknowledging the presence and relevance of Darwinian behavioral proclivities in the workplace enable corporate managers to direct their companies more effectively

The Big D's research base

Darwin evolution

Brown, A. (1999) *The Darwin Wars: The Scientific Battle for the Soul of Man* (London: Simon & Schuster).

Darlington, C.D. (1959) "The Origin of Darwinism," *Scientific American*, May 1959: 60-66.

Darwin, C. (1859) *The Origin of Species: By Means of Natural Selection or The Preservation of Favored Races in the Struggle for Life* (New York: Modern Library).

Darwin, C. (1871) *The Descent of Man: And Selection in Relation to Sex* (New York: A.L. Burt Publishers).

Eiseley, L.C. (1959) "Alfred Russel Wallace," *Scientific American*, February 1959: 70-84.

Futuyma, D.J. (2005) *Evolution* (Sunderland, MA: Sinauer Associates).

Mayr, E. (2000) "Darwin's Influence on Modern Thought," *Scientific American*, July 2000: 79-83.

Ruse, M. (2009) *The Evolution Wars: A Guide to the Debates* (Millerton, NY: Greyhouse Publishing, 2nd edn).

Other types of evolution

Annila, A., and E. Annila (2008) "Why Did Life Emerge?" *International Journal of Astrobiology* 7: 293-300.

Fox, R.F. (1988) *Energy and the Evolution of Life* (New York: W.H. Freeman).

Lima-de-Faria, A. (1988) *Evolution without Selection: Form and Function by Autoevolution* (Amsterdam: Elsevier).

Lima-de-Faria, A. (1995) *Biological Periodicity: Its Molecular Mechanism and Evolutionary Implications* (Greenwich, CN: JAI Press).

Schneider, E.D., and D. Sagan (2005) *Into the Cool: Energy Flows, Thermodynamics, and Life* (Chicago: University of Chicago Press).

Sterner, R.W., and J.J. Elser (2002) *Ecological Stoichiometry: The Biology of Elements from Molecules to the Biosphere* (Princeton, NJ: Princeton University Press).

Williams, R.J.P., and J.J.R. Frausto da Silva (2006) *The Chemistry of Evolution: The Development of Our Ecosystem* (Amsterdam: Elsevier).

Natural Corporate Management

Deal, T.E., and A.A. Kennedy (1982) *Corporate Cultures: The Rites and Rituals of Corporate Life* (Reading, MA: Addison-Wesley).

Frederick, W.C. (1995) *Values, Nature, and Culture in the American Corporation* (New York: Oxford University Press).

Frederick, W.C. (2004) "The Evolutionary Firm and Its Moral (Dis)Contents," *Business, Science, and Ethics* 4 (Ruffin Series of the Society for Business Ethics): 145-76.

Herr, P. (2009) *Primal Management: Unraveling the Secrets of Human Nature to Drive High Performance* (New York: American Management Association).

Lawrence, P. (2010) *Driven to Lead: Good, Bad, and Misguided Leadership* (San Francisco: Jossey-Bass).

Lawrence, P., and N. Nohria (2002) *Driven: How Human Nature Shapes Our Choices* (San Francisco: Jossey-Bass).

Martin, J. (2002) *Organizational Culture: Mapping the Terrain* (Thousand Oaks, CA: Sage).

Nicholson, N. (1997) "Evolutionary Psychology and Organizational Behavior," in C.L. Cooper and S.E. Jackson (eds.), *Creating Tomorrow's Organizations* (New York: John Wiley & Sons).

Nicholson, N. (1998) "How Hardwired is Human Behavior?" *Harvard Business Review*, July–August 1998: 135-42.

Nicholson, N. (2000) *Executive Instinct: Managing the Human Animal in the Information Age* (New York: Crown Publishers).

Nicholson, N., and R. White (2006) "Darwinism—A New Paradigm for Organizational Behavior?" *Journal of Organizational Behavior* 27: 111-19.

Ridley, M. (2010) *The Rational Optimist: How Prosperity Evolves* (New York: Harper-Collins).

Vermeij, G.J. (2004) *Nature: An Economic History* (Princeton, NJ: Princeton University Press).

White, R., and B. Decker Pierce (1999) "The Evolution of Social Structure: Why Biology Matters," *Academy of Management Review* 24.4: 843-53.

4

The **Big G ≈ Gene**

The long reach of the gene knows no obvious boundaries.
Richard Dawkins

"Chocolate lovers of the world, unite! You have nothing to lose and everything to gain! A new and improved chocolate flavor is on the way! Appearing soon—well, in a few years—at your local sweets shop." The potentially good news came from Mars—no, not the planet nor any leftover revolutionary gang—but from a well-known American candy company. The Mars Corporation, joined by IBM Corporation and federal agriculture regulators, was telling the world in 2010 that the cacao tree—whose seeds yield chocolate—was about to let the entire world in on the secret of how it makes chocolate and what might be done to improve the quality of that ever-so-sweet flavor. And how? By mapping all of the genes—the entire genome—of the cacao tree. A similar effort by rival Hershey chocolate company was also under way.

Just down the street, so to speak, another U.S. corporation, AquaBounty, was expecting approval by the U.S. Food and Drug Administration of its genetically engineered salmon. By inserting DNA segments from a larger salmon into the well-known Atlantic salmon, the newer version (called the AquAdvantage® salmon) grows twice as fast, thereby increasing the farmed "catch" along with the company's profits. Modifying the genomes of other food sources—rice, corn, soybeans, pigs, sugar beets—greatly increases the world's food stocks for a rapidly expanding human population.

Yet another business locale where genes may be active is in workplace violence, especially between Darwinian-entwined sexual partners acting out the quest for sustenance, sex, and security. One-fifth of full-time employees in the U.S. are victims of direct or indirect aggression by spouses or domestic partners. Three-quarters of those abused or harassed say it happens on the job. Two-thirds report it affects the quality and quantity of their workplace productivity. It happens in all business sectors, taking a big toll on national economic productivity, not to speak of costs and safety risks for all employees. Is it possible that human genes are somehow complicit in such violent, aggressive behavior? Just how genes might be a causal factor in workplace violence has become a major focus of recent research into human behavior (Cluss *et al.* 2010: B-1, B-4).

This chapter probes these and other intriguing gene-related opportunities and questions confronting today's corporate managers.

Darwin meets Mendel's ghost

Genes—the organic drivers of Darwinian biological evolution—have been around for over 3.7 billion years, but they were discovered and named only a little over a century ago. Darwin had an intuitive hunch they were present and were involved in natural selection, but they eluded his grasp. One of Darwin's contemporaries—an Austrian monk who doubled as a natural historian—came even closer to ripping the cover off these strange entities that seemed responsible for the inheritance of parental traits.

Augustinian monk Gregor Mendel was well educated in the sciences of his day and when not attending to monastic duties, he made meticulous studies of . . . yes, peas! From so humble a beginning, Mendel traced the peas' inherited traits: color and shape of the peas, their pods and flowers, whether the plants were short or tall, and how these varied from crop to crop. It is not recorded whether Mendel's fellow monks shared his appetite for peas, but one thing became apparent to this monasterial pea detective: parental plants passed their traits along to the next year's crop in a definite pattern that caused some traits to be dominant while others were "laid back" (or "recessive," as scientists now say) although they could reappear the following year in lesser numbers. Something—some quality ingrained inside the pea organism, some rule—had to be causing this inheritance pattern to evolve as the generations rolled on. Some traits survived, others dropped aside. If that sounds a bit like Darwinian natural selection, you are on the right track.

In the ways of science, Mendel shared his findings with fellow scientists by publishing the results of his research in 1866, just five years before Darwin published *his* second book, *The Descent of Man.* Alas, Mendel's report was ignored by nearly everyone and was forgotten until several years after his death in 1884 (Darwin had died two years before then). Without knowing it, Mendel had laid the foundations of modern genetics, which subsequently expanded and enriched Darwin's theory of natural selection. Another irony: Darwin did not know of Mendel's research, nor was Mendel aware of Darwin's work. One wonders what might have been the outcome if these two creative thinkers had met and exchanged their equally fertile ideas. But it was to be only a ghostly reunion, hosted by others, after both were dead.

So, what *are* these elusive genes, what do they do, and how do they do it? Here are the basics you need to understand what all the fuss is about. Warning: It's highly chemical in nature.

- Genes are DNA: <u>d</u>eoxyribo<u>n</u>ucleic <u>a</u>cid. That's right, an acid, a chemical substance, which resides in the cells of all plants and animals, yours included. Sounds simple enough until you realize all of its potentials. It's what genes can do that's important

- A single gene is a short segment of DNA that activates or controls one or more traits of an organism

- In doing so, genes may act singly or in concert with other genes

- Genes are an organism's hereditary mechanism (the one that Darwin and Mendel sought, in vain) that determines an organism's size, form, function, life cycle, and behavioral characteristics—all inherited from parental stock

- A new organism created by sexual reproduction inherits half of its genes from one parent and half from the other parent. The two halves are joined together as a double helix, which is a spiral or coiled form like a corkscrew

- Genetic function involves the interactions of various chemical components within the cell—exotically called chromosomes, RNA, nucleotides, amino acids, proteins, and enzymes. Combined in an intricate process, they spell out the types of organic traits that are to be passed along from parent to offspring. In simpler words, genes make bodies which then house them

- Genes are long-lived and stable, promoting an organism's survival (usually)

- However, an organism's genes do change (called mutations) partly in response to changes in the organism's environment, thus adapting the organism to the new conditions. Population geneticists also identify genetic changes that are independent of natural selection pressures in the environment: random mutations, genetic drift over time, and the genetic intermixture that can occur as different populations merge (Klug and Cummings 2005: 532)

Technicalities aside (which are not needed for our purposes), that is what the gene is and does. It is a prime agent of organic evolution, actually generating, activating, and (literally) animating the emergence of new or modified organisms while stabilizing the lives of existing organisms. It sets the patterns of life found in all living creatures. It is the hereditary material passed from parent to offspring that sustains a continuity of life through time. It is the missing key sought by both Darwin and Mendel.

As this chapter's discussion continues, it might be helpful to add a few terms often encountered in the gene world:

Genome. The complete set of genes in an organism. The human genome has around 20,000 to 25,000 genes

Genotype. The genetic makeup of an organism or of a population with a common genetic trait

Phenotype. An organism's physical body or structure as determined by its genes

Gene expression. Carrying out a gene's function

Double helix. The two intertwined strands of DNA and associated chemicals, which takes the classic spiral shape or form of DNA. This chapter's icon depicts the double helix.

Now it is time to move onward from the scientific technicalities to pursue this chapter's key question: What do genes have to do with corporate management? In seeking the answer, keep in mind that we are dealing with the fourth phase—the **Big G ≈ Gene**—of the **Evolutionary Cascade** that flows directly toward and into the operations of the modern business corporation. Remember also that each cascade level exerts an influence on all succeeding levels. That means that the gene is an expression of energy evolution, life in ecosystems, and Darwinian evolution—and will then pass its own unique impacts along to the other cascade levels. The **Evolutionary Cascade** is an entangled, yet orderly, pathway toward **Natural Corporate Management**.

Darwin meets the selfish gene

In the mid-1970s, an articulate young Oxford University Lecturer, Richard Dawkins, startled the world's scientific community by suggesting that Darwin had not told the entire story of evolution by natural selection. The Darwin master had left out a—or perhaps *the*—key that unlocks a hidden evolutionary code. The missing key was what Dawkins famously called the "selfish gene." The genes in each of the billions of organisms found throughout the Earth have one central, overriding function: to perpetuate themselves, not just today, not just tomorrow, not just next year but forever and ever. This overriding function—to replicate themselves endlessly and thereby to preserve their own existence from one generation to the next generation through all time—is the genes' central role in evolution. It was indeed the key to the inner workings of natural selection that had eluded Mendel and Darwin. By functioning solely and exclusively to preserve themselves in perpetuity—to survive in the best Darwinian tradition of natural selection—genes exemplify self-centeredness on the grandest, if not perhaps the most admirable, scale.

Dawkins' own vivid, riveting language conveys his astonishing central message:

> One way of sorting this whole matter out is to use the terms "replicator" and "vehicle". The fundamental units of natural selection, the basic things that survive or fail to survive, that form lineages of identical copies with occasional random mutations, are called replicators. DNA molecules are replicators. They generally . . . gang together into large communal survival machines or "vehicles". The vehicles that we know best are individual bodies like our own. A body, then, is not a replicator; it is a vehicle. Vehicles don't replicate themselves; they work to propagate their replicators. Replicators don't behave, don't perceive the world, don't catch prey or run away from predators; they make vehicles that do all those things (Dawkins 2006: 254).

The gene (the "replicator")—not the organism's physical body (the "vehicle")—is responsible for, and the driver of, evolution. Move over, Charles Darwin. Dawkins says that the key to natural selection is genes, not bodies. Recall from the Big L ≈ Life chapter that natural selection is a process of *weaving adaptive behaviors into* an organism that lives in an ecosystem. From the Big D ≈ Darwin chapter, we learn that natural selection is *a weeding out of maladaptive traits* that hinder the organism's survival. Dawkins' response is, Yes, but such organic adaptations are a function of an underlying and more basic *genetic* process. An organism's genes are the ultimate decider of an organism's fate, its life path, its behavior, its life cycle. Simply put, the gene is the *active organic agent* of Darwinian evolution by natural selection.

And this gene driver is forever. According to Dawkins: ". . . the gene . . . does not grow senile; it is no more likely to die when it is a million years old than when it is only a hundred. It leaps from body to body down the generations, manipulating body after body in its own way and for its own ends, abandoning a succession of mortal bodies before they sink in senility and death. The genes are the immortals . . . [and] have an expectation of life that must be measured not in decades but in thousands and millions of years" (Dawkins 2006: 34).

Let's be clear about that "immortality" claim for genes. What is passed from generation to generation is particular sets of DNA molecules that translate into specific bodily traits and functions. DNA by itself is only a chemical substance, an acid capable of being transformed into an active agent inside an organism's body. The genetic *function* of DNA—what it *does*—is Dawkins' "immortal coil." A newborn organism comes with its *own* particular set of genes, which are not identical to the parents' individual DNA molecules but are only a combination of parental genomes. Some traits will be the same, others not, so some variation from the parents' DNA is unavoidable. Gene "immortality" is more about what adaptive effect the genes have on body and behavior than about the DNA itself which varies generationally. The gene outlives any specific organism when it is sexually reproduced or otherwise transmitted generationally.

Look for both variability and stability in gene evolution. Long-term genetic continuity produces immense stability within whole ecosystems, even in the presence of much organic diversity. On one hand, genes are the cement of ecosystem viability, continuity, and resistance to change. However, genes themselves undergo change over long time periods as a result of mutations, occasional DNA copying errors, genetic drift, migration, and various natural-selection environmental forces. In these ways, new species—new organic "vehicles" housing new combinations of "replicator" genes—do emerge from large populations, as Darwin had said long before the gene was discovered. It took Dawkins to show how.

In an intriguing echo of what was encountered in the Big E ≈ Energy chapter, Dawkins goes on to say that ". . . the individual body, so familiar to us on our planet, did not have to exist. The only kind of entity that has to exist in order for life to arise, anywhere in the universe, is the immortal replicator" (Dawkins 2006: 266). That sounds eerily like something said in Chapter 1 by physicist Arto Annila that life itself is not needed for thermodynamic (energy) evolution to proceed apace. Could the biologist and the physicist be finding common ground in elucidating evolution's pathways? Perhaps they are, so stay tuned for the answer that emerges in chapters to come, for it is critical for an understanding of the modern corporation's operations.

Does the selfish gene apply to the business firm?

A similar question was posed in the previous chapter: whether evolution by natural selection shapes corporate actions and policies. The answer there was, No, because the corporation is not an organism but a culturally sanctioned legal entity, possessing none of the vital organic survival traits of naturally evolved organisms and their ecosystems. The same answer can be given for the selfish gene and the business firm. Companies have no genes of any kind—selfish or otherwise—because firms are not composed of cellular organisms where DNA resides. However, while there is no *corporate* or organizational DNA, the firm does house a large collection of human organisms, each of whom displays a wide suite of DNA-derived behaviors and attitudes—all exquisitely attuned to promote the survival of their respective individual carriers. This need not mean that either the corporation or its employee population is "selfish"—it says only that the firm's human constituents are survival-oriented. Self-centered, yes; selfish, not necessarily. *The genes are the selfish components*, not necessarily the human bodies that carry them around in the workplace.

Does that let all parties off the hook of promoting selfishness in the marketplace, including owners, executives, and employees? Not at all! The multiple, diverse genetic agendas of survival that are operative in the workplace—housed collectively within the firm's legalistic shelter—can, and have repeatedly in past and present years, combined to exert devastating, ruinous impacts on the lives of individuals, their communities, and their life-sustaining ecosystems. Catastrophic instances abound: the BP Deepwater Horizon explosion in the Gulf of Mexico that contaminated coastal and deep sea areas and impacted coastal economies negatively; and the release of toxic wastes by a Hungarian aluminum company which poisoned one of Europe's major rivers, the Danube. Did either firm consciously seek such an outcome—was it "selfish" in that sense? There is little or no evidence that either firm actively promoted such a goal. The consequences in both cases were costly and hardly conducive to the firms' own survival. Well, was it the fault of the firm's workplace population—a case of collective guilt or selfishness on a corporate scale, stemming from their respective personal urges to survive in a Darwinian sense? To conclude such would be another stretch beyond the meaning and function of organic evolution. Worker carelessness, incompetence, lack of focus, managerial ineptitude or inattention, and lax regulatory oversight are perhaps part of the answer but they have nothing to do with selfishness per se. The conclusion is as unavoidable as it is astonishing: *there is no one to blame if we seek to lay the selfishness and guilt on an organic body or even a collectivity of organic bodies!* According to Dawkins, *the genes in* those bodies are the guilty party; they are the literal embodiment of genetic self-centeredness. Genes tell bodies what to do. Genotype dictates phenotype. Case closed. Or is it?

Truth to tell, Dawkins has played a rhetorical trick on his readers. The gene is simply an organism's plan of life interlocked within an ecosystem, nothing more. It is a survival mechanism, neither consciously "selfish" nor purposely "immortal." To be "selfish" is to be consciously aware and deliberately purposive in pursuing a self-interested goal. Genotypes are neither conscious nor purposive, as Richard Dawkins admits; only phenotypes (bodies) act purposively and deliberately, even though their genes may propel them, though mindlessly, in such pathways. Charles Darwin was right, after all: each form of organic life is focused on its own preservation within the opportunities and bounds made possible by—but not exceeding—its genetic potentials.

Genotypes, phenotypes, and cognotypes

Something seems to be missing from this line of reasoning. Admittedly, it makes evolutionary sense, given the respective functions of both organisms and genes. But Dawkins himself was not completely satisfied that the gene told the entire story, saying rather remarkably that "Darwinism is too big a theory to be confined to the narrow context of the genes." In the final chapter of *The Selfish Gene*'s first edition, the author hedged his genetic bets by toying with the idea of the gene's cultural twin, which he labeled the "meme" (rhymes with gene). A meme, he said, was any item of *learned, acquired* human behavior that could be passed from one person to another by imitation, paralleling the way genes are transported by heredity from parent to offspring (see also Blackmore 1999). Such meme transfers were said to take place via the human brain. Dawkins acknowledged the seeming parallel to be completely analogical, not confirmed by scientific research as was true of gene information. He even went so far as to say in a later edition of the book that "our brains are separate and independent enough from our genes to rebel against them" (Dawkins 2006: 332). What are we to make of this? Are selfish genes then to be replaced by selfish memes? Are we shifting from biological determinism to cultural determinism?

This puzzle of evolutionary precedence needn't be explored in detail here, although there will be a return engagement in a later chapter when we encounter the **Big B** ≈ **Brain**. For now, a simpler three-step solution clarifies the distinctions, as well as the links, between hereditary organic traits and culturally learned traits.

- Darwin's theory explains the evolution of **phenotypes**—organic bodies such as our own

- Dawkins' selfish gene theory explains the evolution of **genotypes**, i.e., the genes that live inside an organism's cells and are housed in phenotypes

- Brain research explains the evolution of **cognotypes**—the human brain's complex neural system that makes learning possible. A cognotype generates behavior, attitudes, and beliefs that reinforce (and sometimes counteract) the survival impulses of phenotypes and genotypes. Do not mistake cognotype with the now-questionable idea of the brain as a blank slate on which culturally learned instructions are written; the human brain is a thoroughly natural phenomenon evolved independently of cultural influence. The substantive meaning and functions of a cognotype are further clarified in the next two chapters on the evolutionary emergence of the *Homo* genus and particularly the brain of *Homo sapiens*[1]

As Dawkins' meme concept implies, these three evolutionary entities—phenotype, genotype, and cognotype—are simultaneously linked while also distinct from one another in a swirling, giddy, whirlwind dance of evolutionary change. We'll rejoin the ball in later chapters.

---

1 The term "cognotype" is offered here as an original coinage, although I would not be at all surprised to learn of its earlier usage by others. For a variety of reasons, I believe cognotype is a more accurate and research-based concept than Dawkins' meme concept. Cognotype is derived obviously from cognition, meaning the ability to know, perceive, understand, and recognize aspects of the pragmatic, empirical, factual world. More is said about the cognotype in a later chapter on the human brain.

Darwin meets the competitive gene

The selfish gene story doesn't end with Dawkins. It gets only more complicated—and even begins to sound a bit more familiar and business-like in its ramifications for corporate behavior. Genes *compete with each other for dominance within an organism's genome*. It's not quite a genetic marketplace, but it tends to act that way.

Many of these competitions are described by two leading biologists, Austin Burt and Robert Trivers (the latter famous for his concept of reciprocal altruism, to be discussed in the next section of this chapter). Unlike Dawkins, they claim that genes in conflict with one another are so selfish that they often work *against*—not in favor of—an organism's survival interests. That is selfishness carried to an extreme and potentially fatal outcome for both genotype and phenotype. How can this be?

". . . selfish genetic elements [are] stretches of DNA . . . that act narrowly to advance their own interests—in other words, replication—at the expense of the larger organism . . . [Although] most genes are cooperative . . . some genes have discovered ways to spread and persist without contributing to organismal fitness . . . [and] are diametrically opposed to those of the majority of genes . . . Selfish genes appear to evolve because they benefit themselves directly, with all other unlinked genes in the individual harmed or (at best) unaffected" (Burt and Trivers 2006: 2, 3, 16, 448).

Gene competition and the genomic conflicts it causes occur mainly as parental genes are passed to offspring during the childbirth process and early-stage child development, thereby affecting a wide range of behaviors, including: "in our own species . . . intense internal conflict over early development [of the young], and later internal conflict over juvenile and adult behavior . . . The unity of the organism is . . . undermined by these continuously emerging selfish elements with their alternative, narrowly self-benefiting means for boosting transmission to the next generation" (Burt and Trivers 2006: 475).

Citing many genetic conflicts and their ruinous effects, a trio of French biologists point to the genes' contradictory behavioral significance: "genome conflicts might explain some of the imperfect ways in which individuals function and even some of life's other contradictions" (Gouyon *et al.* 2002: 175). In other words, a person's genes can both help and hinder getting through life safely and securely.

Obviously, all is indeed not well in the genetic world, which displays a virtual warfare among self-directed genes. Unlike Dawkins' cool picture of genotype driving phenotype in ways beneficial to both, the actual sphere of genetic action can be disorderly, chaotic, dysfunctional, and potentially fatal. The evolutionary pilot drives rather like a drunk, threatening not only the driver but all others along the way.

This competitive/conflictual feature of genetic evolution may hint at, or be a harbinger of, great significance to corporate managers who daily cope with organizing workplace employees, securing a niche in competitive markets, and strategically achieving the firm's goals. If genetic competition and conflict are embedded deeply into the genomes of workplace employees, market competitors, and the managerial corps itself—as they surely must be—the stakes for the firm are unbelievably high, in fact, little short of its very survival. An illustrative example is the high incidence of workplace violence between reproductive partners, mentioned at the beginning of this chapter (Cluss *et al.* 2010: B-1). These and other such managerial challenges are revisited at later stages of the on-flowing **Evolutionary Cascade**, specifically in the **Big O** ≈ **Organization**, the **Big M** ≈ **Market**, and the **Big C** ≈ **Corporation**, where the positive and negative effects of competition and conflict are examined more closely.

Darwin meets the collaborative gene

Rivalry and selfishness do not entirely dominate the genetic landscape because genes also have a tendency to produce life-supportive cooperative behaviors in their phenotypic carriers. In other words, genes underwrite the ability of organisms—humans and other species as well—to live in socially cohesive ways. We encountered several of these adaptive patterns in the Big L ≈ Life chapter: symbiotic linkages and mutualisms that tend to lace together the organic diversity found in ecosystems, generating comprehensive adaptive webs and networks to support a wide range of organic life.

Darwinian natural selection has apparently generated two forms of genetic collaboration that are of particular significance for *Homo sapiens*, although other species also enjoy such adaptive consequences in varying degrees. "Kin selection" and "reciprocal altruism" are the labels given to these collaborative gene-based behaviors. Both give a big adaptive lift to human life, although perils lurk in the background of each.

Kin selection

Genetic kinship, established through reproductive sex, can and usually does generate life-supportive behavior toward parental offspring and other relatives (Hamilton 1964). It is called kin selection because children—bearing half of each parent's DNA—are helped to survive natural selection pressures by receiving parental care and protection. Though supported by parental collaboration, kin selection is also consistent with Dawkins' selfish gene concept because it activates a strategy of parents' selfish genes to protect and extend their own respective DNAs which are passed along to their offspring. The offspring's DNA, composed of half the DNA from each parent, is not only *not* an exact copy of parental DNA but also experiences additional genetic variation that occurs during cell division in the embryo. That's why you are not an exact genetic clone of your parents but possess a distinctive set of genes of your very own.

The positive natural selection boost one gets from parental support occurs in each successive generation, so the adaptive kin benefit is repetitive, cumulative, and additive in the number of kin (phenotypes) involved. This life-supporting influence exhibits a historical genetic continuity beginning in the distant (ancestral) past with a founding parental pair. Today's newborn inherit their parents' DNA, who inherited *their* parents' genes, who did the same, and on and on through many parental generations, thereby exerting the cumulative effects of different, though related, sets of intertwined DNA sequences. This leads to extended family kinship categories: brothers, sisters, cousins, aunts, uncles, etc., displaying varying degrees of DNA kinship. In any extended family, the collaborative kin selection mechanism—the all-important protective genetic impulse—weakens as kinship closeness diminishes. This lessening of genetic impulsive behavior throughout an extended family clan may nevertheless sustain and strengthen a kinship identity and familial awareness across many generations—and even across wide areas of the Earth (Sykes 2001).

Reciprocal altruism

Another gene-driven, collaborative behavioral impulse can occur when an organism (human or otherwise) compromises, forgoes, or sacrifices its own evolutionary fitness (reproductive ability) by promoting, protecting, and securing the evolutionary fitness of one or more other organisms. Because it bestows a benefit on the recipient(s), such an act is a form of organic or biological altruism. In extending such an evolutionary advantage to another organism, the altruist usually expects to be treated similarly in some future encounter. Hence, the behavioral impulse is called "reciprocal altruism": a self-imposed fitness cost that conveys a fitness favor to another organism, followed later by a reciprocal response of similar evolutionary significance (Trivers 1971).

Such a risky collaborative transaction is not just an expansion of Darwinian evolution by natural selection but is also consistent with Dawkins' selfish gene. The reciprocal setup is only another selfish-gene strategy of evolutionary survival by acquiring a future fitness favor by imposing on oneself a present fitness cost. The collaboration benefits both altruist and receiver of the altruistic act, as would be expected of a selfish-gene behavioral impulse as each participant gains a benefit for itself. Thus, reciprocal altruism can be seen as a strictly gene-based, dyadic, behavioral inclination, operative without reference to conscious, learned behavioral conventions or group interactions and intentions.

However, there is a broader issue to face: Is gene-driven reciprocal altruism also activated by learned—not inherited—cultural habits and traditions? Unlike kin selection where close relatives extend gene-based, life-supportive aid to one another, reciprocal altruism can occur among non-kin, provided there is continuing contact between the altruist and the recipient of the altruistic act which permits a subsequent reciprocation that balances out the long-run benefits and costs to both participants.

Such conditions were likely to have been present in ancient, small hunter-gatherer groups, clans, and close-knit or isolated tribal villages. Contemporary game theorists present evidence that a similar type of behavioral reciprocity rule operates in present-day exchanges between humans—and must have evolved from ancestral times. The operative exchange rule is fairness or balance in exchanges, especially among strangers and especially if continuing contact is uncertain. Exchange partners who break the reciprocity rule and gain from another's loss are considered to be rule-breaking cheaters subject to punishment. Since this "strong reciprocity" cheater-detection rule has been found cross-culturally, it can be interpreted as a behavioral outcome of evolutionary natural selection, made possible by the human brain's ability to calculate and balance exchange costs and benefits (Henrich *et al.* 2005: 795-855). Carried further, it may well be the natural basis of social contracts and market exchanges (Frederick and Wasieleski 2002; Wasieleski 2008: 1,777-79). All of this seems to imply that non-kin reciprocal altruism is not only gene-based—a behavioral derivative of collaborative genetic impulse— but also has a basis in culturally learned behavior, i.e., that both "nature" and "nurture" activate the collaborative acts (Hammerstein 2003). So, we enter a blurred zone between gene and culture, nature and nurture, hopefully to be clarified in the chapters that follow.

The answers will be powerfully significant for corporations and their managers who seek not just to excel in competitive markets, but also to find cooperative, collaborative pathways toward economic success.

Darwin meets the horizontal gene

You might well ask: What in the world is a "horizontal" gene? Well, it's a plain ordinary gene, sometimes just pieces of them, or even an organism's entire genome, which is transferred from one organism to another in a non-Darwinian way. Darwin's mode of passing genes along from one generation to the next is the familiar sexual reproduction that halves the parents' DNA going to the offspring. The new organism then *inherits* its features from its parents, who had inherited their traits from their parents, who did the same from their parents, and on and on from one generation to another. Looking backward in time through this line of inheritance is like envisioning a *vertical* lineup of one's parents, grandparents, great grandparents, etc., each one above the other, with the oldest ones at the top—a ladder of successive generations. As Mendel and Darwin had proposed, the inherited characteristics are passed *down* this generational ladder from one's older relatives until they reach the present generation on the ladder's bottom rung. In classic Darwinian theory, it is all accomplished through sexual reproduction.

By contrast, *horizontal* gene transfer (HGT) occurs in an entirely different way—actually in numerous and often strange ways. Also called "*lateral* gene transfer," genes move *sideways* or *horizontally* from one organism to another—and right away, without waiting for the next generation. Even more remarkably, it need not involve a parent-and-offspring link at all, nor does the gene's sideways movement require sexual reproduction (Sapp 2005). Strange, indeed. What's going on, and how can this happen? It's certainly not what Darwin had in mind. Besides, is it actually something that today's corporate managers really need to know? You bet it is.

Horizontal gene transfer occurs primarily in the bacterial world, among the world's tiniest and most primal organisms. They have had several billion years to evolve this manner of moving genes around. In one sense, it is Darwinian at least in spirit because it helps bacteria to survive and has obviously proved itself a wildly successful technique for adapting to their surroundings. One needs to place the world's bacterial groups into a perspective that can reveal their overwhelming significance for life on Earth. Bacteria are estimated to number in the billions or trillions. Taken together, their collective biomass far outweighs all other forms of life combined. They occupy literally all parts of our planet: land, sea, air, including the bodies of all living creatures. They are responsible for the existence and quality of the Earth's breathable oxygen atmosphere. They help regulate the planet's surface temperature. Bacteria are the principal source of organic diversity which underlies and sustains the world's ecosystems—the basis of all life as described in Chapter 2, "The Big L $\approx$ Life." For all these reasons, what bacteria do, how they do it, and how they affect their own and other organisms' lives—but particularly how they pass their traits along to others by gene transfer—can hold the key to continued life as we know it. Darwinian evolution by natural selection pales by comparison with horizontal gene transfer's pace and frequency of evolutionary transformation.

The repertoire of the traveling horizontal genes is truly amazing as they move from one organic body to another. Listen to one authority, Lynn Margulis, whose original research on symbiogenesis charted new directions for evolutionary change some 30 to 40 years ago: "How are whole new genomes acquired by any organism? Predator bacteria engulf their prey. Other actively feeding bacteria produce . . . adhesive materials. Still other bacteria are gobbled up by [simpler organisms]. These behaviors lead to *acquisition, attachment,* and sometimes to *fusion* [of genomes] ... Organisms also gain new hereditary traits by *accumulation of viruses,* or of *plasmids* or other *short pieces of DNA.* They acquire long pieces of DNA, many genes at once, by *bacterial mating* and by legitimate *sexual mating with distant relatives*—that is, by *hybridization* ... Attraction, merger, fusion, incorporation, cohabitation, recombination ... are the main sources [of horizontal gene transfer]" (Margulis and Sagan 2002: 74, 75, 205, emphasis added).

Yet another phylogenetics expert, Jan Sapp, testifies that "the fundamental conception of [Darwinian] evolution itself ... is contradicted by evidence that most genes are transferred laterally" (Sapp 2009: 317). Margulis and Sagan sum it up: "Microbes have uniquely capable complete genomes. *They, not selfish genes, or combative male mammals, are the motors of evolutionary change*" (Margulis and Sagan 2002, 87, emphasis added). Take that, Richard Dawkins and Charles Darwin! You are being told that the bacterial world operates by a different set of evolutionary rules than the rest of the organic world. This threatens to turn Darwin's widely accepted theory of evolution by natural selection on its head. Or less dramatically, it introduces a more complex picture of how organic evolution proceeds. Both ways are important.

This abstruse scientific research delivers two practical messages to modern corporate management: opportunities abound; dangers lurk.

- Horizontal genetic changes of far-reaching significance to corporations, especially companies in the healthcare business, can occur rapidly and produce unexpected results, both positive and negative. Because bacterial lives and generations are very short, their horizontal gene transfers can create nearly instantaneous results such as a new bacterial gene resistant to antibiotic medicines. One such gene, labeled a "superbug" which caused health havoc in India, threatened to spread to other countries through "medical tourism" as foreigners sought less expensive medical treatments there. One expert said, "You take very common bacteria that live in all of us and can travel from person to person, and you introduce into it (through HGT) some of the nastiest antibiotic-resistance mechanisms there are." Another said, "It's an acute example of how bacteria can outwit people" (Stein 2010: A-3). Pharmaceutical corporations, an enormous industrial empire, devote large research budgets to such medical dilemmas, many of them a result of short-term horizontal gene transfers among bacteria

- Recombinant genetic engineering, which mimics the natural process of lateral gene transfer, is producing countless opportunities for economic gain by corporations. The engineered salmon and the search for the genetic secrets of the "chocolate tree" mentioned at the beginning of this chapter demonstrate the economic potentials of imitating nature's way of shifting genes around (Naik 2010: A1; Yang 2010: A-2). Another is an unexpected positive "halo effect" from planting corn that has been genetically modified to fight off the deadly corn borer pest. The genetically inserted insecticidal proteins spread their benefits to adjacent corn fields not yet treated—a dividend from the microbial world of gene transfer, worth around $1 billion per year.

Corporate managers, take note. Remember Chapter 2's central message: "Heed life!"? Well, genes—especially those tiny microbes with all the tricks of horizontal gene transfer—are saying the same thing: "Ignore us at your corporation's peril! There's [corporate] gold in 'them thar hills'."

The energetics of gene evolution

The portrait of the gene painted by scientific research and theory can easily leave one in doubt about the gene's true nature and character. Portraitist Rembrandt, a master of artistic character portrayal, would not be satisfied nor would others, including scientist Darwin. Is the gene essentially selfish? Competitive? Collaborative? Inherited long-term? Acquired short-term? All of the above? Some but not others? What is one to make of this fractious scientific portrait?

A possible solution—a way to unify and reconcile the clashing hues and patterns on this contemporary genetic canvas—may well be within reach. Each brush stroke, however inconsistent and contradictory of others, can be harmonized with the whole—and in ways pleasing to a recognized master, whether the Dutch Rembrandt or the English Darwin. The unifying theme is an old friend: Energy.

The gene, like all organic agents, is responsive to energy flows, particularly those that carry energy toward an entropic equilibrium, as described in Chapter 1, "The Big E ≈ Energy." The physicist Arto Annila and colleagues propose that the genome is such a thermodynamic system that performs precisely that kind of energy flow. In fact, the gene was probably brought into existence by continuing inflows of solar energy that set up energy gradients: "The external energy provides the potential gradient that is consumed in raising the concentrations of complex entities, such as genes, beyond those at equilibrium ... They exist due to their functional properties that contribute to the consumption of free energy in the quest for stationary state [entropy] in their surroundings" (Jaakkola *et al.* 2008: 233). So, the master artist of the genetic canvas is none other than the gene itself—it's a self-portrait of the artist busily reducing energy gradients in the direction of entropy.

The energy-processing talent of the gene is centered in a cell's mitochondria, which are small but powerful components within an organic cell's nucleus. These tiny energy factories generate all the energy needed to continue the cell's life. Interestingly, mitochondria possess a set of genes that are different from the cell's main genome, suggesting what scientists now agree was an ancient horizontal joining-together of genes (HGT) from two different primitive organisms. Hence, from early on, the main business of the mitochondrian gene has been energy production generated by biochemical processing of sunlight (free energy) flowing in from the Sun (Allen and Cowling 2011: 6-8, 24-26; Lewis 2012: 25). The positive result supports not just cellular life but entire organic ecosystems, as described in Chapter 2, "The Big L ≈ Life."

This conclusion that genes are central participants in energy evolution stemming from the Big Bang may allow each of the diverse patterns woven into the genetic painting to harmonize the gene's seemingly fractionated portraiture. Here's how.

The *selfish* gene—as an energy transduction mechanism—is favored by energy evolution for its ability to reduce energy gradients on into the far-distant future. The *competitive* gene is a hyped-up version of the selfish gene, fighting fiercely to promote its own competitive place, regardless of any negative impacts on its host phenotype. As a very efficient energy transformer, the competitive gene also promotes maximum entropic equilibrium, even though in doing so it may jeopardize its own existence by being excessively competitive. The *collaborative* gene is yet another potentially more powerful genetic way of pushing incoming solar energy from higher to lower levels, as it recruits fellow genes to join together in cooperative schemes that require and consume even greater stores of free energy inflows than do individual, isolated efforts. Examples are families and close-knit clans that become powerful, dominant collaborators (remember the Godfather!) controlling huge energy accumulations in the form of monetary wealth. The *horizontal* gene may be the superior energy transformer of all by producing results quickly and over widespread areas, gobbling up the needed energy in small but potent amounts. And the horizontals have been around far longer than other gene types, affecting far greater numbers of organisms, which is testimony to their talents in taking in energy and moving it toward entropy. All four types of genetic activity—selfish, competitive, collaborative, and horizontal— are little more than expressions of a far more ancient and more encompassing evolutionary force: the Big Bang's continuing explosive spread of energy into all corners of the Universe. It turns out that the gene is little more than an avatar—an organic manifestation—of energy evolution. So in the end, it is indeed an "Old (very old) Master" who created the gene's portrait—none other than the Big Bang itself.[2]

2 There is no necessary, direct, one-on-one causal relationship between the actions of genes (as selfish, competitive, and collaborative) and parallel behavioral traits observed in members of the *Homo* genus. Although genes are self-centered and they sometimes compete and/or cooperate *with one another*, these gene-level actions may or may not be translated into similar kinds of human behavior. *Homo sapiens* is not simply a genetic automaton responding directly and automatically to genetic signals. This is presumably what Dawkins meant when he said (above) that "Darwinism is too big a theory to be confined to the narrow context of the genes" and that "our brains are separate and independent enough from our genes to rebel against them." In other words, you can't use the excuse, "My genes made me do it" to justify all aspects of your behavior. The human cognotype, as manifested in today's *Homo* brain, when combined with human neuro-organic culture, can indeed reinforce but also can override, modify, or even cancel a range of genetic effects passed from previous generational sources to later ones. Just how this DNA–brain interaction occurs is explained in the following two chapters.

Natural Corporate Management and the gene

Two questions about the gene's place in corporate affairs are worth asking: Can the gene be "managed"? And can the gene be modified for corporate purposes? The answer to the first query is almost certainly, "No," while curiously, the second question can perhaps be given a "Maybe" response. Let's take them one at a time.

If "managing the gene" were to mean eliminating or reversing its basic cellular organic functions—protein production, transcription, translation, sequencing, coding, energy processing, cell division, replication, reproduction, etc.—the answer is clearly negative, given the present state of scientific knowledge. Nor is there any particular reason for attempting to do so inasmuch as genetic activity is the essential basis of all organic life on Earth in all of its manifestations, from tiny microbes to global ecosystems and, indeed, in all realms of Earth's biosphere. Plant, animal, and bacterial population size alone, not to speak of genetic diversity worldwide, render any such attempts doubtful, foolish, and a form of pseudoscientific fantasy. Count on it: the gene is here to stay.

It is a bit like asking yourself: Can volcanoes be "managed"? Typhoons? Earthquakes? Plate tectonics? Oceanic temperatures? Hurricanes? Droughts? Sunspots? Cosmic rays? Of course not, and why? These are among the most powerful planetary forces in existence, each one an expression of the energetics of our Earth and of large-scale astrophysical forces at work beyond our planet. They existed long before life itself or the gene put in an appearance on Earth—and certainly before *Homo sapiens* came along, posing such outlandish questions while wishing occasionally for a positive answer. Again, don't expect these intractable natural events to go away anytime soon.

Well, then, what about the less grandiose prospect of modifying the gene for human and corporate purposes? Will genetic tinkering work, tweaking the genome here and there, giving corporations a leg up in the natural world? Now you're talking about something real and reachable—and why not? Recombinant DNA technology—another name for genetic engineering—has already carved out a place in several fields of human endeavor including cloning techniques (remember Dolly, the first cloned sheep?), pest-resistant wheat, soybean, and corn varieties, fatter pigs, greater milk production, and other genetically tweaked plants and animals, along with new pharmaceuticals that detect and control diseases—a virtual bonanza of corporate opportunities. Recall also the Mars Corporation's and Hershey's plans to map the complete genome of the cacao tree, as a way to enhance its productivity of the chocolate-yielding bean. Or AquaBounty's genetically engineered salmon that grows faster and gets to market quicker. Such a burgeoning genetic frontier creates many challenges—and not just a few risks—to confront the alert, informed corporate manager. Grasping the genetic nature of those opportunities—and especially their evolutionary origins and limitations—is a key element of **Natural Corporate Management** to be explored further in the following chapters.

The Big G's pivotal points

- Genes, whose technical scientific name is deoxyribonucleic acid (DNA), are the cellular components that create, activate, and direct the shape, behavior, and life functions of an organism. As such, the gene is a prime agent of organic evolution

- The gene was undiscovered and unknown to Gregor Mendel and Charles Darwin and therefore was not part of Darwin's theory of evolution by natural selection

- The evolutionary function of selfish genes is to perpetuate themselves by creating and activating successive life plans of the organisms whose cells they inhabit

- Selfish genes cannot explain the operations of non-organic business firms that have no cellular genes, although individual members of the firm's collective human (organic) workforce are capable of being behaviorally influenced to some extent by their own respective selfish genes

- Some genes are competitive, generating conflict and negative effects in the formation and functioning of organisms. Conflictual genes may exert serious long-run impacts on ecosystems and the lives and health of workplace populations

- Collaborative interactions among some genes can produce cooperative group behaviors such as kin selection and reciprocal altruism

- Horizontal gene transfer between bacterial microbes is a significantly different way of acquiring organic genomes than by Darwinian inheritance of parental genes

- Genes are effective energy transduction mechanisms using and driving solar energy inflows toward entropy

- While the gene, the genome, and the genotype cannot be wholly transformed or "managed" by human actions, it is possible to modify some genetic effects and functions. The reciprocal interplay of gene and the business corporation grants limited power to each

The Big G's research base

Allen, T., and G. Cowling (2011) *The Cell: A Very Short Introduction* (New York: Oxford University Press).

Anholt, R.R.H., and T.F.C. Mackay (2010) *Principles of Behavioral Genetics* (Amsterdam: Elsevier).

Blackmore, S. (1999) *The Meme Machine* (New York: Oxford University Press).

Burt, A., and R. Trivers (2006) *Genes in Conflict: The Biology of Selfish Genetic Elements* (Cambridge, MA: Harvard University Press).

Cluss, P., J. Hill-Finegan and G. Peaslee (2010) "Employers vs. Partner Violence," *Pittsburgh Post-Gazette*, September 19, 2010: B-1, B-4.

Dawkins, R. (1982) *The Extended Phenotype: The Long Reach of the Gene* (New York: Oxford University Press, 1999).

Dawkins, R. (2006) *The Selfish Gene* (Oxford, UK: Oxford University Press, 30th anniversary edition).

Frederick, W.C., and D.M. Wasieleski (2002) "Evolutionary Social Contracts," *Business and Society Review* 107.3: 283-308.

Gouyon, P.-H., J.-P. Henry and J. Arnould (2002) *Gene Avatars: The Neo-Darwinian Theory of Evolution* (New York: Kluwer/Plenum Publishers, original publication: *Les avatars du gène: La théorie néodarwinienne de l'évolution*, 1997, Berlin: Editions).

Hamilton, W.D. (1964) "The Genetical Evolution of Social Behavior," *Journal of Theoretical Behavior* 7: 1-52.

Hammerstein, P. (ed.) (2003) *The Genetic and Cultural Evolution of Cooperation* (Cambridge, MA: MIT Press).

Henrich, J., R. Boyd, S. Bowles, C. Camerer, E. Fehr, H. Gintis, R. McElreath, M. Alvard, A. Barr, J. Ensminger, N. Smith Henrich, K. Hill, F. Gil-White, M. Gurven, F.W. Marlowe, J.Q. Patton and D. Tracer (2005) " 'Economic Man' in Cross-Cultural Perspective: Behavioral Experiments in 15 Small-Scale Societies," *Behavioral and Brain Sciences* 28: 795-855.

Jaakkola, S., S. El-Showk and A. Annila (2008) "The Driving Force behind Genomic Diversity," *Biophysical Chemistry* 134: 232-38.

Klug, W.S., and M.R. Cummings (2005) *Essentials of Genetics* (Upper Saddle River, NJ: Pearson Prentice Hall, 5th edn).

Lewis, R. (2012) *Human Genetics: Concepts and Applications* (New York: McGraw-Hill, 10th edn).

Margulis, L., and D. Sagan (2002) *Acquiring Genomes: A Theory of the Origin of Species* (New York: Basic Books).

Naik, G. (2010) "Gene-Altered Fish Close to Approval," *Wall Street Journal*, September 21, 2010: A1ff.

Ridley, M. (1999) *Genome: The Autobiography of a Species in 23 Chapters* (New York: HarperCollins).

Sapp, J. (ed.) (2005) *Microbial Phylogeny and Evolution: Concepts and Controversies* (New York: Oxford University Press).

Sapp, J. (2009) *The New Foundations of Evolution: On the Tree of Life* (New York: Oxford University Press).

Stein, R. (2010) " 'Superbug' Problem Small but has Potential to Become Larger," *The Washington Post*, reprinted in *Pittsburgh Post-Gazette*, October 13, 2010: A-3.

Sykes, B. (2001) *The Seven Daughters of Eve: The Science that Reveals Our Genetic Ancestry* (New York: W.W. Norton).

Trivers, R.L. (1971) "The Evolution of Reciprocal Altruism," *Quarterly Review of Biology* 46: 35-57.

Wasieleski, D.M. (2008) "Reciprocal Altruism," in R.W. Kolb (ed.), *Encyclopedia of Business Ethics and Society* (Vol. 4; Thousand Oaks, CA: Sage): 1,777-79.

Yang, J.L. (2010) "With DNA of Chocolate Nearly Decoded, Could Sweeter Treats Be Ahead?" *Washington Post*, reprinted in *Pittsburgh Post-Gazette*, September 19, 2010: A-2.

5

The **Big H** ≈ *Homo*

Homo. A human being. The genus to which human beings and
certain of their fossil ancestors belong.
Oxford English Dictionary[1]

In the vast, ancient evolutionary panorama of life on Earth, where do
humans fit in? They are, after all, a form of organic Life, and they dwell in
life-sustaining ecosystems. They are adept at acquiring, using, and even
creating new forms of Energy: hence, a model of thermodynamic evolution. They have passed the rigorous tests of Darwin's natural selection to
populate the global biosphere with billions of their own kind. Their genes
have propelled them forward in time—molding and directing their bodies, minds, and behaviors into adaptive channels. They seem to have met
all of the demands placed upon them by an evolving naturosphere—at
least, thus far.

---

1 *Homo*, derived from Latin, is the standard scientific term designating the
   human genus, usually followed by the name of a specific species, e.g., *Homo
   sapiens* or sometimes abbreviated as *H. sapiens.*

So *who* are they? *Where* did they come from? And *when*? *What* was novel about them? *How* did they live? And perhaps of even greater interest, *why* did they appear at all? Answers to these who-where-when-what-how-why questions are explored in this chapter, drawing on contemporary understandings based in scientific research and grounded theory.

In doing so, we shall heed, while going beyond, that ancient Greek aphorism—Know thyself—to reveal behavioral realms of central importance for the successful management of today's business corporations. Anticipate finding in these realms of antiquity the evolutionary source of such modern business traits as competitive drive, sparkling innovative technology, entrepreneurial initiative, near-term strategic perspective, and a pragmatic get-it-done-now attitude. The **Evolutionary Cascade** flows onward, revealing the basal traits of human—and business—behavior.

The *Homo* profile: Who, when, where?

Homo showed up a *long* time ago, emerging gradually from even earlier ancestral beginnings. There was no magical moment or year or century when one could say, "Humans are here now but weren't around yesterday." That's the nature of evolution: a long, slow process of change and modification, with each form of life derived from earlier organically related forms, carrying most but not all of the ancestors' traits. That also means the newest evolved bunch of humans needn't look or act exactly like Grandpa either.[2] Here is the story of *Homo*'s appearance on Earth.

Pre-*Homo*: *Australopithecus*

We could—but won't—begin looking for the first human ancestors 45 million years ago. That's when the tiny "dawn monkey," *Eosimias* (about the size of your thumb) lived. It stood at the branching point of the primate order that eventually led to modern *Homo*. Competing claims have been made for the very earliest human-like beings dating to some 6 or 7 million years ago. However, we'll skip ahead to more "recent" times, say,

---

2 If you've never heard the country song, "I'm My Own Grandpa," you've missed a musical gem with evolutionary implications.

just 4.5 million years ago; that's when *Homo*'s great-great-great[(X)] grand-parents bowed in. They didn't look much like us but had some of the key features—a partially erect posture and human-like teeth—that would carry through into modern times, allowing us to claim a distant kinship with them. They were the *Australopithecus* genus, meaning "southern ape" because they were found in South Africa (also in East Africa). All in all, they were apelike in behavior, living mostly in trees, not (much) like your Uncle Joe or cousin Bob (although it's true that the Australopith brain *was* only half the size of today's average human brain, so draw your own familial kinship conclusions). Stop and think about that date for a moment: 4.5 *million* years ago. Sounds rather old until you recall from Chapter 2 that life on Earth originated 3.75 *billion* years ago. Obviously, it took *Homo*'s even oldest ancestors quite a while to show up—but, as the saying goes, better late than never.

Organic nature being what it is and how it evolves, the Australopiths branched out into several different species—at least five in all, plus a couple or three closely related cousinly varieties. They lived their lives in the African jungles over an immense span of two and a half million years. Let that longevity sink into your consciousness. It had to mean they were enormously successful adapters to their respective ecosystems. They met Darwin's challenges by being naturally selected for continued life. Their diets enabled them to gain the energy needed to overcome the ever-present entropic trend toward extinction, and their reproductive practices produced generational growth and development. Their genes directed them in life-sustaining ways. From this hardy stock of ancient Australopiths—apelike creatures of the African jungles—the entire *Homo* genus was to evolve until it produced modern human beings: ourselves. But even that evolutionary eventuality was to consume yet another 2 million years, producing still more organic variety in the form of varying *Homo* species and sub-species along the way. It was, as one expert said, "not a single, linear transformation of one species into another but rather a meandering, multifaceted evolution" (Tattersall 2000: 60).

Homo: The human genus

That meandering evolutionary pathway is nowhere better illustrated than by the appearance of the *Homo* brand of humanity. Among the certainties agreed on by most experts, the timeline is reasonably secure: by around

2 or 2.5 million years ago, a new, more humanlike creature shows up in the fossil record. Compared with apelike ancestors, it has a somewhat larger brain, a more-or-less upright stance, a skeletal and muscular framework much like those you see today when you work out in your local health club. These physical traits, particularly brain size, continued to develop and expand over another 2-million-year era, leaving far behind their ancestral forebears.

Paleoanthropologists—popularly known as fossil hunters—are a quarrelsome, though dedicated, lot. Their differing interpretations of the evidence they dig out of ancient sites range from furious to downright mean-spirited. They all want to be the one who finds the oldest, the first, the most convincing sign of early *Homo* types. It's a bit like a NASCAR race with every driver speeding toward the finish line, as described vividly by science writer Ann Gibbons in *The First Human: The Race to Discover Our Earliest Ancestors*, written by a hands-on evolution expert who has visited the main sites where the very earliest fossil finds were made (Gibbons 2006). So, competitive professionalism is partly responsible for lack of agreement on the finer details of the search for *Homo*'s first appearance. Perhaps more important, though, is the continuing search undertaken by each new generation of specialists who, often armed with better equipment, more efficient ways of analyzing evidence dug out of the ground, and a wider geographic area to search, can and do indeed discover what eluded earlier fossil hunters. In spite of such argumentative differences—some good, some not so helpful—there is broad agreement on the overall pattern of human evolution. Here is the way it looks.

Consistent with Darwin's natural selection process, and driven by genetic mutations, several *Homo* species evolved from the earlier world of the Australopiths—and lived for surprisingly long periods (Klein 2009: 280). By comparison, *Homo sapiens*—modern humans—are not just youngsters but have a long way to go to out-survive our ancient *Homo* ancestors. Starting with the oldest ones, here is the lineup.

- *Homo rudolfensis*   ~ 2 million years ago
- *Homo habilis*   ~ 2 million years ago
- *Homo ergaster*   ~ 1.5 million years ago
- *Homo heidelbergensis*   ~ 1 million years ago

- *Homo erectus*   ~ 0.5 million years ago

- *Homo neanderthalensis*   ~ 0.25 million years ago

- *Homo sapiens*   ~ 0.1 million years

Their technical scientific labels and precise dates are less important than their changing bodily and behavioral traits, which presumably carried them through extremely long periods of survival within habitats not easily traveled. The emergent *Homo* evolutionary markers were body type, bipedal gait, increasing brain size, and stone tools that made possible a more carnivorous diet that slowly replaced their predecessors' preference for vegetation. More is said about each of these evolutionary advances in following paragraphs.

Intriguingly, it is quite probable that several of these species—*Homo* and pre-*Homo* alike—coexisted, as attested by Ian Tattersall's haunting phrase, "Once we were not alone" (Tattersall 2000). There is little doubt that Neanderthals lived for thousands of years in proximity to modern *Homo sapiens* in the Middle East as well as in Europe, even apparently interbreeding to some extent (Gibbons 2010: 680-84). Tattersall, one of the world's leading paleoanthropologists, puts the matter of coexistence among *Homo* species neatly: "Over the past five million years, new hominid [pre-*Homo* as well as *Homo*] species have regularly emerged, competed, coexisted, colonized new environments and succeeded—or failed" (Tattersall 2000: 61). We shall then have to explain, or conjecture, just why only one species among the 20 or more hominid types has managed to outlast all the others who, after all, survived far longer—1 to 2 million years on average—than modern *Homo sapiens*'s rather puny longevity record, which is far less than half a million years so far.

With the *Who?* and *When?* questions now answered on the basis of the best expert knowledge available, it's time to move on to the question of *Where?* Experts are generally agreed that *Homo*'s original home was Africa, in the far south and along the famous Rift Valley in the east and quite possibly well over into north-central Africa. The Australopiths had also occupied those same areas, thereby lending additional credence to the long-distance kinship link of these two kinds of hominid life. Geneticist Rebecca Cann sums up the dominant view: "Africa has apparently acted as a source population throughout the history of our species, where humans achieved high rates of reproductive success that allowed them to expand and fill an abundance of ecological niches, even those held for millions of years by other numerically abundant taxa [groups] such as apes and monkeys" (Cann 2001: 1,744). It should not be overlooked, however, that other well-qualified specialists argue the case for more widespread multiregional origins of *Homo* (Thorne and Wolpoff 1992: 76-83)—a controversy we shall forgo here in favor of the more currently accepted belief in the Out-of-Africa hypothesis.[3]

The Long Trek

It might well have been called the Long Trek—long in distance covered and in time to complete the journey to distant lands. It began in the deepest, most remote southern parts of the African continent until it reached the Great Rift Valley stretching along vast regions of the eastern part of that continent, and then the walk veered up and into the central northern areas of this primeval block of land that had been positioned by eons of continental drifting. Once the African gateway was opened, most probably in the uppermost northeast corner, *Homo* spilled out and moved onward until reaching unimaginably faraway places in the vast regions of Asia—central, eastern, southern—pushing onward, now southeasterly even across forbidding oceanic barriers onto the nearby archipelagos and eventually into yet another continent, Australia.

Trek indeed: getting there meant *walking*, over endless plains, across rugged mountains, through riverine valleys carved out over the millennia, skirting arid deserts, finding ways to cross wide rivers or to circle around big lakes, always on the lookout for edible game and vegetation while avoiding new and unknown predators—all of this amidst an ever-changing physical environment filled with volcanic eruptions, mountain building, splitting of earth into rift zones, furious storms of sand, wind, rain, snow and ice, monstrous floods and monsoons, tornadic furies, blazing forests and plains. Think of it: no GPS, map, or prior history as guides; no wheeled vehicles, no pack animals—nothing but pure human muscle

3 Fossil hunters in Asia have found 38-million-year-old remains of a small monkey-like creature that closely match similar proto-monkey fossils discovered living in Africa at a later time, raising the possibility that Asia, not Africa, was indeed the original home of human ancestors (*Pittsburgh Post-Gazette* 2012: A-2). For a comprehensive update, see Bower 2012b.

power, aided of course by those Darwinian evolutionary gifts: the grasping hand and an erect posture enabling the needed long strides.

The distances marched are almost unthinkable. From South Africa up to the northeastern African "gateway": 5,000 miles. From that gateway far over to Southeast Asia: another 5,000 miles plus yet 2,000 additional miles to enter Australia. To attain central Asia (today's China) from the African gateway consumed 5,000 miles, and to far northern Asia (Russia and Mongolia), a 7,000-mile pathway. The European trip was shorter, "only" 5,000 miles to the far western edge (today's United Kingdom), although if the Straits of Gibraltar gateway was used, it was a "day trip" of just 2,000 miles. And then the much later adventures from northern Asia into the Americas were even longer, 12,000 miles to South America while only 4,000 miles to coastal North America and beyond.

Obviously, no single individual or tribal group covered such long-distance ground, because migrant groups were small-scale, their movements gradual and limited by the surrounding terrain, climate forces, and findable food sources. We are speaking here of population movements that occurred over millions of years—a long walk if ever there was one. Think of it more as a slow-motion Olympic-style relay race as one species handed the baton to another close kin successively over vast stretches of time and area, moving along the ever-extended evolutionary chain of life. The Australopithecines—*anamensis, africanus, afarensis*—hardy inhabitants of South and East Africa—carried the torch during the 4-million to 2.5-million-year era, handing it off to the early *Homo*s: *habilis, rudolfensis, ergaster* for a half-million-year run, who in turn welcomed the outstretched hands belonging to new teams of *Homo* kin: *erectus, heidelbergensis, neanderthalensis,* and finally *Homo sapiens* who was left to seek the finish line, if indeed there was to be one. But of course the race goes on, the prize going to the species most able to secure an ecological niche, to measure up to Darwin's natural selection criteria, to inherit a genome that drives toward its own unlimited life, and a body and mind possessed of an energetics process that holds life-ending entropy at bay.

One wonders, why did they do it? Why make the journey? Why not stay home?

These questions and their answers may seem to you to be pretty remote from today's corporate managers which is what this book is about—and that's understandable. But keep in mind that we are talking here about the earliest formation of what would later become today's business behavior—the life, the motives, the personalities, and the skills of people who today own businesses, manage them, work in them as employees, and buy their products and services. Business managers—and all the rest of us—are uniquely identified as the most recently evolved members of the *Homo* genus. Knowing their background and how they got here gives you a great heads-up on how they behave today.

The *Homo* profile

There has long been—since the very beginning of organic life on Earth—a close interplay of organism and environment, which together make up what we now call ecosystems. From such a surround of chemical compounds, the earliest life forms managed to soak up and process enough energy flowing in from the Sun to sustain themselves over repeated life cycles. From there, as told in a previous chapter, more complex cellular components evolved into multicelled organisms even more efficient at energy acquisition. The entire life process has been one long story of organism–environment interaction. Natural selection is nothing but an adaptive form of that interactive process. Genomes (an entire set of genes) living within phenotypes (physical bodies) are highly sensitive to both positive and negative ecosystem forces.

Why then expect anything different in the case of *Homo* creaturely life? Their physical bodies are witness to the marvels of natural selection: larger brains than their forebears; more flexible hands adaptive for multiple uses; extended leg and foot bones enabling upright posture and bipedal walking; teeth and jaws capable of masticating both meat and vegetation; a bulging skull positioned to house a complex brain atop an erect posture; bifocal vision and keen hearing to discern and interpret the plethora of sights and sounds emerging from the flora and fauna in which they lived; a digestive system adaptable for carnivory and herbivory; testes, ovaries, and gender characteristics enabling reproduction of successive generations; skins and hair coverings suitable for varying climates—every single one of these physical traits a heritage from earlier beings and times. All were to drive forward this rather unique newcomer onto the Earthly stage of life, a result of natural selection that simply expresses the intertwined forces of organism and environment, nothing more needed beyond an elaboration of each.

How *Homo* evolved and survived

Key evolutionary strides converted early *Homo* types into what was to become the recognizably unique being we are today, scientifically labeled *Homo sapiens sapiens*.[4] Each step of the way to modernity was taken on and over the backs of our progenitors who had discovered how to travel in these ways long before *Homo sapiens* showed up on the evolutionary horizon. Taken together, these new behaviors became the basal infrastructure of an evolving organic human culture. This is *how* they did it.

Tools and tool use

Tool-making and tool use were once believed to be the singular marker of human beings; "man, the tool-maker" was a popular phrase to proclaim this evolutionary truth (Oakley 1961). However, deeper digging (literally) into the past revealed a different, far more sophisticated plot of *Homo* development. Tools remain today as testament to a skill indispensable for an extended life. However, tools appeared in nature long, long before our kind and were wielded by all kinds of creatures in all kinds of ways for all kinds of purposes. Keep firmly in mind an important chronological perspective: other animals do not display humanlike tool use; it's the other way around: humans came late to the practice so we seem to mimic the tool traditions and practices of our many organic predecessors. *We* adopted (and adapted) *their* tool traits, not they ours.

But first, let's be clear about what we mean by a "tool." It's not so simple as talking about everyday items such as hammers or kitchen knives. Tools in an evolutionary sense need to be seen in relation to the organic users who employ them. Think of tools as a kind of extended aid to natural actions taken by their user. They multiply an organism's muscular power,

4 Literally, "man the wise" but also conveying the notion of knowing and understanding. An anthropology professor of mine, Gilbert McAllister, often smirked cynically in referring to modern humans as "wise."

as hammers and knives assuredly do, and can enhance other senses as well as cognitive awareness and performance. Tools are external to organic bodies though in service to those bodies' organic functions. Put another way, they are behavioral aids, promoting practices not otherwise attainable. The array of things tools can do is astonishing, particularly when one thinks of their earliest adoption by our ancestors: cut, carve, dig, break, scrape, hit, puncture, pierce, drill, hook, grind, saw, whittle, crush, crack, tear, reach, pull, push, propel, repel, stretch, probe, reshape, join, reinforce, strengthen, expand, extend, retrieve, elevate, press—add any more you might think of. Tools are capable of rechanneling or repurposing the original forms of inorganic (stone) and organic (wood, bone, sinew) materials, turning them toward new and different uses. Even more fascinating is that tools are nothing more nor less than simple extensions of natural processes in service to their users—just another form or manifestation of organic life serving the Darwinian triad: sustenance, sex, and security.

As with all things evolutionary, tools came along gradually. Our most closely related hominid cousin, the chimpanzee, displays "diverse and regionally varied repertoires of tool-using [and] tool-making" while "*Cebus* monkeys [a much more distant kin] are considered prolific tool users but exhibit no understanding of cause and effect, or of the difference between appropriate and inappropriate tools" (Ambrose 2001: 1,748). Note also how chimpanzee tools are more "nature-made" than "chimp-made": "Chimpanzees make and use several kinds of tools for extractive foraging, including leaf sponges, termite and ant fishing wands and probes, marrow picks, levers, pestles, stick brushes for honey extraction, leaf scoops, and hooked sticks to extend their reach. West African chimpanzees use wood and stone hammers and anvils for cracking nuts." And note the narrow gap between chimp and human stone tool use: "Repeated use produces shallow dimpled and pitted anvils and hammers *resembling those made by humans*. Sharp-edged stone chips (flakes) are occasionally produced *but are not used*", which means chimps did not quite cross the threshold into human technological culture. But even this primeval form of technology had a long history. It is probable that "the minimum level of technological capacity of hominids between 5 and 2.5 million years ago (Ma) was comparable to that of chimpanzees" (Ambrose 2001: 1,748-49).

The limiting factor of pre-*Homo* tool use was twofold: a hand shape and arm and wrist inflexibility not adapted for the making of stone tools, and a brain not sufficiently developed to cope with the skills and logic required to shape the stones and other materials for specific purposes. The line between "organic" or "natural" tools and deliberately shaped stone tools is indefinite but most authorities agree that the date was around 2.5 million years ago. That's when the African Australopithecines were active but also when early *Homo* types were emerging in the same areas. But drawing the line's locus in time is less important than understanding the enormous evolutionary advantage incurred by those ancient inventors who literally thrust into the hands of all succeeding *Homos* an unparalleled device that continues even today to support human life in ever-expanding ways.

The practical usefulness of these early stone tools is indicated by their longevity of over 2 million years, with only relatively minor modifications and improvements. Stone was supplemented by the use of bone, antler, wood, and ivory plus more perishable materials made of fibers, vines, and leaves. Beyond using stones (cores) to make other stone tools, their uses were many: hunting animals, digging tuberous roots, slitting and scraping the hides of animal prey, butchering, chopping and breaking bones (for marrow), cracking nuts, grinding wood and bone, cutting vegetation, and—perhaps as vital as any other—defending against predators who sought them for food or others of their kind or kin who competed for mates or who invaded clan territory. Perhaps the greatest advantage conveyed by a *Homo* tool tradition was the greater opening it created for adding meat to the human diet, which greatly increased the protein intake that is believed to have been a major influence in enlarging the human brain, which in turn supported even more tool improvements—a ratcheting effect. On that long trek outward toward far-flung lands, tools magnified manifold the potential food sources to sustain the *Homo* march: scavenging, hunting, digging, gathering, fishing.

Nor were some of these primitive denizens hesitant about eating their own kind. While not rife, cannibalistic practices have been documented from fossilized human bones and skulls, broken open and scraped for their nutritious contents, marrow and brain, as early as 700,000–800,000 years ago. Though most such ancient sites were in Europe and Africa, similar practices existed among the Anasazi Indians who lived in what is now the southwestern United States (Johanson and Edgar 1996: 93; Wilford 2000; White 2001); 15,000-year old skull-cups, made of the hollowed-out human brain case, were used by Indo-European warriors for sipping the blood of enemies and other tasty morsels, and some 19th-century oceanic island communities were known to make and use human skull-cups (Bhanoo 2011). Most will agree that's taking tool use to a pretty low level.

As these tool-wielding *Homos* picked and packed and hacked their way outward from ancestral territories, all ecosystem inhabitants in their path might well have been forewarned about this creaturely crawl moving toward them at a deliberate pace, armed to the teeth (literally) with extra-bodily tools and weapons, seemingly determined to claim a place for themselves.

Keep this early ancestral tool-use in mind as we explore in later chapters the importance of advanced technology for the success of the modern business corporation. In time, tools became one of the key features of a corporation's culture and its way of doing business.

Shelter and clothing

Our human ancestors, like most ecosystem inhabitants, spent the great majority of their lives in the open without constructed havens. Limestone caves proved useful if bears, reptiles, bats, and other occupants could be evicted and kept out. In this sense, *Homo* lagged far behind some ecosystem neighbors—ants, termites, bees—who erected elaborate, long-lasting nests, while birds, squirrels, apes, and others leaned toward annual, temporary shelters for sleeping, birthing, and protection. Donald Johanson reports that "our ancestors lived without building themselves shelters for most of our evolutionary history . . . only around 60,000 years ago does evidence for the construction of shelters become apparent (Johanson and Edgar 1996: 97), which translates into more than 2 million years of outdoor living.

Human clothing was even slower to appear, but for good reason: "early humans had no need for clothing during most of their evolutionary history. They occupied tropical and subtropical regions and, at least until *Homo ergaster* and *Homo erectus* appeared, probably had a healthy coat of body hair . . . The earliest hominid that is likely to have had attire is *Homo neanderthalensis*," although specific evidence does not appear until just around 25,000 years ago" (Johanson and Edgar 1996: 99). So, that left the chic salons of France, Italy, and other style centers ample time to create their sought-after fashionable designs for today's big *Homo* events.

Fire

Of all the formative features of an evolving organic *Homo* culture, fire and its control for human purposes was certainly at the forefront, equally important to tool use. But it too came along surprisingly late, i.e., more recently. Here again, the scientific authorities split up into warring camps, some saying fire pits and hearths appeared between 400,000 and 200,000 years ago, others testifying that "if you want hard evidence for fire in the form of stone hearths and clay ovens, you are in the last 250,000 years." Another paleoarcheologist group pushed use of controlled fire back to 1 million years ago (Bower 2012a: 18). Perhaps the leading expert is Richard Wrangham, author of *Catching Fire: How Cooking Made Us Human*, whose research leads him to conclude that pre-*Homo* Australopithecines had gained control of fire and began cooking tubers in East Africa around 1.9 million years ago (Wrangham 2009). The major gain was a more varied diet, especially cooked meats which nourished an expanding brain; but fire also helped repel predators and provided heat in cold climes. Holding that primeval torch ahead of them, ancestral humans marched steadily onward toward more promising—though not promised or guaranteed—lands.

Ancestral behavioral patterns and networks

Equally important to the *how* of *Homo* evolution were adaptive organized behaviors. A large range of modern contemporary organizations— economic, political, social—rely on behavioral infrastructures laid down long ago as *Homo* culture evolved.

Aggression—pure and simple physical force exerted by muscular strength, large size, big groups, and killing tools—was an absolute must for survival in ecosystems filled with both prey and predators (Lorenz 1967). This brutal and ultimately, or at least potentially, murderous trait has often been noted as a present-day holdover operative in various arenas of human interaction, including domestic family life, politics, religion, and symbolically in competitively driven corporations (Seabright 2004).

Reproductive success among *Homo* ancestors was assured by a sexual selection pattern featuring gender dimorphism (large males, small females) which resulted in male dominance, female nurturance, and extended offspring support. No less an authority than Charles Darwin, in *The Descent of Man: And Selection in Relation to Sex*, identified sexual selection as a central behavioral trait of *Homo sapiens* whereby females are attracted to males who display attractive physical or behavioral habits, inferring an ability to sustain the lives of offspring (Darwin 1874). Need one today do more than cast a casual glance around the neighborhood to confirm its contemporary presence?

Extended family, clans, and neighboring groups reflect as well as anything an organizational legacy inherited from preceding *Homo* species. These ancestral groups became the underlayer of human social life, the first stage beyond the nuclear family that initiated humans into the world of cooperative endeavor—an outcome of genetically driven organic functions beginning with reproduction but eventually expanding into group efforts to hunt, gather, scavenge, cultivate, and domesticate foodstuffs. The same cooperative behaviors can be seen in today's corporate workplaces.

Organizational infrastructures extending beyond kinship ties gave *Homo* evolution a further push toward modernity. Life-supporting *economic* practices morphed into long-distance exchanges, mediated by barter and eventually markets. Ever more complex *political* structures emerged taking the varied forms of clans and tribes, regional communities, empires, nations, states, and now inter-regional, international, and global linkages. Such foundation stones of modern society were laid down by our *Homo* ancestors and then built upon by succeeding generations—an evolutionary monument to their ingenuity exercised amidst previously described dramatic, disruptive ecosystem dynamics. Those same organizational patterns can be seen in action within business corporations, as explained in a later chapter.

Why *Homo* evolved and migrated

Why did *Homo* do it? Why make life more complicated, more complex, less manageable? Why migrate to unknown lands? Why increase the pace and scale of movement the longer the journey went on?

Part of the answer—perhaps the larger part—lay in ecosystem changes. Recall the longevity of *Homo* evolution: 2.5 million years from the earliest primitive human types to modern humans. That was a period of great geological upheaval in the *Homo* African heartlands: frequent volcanic eruptions, repeated earthquakes, crustal uplifts that built mountains and split the Earth's surface into deep valleys and wide plains. Torrential rainfall over protracted time periods created new rivers, lakes, washouts, and floods. Long-run climate changes, both cooling and drying, thinned forests and created arid savannas that affected the types of animals and plants available for human consumption (Gibbons 2006: 63). While any given human group or population would not feel the totality of these ecosystem changes, their long-run impact, plus genetic mutations, would begin a process of natural selection pressures gradually modifying behaviors and generating new phenotypes moving in the direction of new *Homo* subspecies. "Experts have suggested that a series of wild global climate swings, which were especially intense about 250,000 years ago . . . forced hominid species to adapt or go extinct" (Balter 2002: 1,225). Even earlier, "The australopiths, the genus *Homo*, and *H. ergaster* . . . each may have evolved abruptly . . . sparked by global climatic change [but subsequently] . . . either niche expansion in *Homo* or climatic change may have extinguished the robust australopiths between 1.2 and 0.7 Ma. Climate change may be more likely." That left *Homo ergaster* as "the first hominin species to invade truly arid, highly seasonal environments" (Klein 2009: 727, 277).

So, why did *Homo* spread outward and onward? Population migrations in the natural world, after all, were not unique then nor are they unknown even in today's natural world. Think of those grandiose yearly migrations of African wildebeest hordes seeking new feeding grounds, or seasonal bird movements from cold to warmer climes, or the thousands-mile swims taken by whales to seek migrating food groups where breeding is more securely accomplished. There is a further history lesson even in the term "wildebeest," a label attached by the Dutch who were themselves migrators to the African continent, along with Belgians, Germans, French, British, and Italians as colonizers of new lands. The spread of Arabian medieval culture thrust deep into Europe, bringing new elements of civilization to these regions, until turned back by countervailing Christian forces. Then there was Genghis Khan and his "hordes" who rode and plundered from Asia to the very gates of an evolving Western society. Current migrations from the underdeveloped South to North, and from East to West continue apace. These more recent human migrations not only reflect an obvious socio-ethnic-economic search for jobs and living space, but they also rest firmly on underlying natural-ecological processes.

All of these massive organic flows of people and animals across wide expanses of an ever-shifting Earthly surface are normal and to be expected: *Homo* was no exception. The immediate drivers were (and are): ecosystem disruption, fluctuating climate, territorial competition, and the universal organic search for those three Darwinian behavioral goals: sustenance, sex, and security. As two experts say, "The driving force for this world-wide spread of modern *Homo sapiens* was probably a gradual increase in population numbers, leading to an outward press of hunter-gatherer territories, and a trickle of advance by a species whose adaptability was no longer measured solely by its potential for genetic and physical change. Where the climate was hostile, they could make clothes and build shelter. What their unaided bodies could not manage, their artifacts, tools, weapons, and collective action could achieve" (Andrews and Stringer 1993: 250). Even larger evolutionary forces were at work behind the immediate scene, which we shall revisit soon.

Homo's Big Bang

As the *Homo* genus continued to evolve, something big began happening between 70,000 and 40,000 years ago, a mere blink in the evolutionary time scale. Tools improved remarkably over cruder predecessors, both in workmanship and complexity, as well as in their application to a wider range of uses. Better-built structures and shelters, some made of large stones and wood, were erected as protection from climatic forces and predators. Stone hearths to support controlled fire began to appear, thus enabling greater consumption of meat and the digestive breakdown of vegetable matter in the *Homo* diet. In more northern climes, clothing made of animal hides put in an appearance. The larger game animals captured, killed, and eaten in ever-larger numbers implied a growth of social cooperation among close family and clan members. The materials used in making tools, shelters, and hearths often came from sites far distant from their place of manufacture, suggesting the presence of exchange networks between different human groups. Even more intriguing was the emergence of what we now call art objects having no obvious practical or instrumental use: small human (usually female) figurines carved from stone, bone, and ivory; wearable necklaces, bracelets, and anklets of shell, teeth, and bone; small objects carved with various geometric designs; human skeletal remains colored with ochre compounds; and the well-known cave paintings of animals commonly hunted by their artistic depicters, plus crudely rendered human figures sometimes armed with hunting weaponry.

Nothing like this sudden upsurge had occurred in the entire evolution of the *Homo* lineage through 2.5 million years. Behaviors, implements, objects, structures, pictorial depictions, and a range of implied group practices never before seen were now becoming commonplace. It should come as no surprise, although an illuminating revelation, that this was the very period when the modern human species, *Homo sapiens*, checked in as the leading and soon-to-be only surviving candidate of *Homo* evolution. The other surviving runners—*Homo erectus* and *Homo neanderthalensis*—were toast by about 25,000–30,000 years ago, pushed to the margins, out-competed, possibly victims of an ancient genocidal purge by the more "modern" *H. sapiens*, or simply overcome by disease or ecosystem disasters and climate change. As Richard Klein points out, "The advanced behavioral traits that blossom after 50 [thousand years ago] . . . provided the competitive advantage that allowed fully modern humans to replace their nonmodern contemporaries" (Klein 2009: 743).

Don't expect to find universal agreement among evolutionary experts about the timing and causes of this upwelling of innovative behaviors and practices. One pair says, "the real roots of modernity could be found long before 50,000 years ago [including] sophisticated stone- and bone-tool manufacture, advanced hunting and fishing skills, and well-developed exchange networks." Yet another pushed the dawn of art back to 77,000 years ago (Balter 2002: 1,223).

Mutations, partly gene-driven, partly in response to ecosystem natural selection pressures, are thought to account for the somewhat radical behavioral shifts. "What could explain this [behavioral acceleration] better than a neural change that promoted the extraordinary modern human ability to innovate?" (Klein 2009: 745). Others agree with this interpretation. "About 50,000 years ago, the human lineage underwent a genetic change that boosted the brain's cognitive powers . . . including language, abstract thought, and symbolic expression" (Balter 2002: 1,223); ". . . we are most sharply distinguished from other denizens of the living world by our behaviours, which are in turn underwritten by a unique cognitive system [and] we deconstruct and re-create the world around us via a mass of mental symbols" (Tattersall 2007: 22).

The new stimulative element was a brain that could lead human behavior beyond simple, immediate, tangible sensing or sense-making into innovative, imaginative, symbolic behavioral realms and thought patterns unknown or only weakly developed earlier. *Homo*, the tool maker, hunter-gatherer, long-distance traveler, invader of unknown lands, controller of fire, builder of shelters, breeder of offspring now moved at an ever-increasing pace toward becoming *Homo*, the innovative symbol user. The **Evolutionary Cascade** seems to have taken a step beyond phenotype and genotype by generating an expansive, creative cognotype (defined in the previous chapter) capable of behavioral feats previously unknown. Just how this newly evolved *Homo* cognotype works its wonders is the subject of the following chapter.

In looking forward, however, one should note Donald Johanson's cautionary reminder of the possible future: "we must understand that we are not the final product of 3 billion years of evolution on Earth" (Johanson and Edgar 1996: 112). That's another way of saying that the **Evolutionary Cascade** moves onward through time and space, with or without *Homo*.

Natural Corporate Management and the emergent business mind

The foundations of modern human behavior are to be found in our evolutionary past. There is no reason to believe that the behavior of corporate managers is an exception, particularly since hints of its presence linger from *Homo* evolution. While today's complex, worldwide, technologically advanced trade networks differ markedly in scale and geographic distribution from ancient practices, many of the evolutionary behavioral leftovers and attitudes honed during *Homo*'s long trek toward modernity stand out. These early behaviors were originally responsible for successfully negotiating the treacherous ecosystem pathways that carried humanity to its present economic state—no small accomplishment, indeed.

The more recently emergent business mind—the one that now is expected to lead giant corporations into innovative, highly productive, economically efficient channels—was born in a time and place where key traits and attitudes were needed if *Homo* was to survive at all. That ancestral Paleolithic mind exhibited all of the following behavioral traits, which were to reappear in the modern business mind. Whether ancient or modern, the *Homo* mind was and is:

- **Aggressive, combative, and competitive** (as noted earlier in this chapter) in its search for food within ecosystems rich with possibilities but filled with predators, both human and nonhuman, seeking their own survival needs. Recall that ecosystems are little more than food chains where the organic totality depends for survival on a reciprocal who-eats-whom system—a cafeteria of sorts where those at the chains' topmost positions tend to be first in line. Getting to that favored spot was mostly a matter of phenotypic and genotypic traits shaped by natural selection. Evolution had driven *Homo* far upward on the food-chain tower, where a fiercely competitive or even combative outlook sought to maintain the benefits conferred by nature and evolution. Now segue to modern times: Does this sound like anything going on in today's competitive markets? Perhaps an evolutionary leftover?

- **Pragmatically and purposefully focused** to solve whatever problems and challenges arose as threats to or opportunities for advancing the survival-sex-security agenda of oneself or close kin. Given the many uncertainties and unanticipated events within evolving ecosystems, the survival prizes went to those most attentive to the habits of one's organic neighbors, with an alert eye focused on possible dangers and unexpected threats. Few rewards went to the slow, the dimwitted, the laggardly, or those not focused on the immediate task at hand. And in our own time, ever hear the workplace refrain "Pay attention, do it right, get it done"? Same refrain now as then, isn't it?

- **Astigmatic, short-sighted, present-oriented** as a pressing requirement imposed by the immediacy of daily needs. Today's hunt is more important than tomorrow's uncertain search for prey. In modern times for a corporation: this quarter's rate of return is more important than longer-run uncertainties, right?

- **Dominant if possible, cooperative when advantageous**. Solitary control of one's search for sustenance and a secure niche often yielded to cooperative work routines. Killing, capturing, and butchering mega-size game animals or hauling and using large stone and wooden construction materials, or making clothes from hides, vines, and leaves encouraged cooperative family, clan, and tribal efforts. Division of labor and specialization necessarily emerged. As capitalist economies began to appear around 200 years ago, wasn't it Adam Smith who emphasized the importance of cooperative division of labor in the growth of capitalist enterprise?

- **Tribally loyal, retaliatory if attacked, and territorially defensive**, particularly if the offenders were non-kin from a strange clan or an unfamiliar tribe found poaching on staked-out lands or fishing sites. Can corporate identity, brand loyalty, and patented logos be far behind?

- **Exploratory, risk-taking, and innovative** as testified by the Long Trek out of Africa to far-flung continental lands, and perhaps even more significantly, the gradual but accelerating pace of tool technology and an accumulating culture of protection, cooperation, and security. Probing the unknown, challenging the odds, blazing a new, entrepreneurial trail, generating a visionary future—all have deep ancestral roots. You are familiar with today's innovative social media language: will u frnd me, steve jobs? pls tweet. fyi b gates did 2. yo!

Noted in the Big D chapter, links between the *Homo* past and the corporate present have been superbly described by Harvard Business School Dean Nitin Nohria and his well-known faculty colleague Paul Lawrence, who discern four managerial skill-sets critical for successful organizational leadership that are embedded in the *Homo sapiens* brain (Lawrence and Nohria 2002; Lawrence 2010). Equally insightful is corporate advisor Paul Herr's description of five seminal "emotional appetites" that are workplace expressions of inherited, gene-driven neural activity. Feeding those intertwined biological and social appetites is a key to effective workplace management—and another clue to modern management's debt to the *Homo* ancestral lineage (Herr 2009).

A hint of the presence and managerial significance of nature-based psychological needs operative in the corporate workplace is found in Abraham Maslow's well-known "hierarchy of needs" (Maslow 1954). Maslow's various levels of human "needs" clearly reflect what subsequent research now identifies as modern "leftovers" of human evolution. The two most basic needs, "physiological" and "safety"—air, water, food, clothing, shelter, sex—are remarkably similar to Darwin's evolutionary trio: sustenance, sex, and security, while also testifying to the entropy-avoiding metabolic survival functions rooted in cellular/organic/genetic life. Even the "love and belonging" needs are suggestive of Paul Herr's "emotional appetites" that well up from within complex neural networks of the human brain. Upper-level needs, such as "love and belonging," "esteem," and "self-actualization" are manifestations of yet another human behavioral realm—symbolic culture—which is explored in a subsequent chapter. Corporate managers, take heed of the core, basal, natural behaviors present in the firm's workforce. They have a direct impact on your company's productivity (Maslow *et al.* 1998).

Our ancestral grandparents[X] stood on the cusp of momentous transitions in the lives and times of all surviving and yet-to-be *Homo* individuals. No group of evolved cousins has been more caught up in this phase of the **Evolutionary Cascade** than the managers of today's and tomorrow's corporations—a story that continues in the following chapters.

The Big H's pivotal points

- The *Homo* genus—human beings—first appeared on Earth around 2.5 million years ago, evolving primarily from an older *Australopithecus* genus. The *Homo* form of life differs from predecessor types mainly by upright bipedal posture, skeletal structure, hand-thumb capability, and brain size

- Paleoanthropologists have documented the subsequent evolution of seven distinct *Homo* species, all but one—today's *Homo sapiens*—now extinct

- The dominant scientific view favors an African origin for all *Homo* types, followed by successive migrations from African homelands into the eastern Mediterranean region, Europe, central, eastern, southern, and northern Asia, and much later to the Americas and Pacific Oceania

- The major markers of *Homo* evolution are tool use, constructed shelters, clothing, controlled use of fire, varied carnivorous and vegetation diets, and more complex behavioral patterns, including the nuclear family, kinship clans, and tribes

- *Homo* migrations were driven by a combination of forces: climate change that modified an ecosystem's life-support networks, increased population pressures on food sources, and a slowly improving material culture supportive of life in varied climes and regions

- *Homo* evolution accelerated around 50,000 years ago during the Upper Paleolithic era, producing a range of material improvements, behavioral traits, symbolic usages, and cooperative networks unknown to earlier species. Experts disagree on the cause of this *Homo* upsurge, whether from population increase and resultant social complexity, or from an enlarged brain generating an expanded range of more complex behaviors

- The behavior of modern corporate managers tracks many of the traits observed in long-term *Homo* evolution, thereby suggesting an evolutionary source for the components of **Natural Corporate Management** and their relevance to current business problems and challenges

The Big H's research base

Ambrose, S.H. (2001) "Paleolithic Technology and Human Evolution," *Science* 291 (March 2, 2001): 1,748-53.

Andrews, P., and C. Stringer (1993) "The Primates' Progress," in S.J. Gould (ed.), *The Book of Life* (New York: W.W. Norton).

Balter, M. (2002) "What Made Humans Modern?" *Science* 295 (February 15, 2002): 1,219-25.

Bhanoo, S.N. (2011) "Skull-Caps in British Cave Conjure an Ancient Rite," *New York Times*, February 16, 2011.

Bower, B. (2012a) "Stone Age Fire Rises from the Ashes," *Science News* 181.9 (May 2012): 18.

Bower, B. (2012b) "Tangled Roots," *Science News* 182.4 (August 2012): 22-26.

Brown, L. (ed.) (1993) *The New Shorter Oxford English Dictionary on Historical Principles* (Oxford, UK: Clarendon Press).

Cann, R.L. (2001) "Genetic Clues to Dispersal in Human Populations: Retracing the Past from the Present," *Science* 291 (March 2, 2001): 1,742-48.

Darwin, C. (1874) *The Descent of Man: And Selection in Relation to Sex* (New York: A.L. Burt Publishers, 2nd edn).

Dunbar, R.I.M., and S. Shultz (2007) "Evolution in the Social Brain," *Science* 317 (September 7, 2007): 1,344-47.

Finlayson, C. (2009) *The Humans Who Went Extinct: Why Neanderthals Died Out and We Survived* (Oxford, UK: Oxford University Press).

Gibbons, A. (2006) *The First Human: The Race to Discover Our Earliest Ancestors* (New York: Doubleday).

Gibbons, A. (2010) "Close Encounters of the Prehistoric Kind," *Science* 328 (May 7, 2010): 680-84.

Herr, P. (2009) *Primal Management: Unraveling the Secrets of Human Nature to Drive High Performance* (New York: American Management Association).

Johanson, D., and B. Edgar (1996) *From Lucy to Language* (New York: Simon & Schuster).

Klein, R.G. (2009) *The Human Career: Human Biological and Cultural Origins* (Chicago: University of Chicago Press, 3rd edn).

Lawrence, P. (2010) *Driven to Lead: Good, Bad, and Misguided Leadership* (San Francisco: Jossey-Bass).

Lawrence, P., and N. Nohria (2002) *Driven: How Human Nature Shapes Our Choices* (San Francisco: Jossey-Bass).

Lorenz, K. (1967) *On Aggression* (New York: Bantam Books).

Maslow, A.H. (1954) *Motivation and Personality* (New York: Harper).

Maslow, A.H., D.C. Stephens and G. Heil (1998) *Maslow on Management* (New York: John Wiley).

Nitecki, M.H., and D.V. Nitecki (eds.) (1987) *The Evolution of Human Hunting* (New York: Plenum Press).

Oakley, K.P. (1961) *Man, the Tool-Maker* (Chicago: University of Chicago Press).

Pittsburgh Post-Gazette (2012) "Possible Human Ancestor Made Perilous Trip from Asia to Africa," *Pittsburgh Post-Gazette*, June 6, 2012: A-2.

Rightmire, G.P. (1990) *The Evolution of* Homo Erectus: *Comparative Anatomical Studies of an Extinct Human Species* (Cambridge, UK: Cambridge University Press).

Sawyer, G.J., and V. Deak (2007) *The Last Human: A Guide to Twenty-two Species of Extinct Humans* (New Haven, CT: Yale University Press).

Schrenk, F., and S. Muller with C. Hemm (2005) *The Neanderthals* (London: Routledge).

Seabright, P. (2004) *The Company of Strangers: A Natural History of Economic Life* (Princeton, NJ: Princeton University Press).

Stringer, C., and P. Andrews (2005) *The Complete World of Human Evolution* (London: Thames & Hudson).

Tattersall, I. (2000) "Once We Were Not Alone," *Scientific American* 282.1 (January 2000): 56-62.

Tattersall, I. (2007) "We Were Not Alone," in G.J. Sawyer and V. Deak (eds.), *The Last Human: A Guide to Twenty-two Species of Extinct Humans* (New Haven, CT: Yale University Press): 18-23.

Thorne, A.G., and M.H. Wolpoff (1992) "The Multiregional Evolution of Humans," *Scientific American*, April 1992: 76-83.

White, T. (2001) "Once Were Cannibals," *Scientific American*, August 2001: 58-65.

Wilford, J.N. (2000) "New Data Suggests Some Cannibalism by Ancient Indians," *New York Times*, September 7, 2000: A1, A20.

Wilson, A.C., and R.L. Cann (1992) "The Recent African Genesis of Humans," *Scientific American*, April 1992: 68-73.

Wrangham, R. (2009) *Catching Fire: How Cooking Made Us Human* (New York: Basic Books).

6

The **Big B ≈ Brain**

> The human brain is the most complex natural system
> in the known universe.
> ***Elkhonon Goldberg***

To ease the undoubted challenge of understanding just how the human brain is a key component of **Natural Corporate Management**, we begin good-naturedly by comparing the human brain with one of America's most popular sports.[1]

---

1 Fans of equally popular team-sports in other nations—soccer and hockey—can insert those sports into the text, although with some minor differences.

American-style football and the human brain

Football		Brain
An organized group of skilled athletes	→	An organized network of specialized neurons
A head coach to direct overall team effort	→	An executive center to direct brain activity
Assistant coaches to manage team strategy	→	Subregions and processes to activate neural signals
Teamwork among specialized players	→	Integration of specialized brain areas
A quarterback to operationalize strategy	→	A neocortex to direct neural signals
Muscular and mental activity	→	Organic and cognitive activity
Support of enthusiastic, loyal fans	→	Support of surrounding ecosystem
Short-term goal: ball control and win	→	Short-term goal: process neural signals
Outcomes for team: win or lose	→	Outcomes for brain: adapt or die
Long-term goal: continuity of franchise	→	Long-term goal: continuity of organism

You might well say, OK, but what does that tell me about how the modern business corporation is managed—and especially what the brain has to do with it? Well, aside from the fact that professional football teams (and some college teams) are indeed sizeable corporate entities—with the salaries of their coaches and players rivaling those of top-tier corporation executives—these parallels between the operations of sports teams and the human brain foreshadow a similar set of relationships between corporation and brain. When you have reached the end of this chapter, I suggest you return to this opening comparison and substitute well-known corporate characteristics for those of football teams. The results may indeed tell you much about the links between the human brain's neural activity and the search for bottom-line results in the modern business corporation.

The human brain: Neurology 101

To understand how the brain influences corporate management, you need to know a little something about its "wiring"—some of the main parts, how they interact with each other, and the results produced. The technical terminology of neuro-speak can and will be avoided, just so long as the brain's basic functions are made clear, which this section attempts to convey in plain-speak.

First of all, the human brain is nothing more nor less than a mass of cells. That's simple enough if you recall from the Big L ≈ Life chapter that living organisms are made up of cells and clusters of cells called organs. The brain is one of those specialized organs: a cellular mass, nothing more. The activity of that concentrated conglomeration of cells is indeed remarkable, intricate, and far-reaching. But it is well to keep in mind that we are speaking here of a rather basic feature of organic life in general, and special only in the brain's cellular density and complexity. It's a bit like learning in the Big G ≈ Gene chapter that DNA, for all its complex functioning, is nothing but an acid, a chemical substance that is just another feature of the natural world.

The brain cells of greatest significance are the **neurons** because they are the activators and generators of all brain action. Every bodily motion, thought, reaction, sight, sound, sensation, memory, anticipation, and idea you ever had or will have are expressions of your own set of neurons. Taken together, neurons are the "nerve center" of your body and mind as they interact with the ecosystem environment. Your perception, comprehension, consciousness, and self-awareness are all indebted to signals originating in that mass of neurons we call a brain.

If your brain had only a few of these key neurons, it might be easy to trace how and where those neuronal signals go but, alas, the brain is as complicated as all of the preceding phases of the **Evolutionary Cascade**, including Energy, Life, Darwin, Gene, and *Homo*. Neuroscientists have never made a full count, but they estimate that the average human skull is home to 100–150 billion neurons. That's 20+ times greater than the entire number of people in the world—and each human has about the same number of neurons, so obviously we're talking big numbers here.

You can imagine the wiring job needed to connect up such a massively complicated neuronal system. The task is done by two kinds of "wire," one outgoing, the other incoming. The signals going out from the neuron cell are sent on an **axon**. When a neuron receives a signal from another neuron, it comes in on a **dendrite**. Both wires are attached to the main body of the neuron. Some axons and dendrites are as long as a meter or more; and while dendrites come in multiple clusters, axons are generally one per neuron. It is not at all critical that you learn or remember these technical terms; just remember that these interconnections allow the brain to work its wonders.

Each of the brain's neurons comes with a built-in energy potential which can be either at rest or active, but when active these potentials are the drivers of everything the brain does. At rest, a nerve cell doesn't do much, but when it receives a signal from another neuronal neighbor, it "lights up" because its basic electric charge has been changed (usually from negative to positive). That causes the stimulated cell to send out its own signal, which travels outward along its axon until it arrives at a junction (called a **synapse**) connecting with its neighbors' dendrites, which then allows the message to reach still other neuronal cells. That can eventually generate some kind of bodily response, such as muscular movement or seeing or hearing or even a mental "Aha!" moment (Purves *et al.* 2001: 43-44). Imagine this happening all over the brain at all hours, every day, as the human body interacts continuously with its surroundings in the normal course of daily living—and you can see why the energy load is enormous. Neuroscientists say that running the brain consumes 20 per cent of the total energy used by the body. We will return to this high energy consumption rate later in the chapter because it is another sign that those who manage the modern corporation do their work in the energy shadows left over from the Big Bang.

Note also that the entire activity of neuronal signaling is nothing but a natural bio-physico-chemico process: the neuron is the biological part; the electric signal is the physics component; and the synaptic connector combines chemical and biological elements. So the final product is a combination of biological, physical, and chemical activity. In other words, brain signaling—the core of all we humans do—is entirely natural. In that sense, the human brain displays its natural evolutionary kinship with Energy, Life, Darwin, Gene, and *Homo*—just another extension of the on-flowing **Evolutionary Cascade** that shapes the actions of the modern business corporation and its managerial cadre. Later in this chapter, we'll explore some of the astounding ways the brain makes possible a corporation's innovative inventions and its almost unending creativity and organizational complexity.

Brain evolution in the *Homo* genus

Recall from Chapter 5, "The Big H ≈ *Homo*," that all of our *Homo* ancestors had larger brains than the earlier apelike Australopithecines. Remember also that our own species, *Homo sapiens*, was the only one around for the "*Homo* big bang"—the sudden upsurge around 50,000 years ago of improved tools, better clothing, safer shelters, the use of fire for warmth, cooking, and security from predators, and even symbolic art—long after most other *Homo* types had gone extinct. Most archaeological evidence and neuroscience research support a causal linkage between these three evolutionary events: increasing brain size, improved adaptive techniques, and survival of the last-standing representative of the *Homo* genus—*H. sapiens.*

However, brain size alone doesn't tell the whole story. As with all evolved, cascading organic traits we have examined so far, it's what the cell, organ, organism, gene, phenotype, ecosystem, or other life component can *do* that counts in evolutionary terms. Can an organism deal with—adapt to—Darwinian natural selection pressures out there in the ecosystem? If so, it lives to see another day. If not, it becomes a museum exhibit. What was happening during the 2+ million years the *Homo* brain was expanding was an ever-so-slow specialization occurring *within* the human brain. New structures, new neural connections, a subtle shifting of functions from one area to another, an emergence of control centers, and a diminution of structures and impulses that had formerly been dominant—these were to be the sources and drivers of new behaviors unknown to our earliest *Homo* ancestors. As we shall see, it made all the difference.

The human brain's architecture did not happen overnight but emerged slowly as part of the related evolution of the brains of non-human organisms. And because the *Homo* line came along rather late in evolutionary time, our contemporary brain reflects many of the earlier features we inherited from those older, more primitive neural systems. The result has been called a three-layered or "triune" brain, with a bottom layer being the oldest, a middle layer having come along later, and the top layer most recently evolved (Cory 1999: 10).

This layered pattern of evolutionary development begins with a very primitive "reptile" brain, followed by a more advanced (but still old) "paleomammalian" layer, and culminates with the appearance of a yet more complex "neomammalian" neural system (which includes the neocortex). In the human brain, the newer layers were simply added to— but did not replace—the older layers. "As brain evolution progressed . . . simple protoreptilian brain structure . . . was not replaced . . . while largely retaining its basic character and function" (Cory 1999: 10). Does that mean that sometimes we act like snakes or apes? Well, let's leave that possibility until later in the chapter when we see the brain in action, particularly in today's business corporation. For the moment, the triune brain idea simply records that the human brain has had a very long evolutionary history and that it retains a capacity to express both ancient and more recently evolved neural impulses.

The neocortex: The brain's management center

Just as a football team needs someone—usually called the head coach—to coordinate the specialized skills of assistant coaches and team players, so too does the human brain have a coordinator function—called the neocortex—to bring together the various specialized parts and systems that are present in the brain. Unlike the coach who has rather complete authority and control—even authoritarian power—over the players' actions, the neocortex's role is a bit more "persuasive" in checking and directing the swarm of electric signals rushing to and fro inside the brain's perimeters. The neocortex doesn't always have the last word as it struggles to direct neural traffic.

Before the cortex part of the brain appeared on the evolutionary scene, some of the most basic organic/neural functions were performed by other means. One leading neuroscientist says, "A number of subcortical structures exist in the brain. In evolution, subcortical structures developed before the cortex, and for millions of years they guided the complex behaviors of various organisms." One such neural substructure, the **amygdala**, "regulates interactions of the organism with the external world that are critical to the survival of the [organism] and the species: decisions to attack or to escape, to copulate or not, to ingest or not. It provides rapid, *precognitive, affective* [emotional] assessment of the situation in terms of its survival value" (Goldberg 2009: 28-29, emphasis added). Note how these survival impulses match up with the Darwinian survival trio of sustenance ("to ingest"), sex ("to copulate"), and security ("to attack or escape") discussed in the Big D chapter. So, unlike the neocortex, this more ancient emotion-generating nerve structure "contributes an automatic component *not under conscious control*," or in other words, a knee-jerk, hair-trigger kind of response to some of life's most basic needs and challenges (Goldberg 2009: 121, emphasis added).

Goldberg continues: "relatively late in the evolution of the brain, the cortex began to emerge . . . [and] the *neocortex* arrived on the evolutionary scene." But since the older neural functions were still in place deep inside the brain and working quite well, this cortical newcomer had to find a new job, which indeed it did by introducing a newly evolved capability. Its appearance: "radically changed the balance of power within the brain. The ancient subcortical structures, which used to discharge certain functions independently, now found themselves subordinated to the neocortex and assumed supporting functions in the shadow of the new level of neural organization" (Goldberg 2009: 29-30). What had been only an automatic reaction not under conscious control gave way to "a more reasoned and consciously controlled 'oversight' over our emotional world" (Goldberg 2009: 121). Knee-jerk began to yield, though slowly and incompletely, to the brain's new "boss," the neocortex. However, those more primitive, basal emotional responses did not disappear entirely (for good reasons, as we will see in a later section) but were subordinated to their human carrier's more adept, subtle survival needs. So, this new brain feature—the neocortex—leads to an interesting adaptive possibility, not just for human beings in general but also for more effective ways of managing corporations, as explained after a closer look at this new aspect of *Homo sapiens.*

The human cognotype

As told in the two preceding chapters—"The Big G ≈ Gene" and "The Big H ≈ *Homo*"—the evolution of modern humans seems to have revealed the emergence of a quite unique organic feature, called the **cognotype**. A cognotype is a significant step beyond the earlier "phenotype" used by biologists to describe an organism's bodily forms and structures, as well as beyond what genetic scientists call a "genotype" in referring to an organism's entire genome. Obviously, not all phenotypes are alike, nor are all genotypes; in fact, that is what evolution is all about as it generates an immense diversity of organic life that one finds in all ecosystems. And since many animals have brains of varying size, form, and complexity, neither are cognotypes equal in what they can do in support of an organism's life.

But it is widely agreed by neuroscientists that the human cognotype is indeed unique in its ability to effectively adapt its human carriers to their environments. In other words, the *Homo sapiens* phenotype and its internal genotype have gained a most helpful adaptive companion in the Darwinian sustenance–sex–security survival game. The human cognotype is built entirely on the human brain's neural foundations, and the term itself simply refers to the cognitive, or knowing, process. Cognition is the neural activity of perceiving, conceiving, recognizing, knowing, and understanding the pragmatic, empirical, factual context in which one lives. It's where the rubber meets the road, or where the sensing organism makes contact with its surroundings.

The human cognotype acts through several behavioral routines that are indeed critical to its welfare.

Primal Darwin drives

Aggression in search of *sustenance*, reproductive drive for *sex*, the search for a *secure life-niche*: these basic Darwinian phenotypic and genotypic impulses are always present and behaviorally dominant. While such cognotypic behavior is adaptively self-serving, much of it occurs in a social context populated by other like-minded self-servers: mates, family members, extended close kin, friends, neighbors, clans, tribes, and citizens of states, nations, empires, etc. Within these human networks, the directly self-centered behaviors of some cognotypes come up against the equally determined and competitive actions of others. Because the survival stakes are so high, this self-and-social borderland offers the prospect of collaborative interactions that are potentially supportive of the adaptive aspirations of all parties. If it is to be done at all, the leading role falls to the brain's executive center that can at times reconcile contradictory signals sent from its own deeply embedded neural centers as well as from a potentially hostile ecosystem setting.

Sensing

The basic human senses—visual (seeing), auditory (hearing), tactile (feeling pain/heat/cold), olfactory (odor), taste (sweet, salt, bitter, sour), balance (stability)—are activated as the cognotype interacts with the ecosystem. Cellular receptors in the skin, eyes, ears, muscles, tongue, and various other internal organs, upon experiencing a sensation sent from an external or internal source, react by initiating signals to the particular part of the brain that then responds with an appropriate action. The resulting human behavior can be either reactive and defensive—as in protective moves—or proactive and positive—as in seeking out food sources. Damage to any of the senses seriously limits the cognotype's ability to adjust and adapt successfully to life's daily rounds.

Inventing, exploring, expressing

The last three human cognotypes—*H. erectus, H. neanderthalensis,* and *Homo sapiens*—who came out of Africa and spread to Asia and Europe did so only by the powers of their larger, more complex brains.

As they took the long trek to unknown lands, they reshaped the organic/inorganic world of nature for their survival purposes: stones became tools; vines were made into ropes; wood, bone, and antler were whittled, chiseled, hammered, and ground into pointed weapons; leaves, tree limbs, and caves became constructed shelter; animal skins were made into the latest stylish clothing; stones were converted into hearths; fire was controlled for warmth, cooking, and predator protection. *Inventing* as they went, their brains constantly met formidable, varying ecosystem challenges, forming ever-newer neural circuits to enrich and expand brain size and complexity even further.

The human cognotype's penchant for *exploration* which found expression in those far-flung migrations was only the tip of a vast "neural-berg" lying just out of sight deep within the brain: an *alertness* for the new and the unexpected that might loom up suddenly from the forest, the sea, the sky; an unquenchable *curiosity* about what might be found in the next jungle, lake, or desert sand dune; an urge to *probe* further into the soil for roots, tubers, and burrowing animals; a constant *search* for new sources of fruit, berries, nuts, fish, and animals as novel regions were explored. Here too one sees a reciprocal interplay between brain and environment, with each reinforcing the other, as new neural circuitry formed in response to ecosystem survival problems.

As important as these basic survival skills proved to be, a far more significant neural capability was astir somewhere within that cognotype cranium: the power of *expressing* one's feelings (anger, fear, pain, pleasure); *communicating* with one's fellow-beings (approval, disagreement, satisfaction); and *signaling* one's intentions, purposes, and goals (to hunt, hide, attack, retreat, mate, cooperate, compete). These emergent expressions would come to exist in a sphere of behavior and cognition beyond the capacity of earlier ancestral kin because *human meaning was to assume a unique form—the symbol*—whereby meaning and intention were conveyed via a neural, and not simply a muscular or organic, dimension. Modulated sounds (grunts, shouts, calls), physical gestures of hands and arms (pointing, silencing, cautioning), bodily posture (upright and dominant, craven and submissive), facial expressions (hostile, accepting)—all of these conveyed meanings and intentions in successfully adaptive ways. The phenotypic muscular-bodily movements and expressions were sending cognotypic neural-based symbolic messages. Could human language—a symbolic phenomenon par excellence—be far behind? Too complex to develop here, the symbol, in all of its astounding manifestations, is given full treatment in the following chapter.

The neural roots of Natural Corporate Management

There is a natural infrastructure that supports the management of the modern business corporation. It includes, thus far, all five major phases of the **Evolutionary Cascade** previously described: energy that activates the corporation as a producer of goods and services; cellular life within ecosystem networks that activates a search for life-sustaining resources; natural selection that favors the more effectively adaptive economic (food-getting) activity of an organism; genotypes that shape phenotypes' bodies to be compatible with their ecosystem's survival pressures; and *Homo* behavioral traits that enabled adaptation, survival, and life-span extension for individuals and families over successive generations—all of these being manifestations of an economic infrastructure capable of supporting and extending the organic status of humankind. These collective natural processes (plus other phases to be discussed in following chapters) constitute a context within which corporate enterprise presently operates. The modern business corporation is a principal means of producing, through an economizing process, a flow of goods, services, and information that nourishes and sustains human organic life. Managing and directing this vital economizing process is what **Natural Corporate Management** is all about.

It is important also to understand another broad contextual reality. Human economies and non-human economies (rainforests, oceanic reefs, savannas) share identical natural functions: the survival, nourishment, and continued life support of their organic participants (Vermeij 2004). Within most, but not all, human economies, the business corporation has become a major player in performing that central natural economic function by producing and distributing life-sustaining goods and services to consumers. The economizing corporation—one that oversees and carries out the conversion of energy flows into organically useful forms—has indeed become the dominant player in an increasingly globalized, planet-wide economy.

In assuming this pre-eminent stature, the economizing corporation frequently encounters both the opportunities and limitations held out by diverse ecosystems, which are home to multitudes of non-human organic denizens. This presents the corporation and its managers with a more complicated agenda than simply pursuing a singular economizing pathway, because **economizing** is compromised by an alternate (complementary) natural process of **ecologizing**, which is the recognition and inclusion of ecological components in corporate operations, decision-making, strategy, and goals. All economies, human and nonhuman, face this double-edged natural sword of organic survival which plays no favorites: life's continuity in all forms depends on a balance and reconciliation of these two natural forces—economizing and ecologizing (Frederick 1995: Chapters 2 and 6).

The managerial function of the modern business corporation is to coordinate and direct the firm's economizing–ecologizing operations to secure a continuing life for the firm and its associated organic participants, whether inside or outside the firm's organizational boundary. The firm's ability to carry out this core managerial function, and the degree of success and effectiveness attained, rests largely on the capability of its managerial cadre. The key to the firm's effective management, the one that unlocks and releases the power of adaptive survival, is to be found nowhere else than within the cellular/neural circuits and networks of the human brain, especially the neocortex.

As explained earlier, the neocortex prefrontal lobe is the brain's executive command post that (usually) resolves conflicting neural signals coming from disparate brain regions. This most recently evolved neural center sets the behavioral patterns of control and direction located not just in the brain but also in members of the management cadre of the modern corporation. Corporate managers are engaged in a similar kind of coordinative activity, which at times is conflictual, as they supervise and direct the company's workforce. In performing this necessary management function, executives are entirely dependent on a coordinative process present in their own individual brain's executive center. Both entities—the organic brain and that organic collectivity of people we call a corporation—thereby attempt to move or evolve toward their respective survival goals. Attaining such goals is made possible by the presence in each entity of a coordinating center: prefrontal lobes for the brain, and an executive cadre for the corporation. No simple analogy, these parallelisms of coordinated activity express an underlying, interrelated organic function essential to the further evolution of both brain and corporation.

The neural roots of **Natural Corporate Management** penetrate deeply and spread widely into the soil and waters of that cascading, evolving natural infrastructure—the **Evolutionary Cascade**—finding life-supportive nutrients there, as well as some resistance, in charting the firm's course. One might imagine (but only metaphorically) that the corporation, through the decisions of its managers, sends economizing signals and neural impulses along the routes of the firm's own axons until they reach the receptive dendrites of ecosystem dwellers who respond reciprocally with signals and economizing impulses of their own. However, we need not rely on metaphorical depictions alone (or at all) to grasp the role of real-life neuronal signals originating in the managerial brains of corporate managers as they direct the economizing–ecologizing activities of their firms. Those neural pathways have already been charted by several pioneers whose works exemplify the operational meaning of **Natural Corporate Management**. Consider the following exemplars.

How nature drives organizational design

As noted previously, building directly on contemporary neuroscience research and evolutionary biology, two seasoned management scholars at the Harvard Business School, Paul Lawrence and Nitin Nohria, identify four basic behavioral drives at the very center of corporate decision-making and organizational design (Lawrence and Nohria 2002).

The drive to acquire is: "a drive to seek, take, control, and retain objects and personal experiences humans value. In the course of human evolution humans have been selected naturally for this drive by survival pressures, based primarily on the basic needs for food, shelter, and sexual consummation" (Lawrence and Nohria 2002: 57). That's just another way of naming the Darwinian 3 Ss: sustenance, security, and sex.

The drive to learn. "Humans have an innate drive to satisfy their curiosity, to know, to comprehend, to believe, to appreciate, to develop understandings or representations of their environment . . . People puzzle over causes and effects. They want to know how things work . . . Over millions of years of hominid evolution, the emerging drive to learn fostered the evolution of additional skill sets: . . . manipulating tools, creating all kinds of mechanical devices, muscular coordination or athletic ability, painting, dancing, creating and performing music" (Lawrence and Nohria 2002: 107). That's the **Big H ≈ Homo** story told in an earlier chapter. This kind of exploratory, pragmatic, symbolic outlook is the very essence of what one finds at the core of business decision-making—a gift of sorts from the evolutionary past. More on symbols is found in the following chapter.

The drive to defend. ". . . humans have an innate drive to defend themselves and their valued accomplishments whenever they perceive them to be endangered . . . The drive to defend has been selected for in the course of evolution as essential for survival of the genes." Richard Dawkins' selfish gene, please stand up and take a bow for guiding today's corporations who must constantly defend themselves from threats posed by market competitors. Moreover, the "signals of external threats of harm [are] fed to the central nervous system through nerves from primitive sense organs" such as the reptilian and paleomammalian brain regions, producing "defensive routines—to hide or fight back—that were activated by chemical signals as well as [electric] ones" (Lawrence and Nohria 2002: 130-31). Those are the same organic links of chemical and energetic impulses that activated early cellular-ecosystem life and that now underlie human behavior—a blend of organic phenotype, DNA genotype, and neural cognotype.

The drive to bond. Lawrence and Nohria (2002: 76) maintain that "all humans share an innate drive to bond . . . to form social relationships and develop mutual caring commitments with other humans." They see it as a kind of organizational cement that secures the necessary cooperation among corporate employees to achieve the firm's goals. This drive, like the others, was essential to the continued evolution of early humans faced with ecosystem challenges requiring cooperative engagement in hunting, scavenging, and protection from predators.

These four behavioral drives, when seen within a corporate context, mean that: "every person, from the CEO to the most junior employee, will bring a predictable set of mental equipment to work each and every day. This mental apparatus will be engaged in every item of behavior that takes place at work. Likewise, all the other people engaged with the focal organization—its customers, its shareholders and creditors, its suppliers, its neighbors and its regulators—will have this same mental equipment" (Lawrence and Nohria 2002: 221). Is there a clearer way to say that the modern corporation and its stakeholders are a contemporary manifestation of ancient evolutionary processes?

Even more compelling is the role played by the brain. Those four behavioral drives, taken together, are "clusters of multiple skill sets . . . interconnected in the prefrontal cortex"—the precise location of the brain's executive center, as described earlier in this chapter. The overlap of ancient and modern neural functions, which are key to the successful management of the corporation, could not be more obvious.

Equally important are the organizational design criteria for creating a successful business enterprise. "Clearly, every job must provide an opportunity to fulfill, to some reasonable degree, all four drives . . . A job that fulfills only one or two drives, no matter how lavishly, would not be a substitute for a job that provides a balanced opportunity to fulfill all four drives. This simple design rule is the fundamental and primary one that should guide the work of the organizational leader" (Lawrence and Nohria 2002: 222).[2]

How nature shapes corporate leadership

In a follow-on book, *Driven to Lead: Good, Bad, and Misguided Leadership*, Harvard Business School professor Paul Lawrence (2010) applies his four-drive theory to leadership in the modern business corporation. Lawrence's views—based on years of organizational expertise and corporate strategy—take on an added weight in elucidating the essence of leadership qualities found in the modern business corporation.

It is also pleasantly surprising to find this dedicated management scholar thoroughly committed to a Darwinian interpretation of this most central facet of corporate theory, and he puts it very plainly: "leadership is an expression of the [Darwinian] survival mechanism, which human beings have evolved." And where is that behavioral trait located? "[T]he brain [is] literally where our capacity for leadership is lodged," specifically in the prefrontal cortex (Lawrence 2010: 12, 33-36). That should sound rather familiar by now to readers of this book's earlier chapters.

Essential to good leadership is an ability to integrate the four basic drives—to acquire, bond, comprehend, and defend—found within a diverse workforce. Every employee, regardless of organizational rank, wants and needs to express these behavioral urges. That includes acceptable pay (drive to acquire), applying one's skills (drive to comprehend), working harmoniously with colleagues (drive to bond), and job security (drive to defend). Effective leaders encourage the full expression of all four drives. Bad or misguided leadership focuses on encouraging only one or two of the drives that are believed by top management to count more than others in achieving the firm's goals, or in some cases when an executive "without conscience" seizes control of policy, goal-setting, and strategy,

---

2   Dan Hill's *Emotionomics: Leveraging Emotions for Business Success* (Kogan Page, 2008) extends the Lawrence–Nohria four-drive model to the area of consumer motivation and marketing, thus demonstrating the operational usefulness of a naturological approach to corporate management.

and pursues a path of power, status, and unconcern for others. The ability of the leader's prefrontal cortex—the brain's executive center—to receive conflicting neural signals and to coordinate them into a survival-oriented set of behavioral instructions enables the emergence and expression of workplace leadership.[3]

How nature's emotional impulses condition corporate management

Another experienced voice beamed directly to the corporate workplace tells us that emotions are at the core, the very center, of management decision-making. "Emotions rule," he says, in "every aspect of human behavior," including the corporate workplace. And why? ". . . because they encapsulate the fundamental survival needs of our species." Well, that sounds familiar, doesn't it? The voice we are hearing is that of Paul Herr, author of *Primal Management: Unraveling the Secrets of Human Nature to Drive High Performance* (Herr 2009: 39, 25-26). Herr, whose background is in engineering, is self-described as "an independent researcher who has spent 30 years trying to reverse-engineer human nature." That means he starts at today's end result and searches backward in time for the factors that led to the contemporary result: modern *Homo sapiens*.

Consultant Herr arrives at his rather unexpected and counterintuitive conclusion about the managerial centrality of emotions by drawing heavily and expertly on what is now known about the brain's inner workings and the legacy of *Homo* evolution. Keep in mind a couple of lessons learned earlier in this chapter: behavioral signals are sent along axon–dendrite pathways; and emotional impulses originate in the brain's evolutionarily ancient protoreptilian and paleomammalian layers. Much emotional dynamism stems from the presence of neurotransmitters and hormones such as dopamine, serotonin, and oxytocin that trigger varied reactions

---

3 Leadership and executive authority are frequently conflated within organizational-behavior theory, implying not just an identity of the two but that an organization's operations are entirely dependent on its being "directed" or "managed" or "led" by an executive cadre. A subsequent chapter takes a closer, somewhat skeptical, look at this presumed organizational necessity and function of both leadership and executive authority.

within key areas of the brain, including the hyper-alert amygdala and the prefrontal cortex (the executive/managerial center).

The evolved result is five key emotion-based "social appetites" centered in the human brain. They are cooperation, competency, skill deployment, innovation, and self-protection. Like all organic appetites, they reflect either pleasure when satisfied, or pain and discomfort when denied. Not only are these emotional urges similar to Lawrence and Nohria's four drives, but in like fashion they track the story of *Homo* evolution based on an expanded, more complex human brain. All five emotions "are aligned with survival—which is what human nature is all about" (Herr 2009: 25). In their modern behavioral form as expressed by employees and managers alike, the five emotional appetites must be satisfied if the firm is to meet its goals. Here are the organic seeds of the firm's technical accomplishment (competency and skill-deployment appetites), entrepreneurship (innovation appetite), organizational solidity and teamwork (cooperation appetite), and collective unity of purpose (self-protection). Executives who fail to cultivate these potentials in their emotion-hungry employees and associates are labeled "value-destroying managers," "poisonous leaders," and "high-functioning narcissists" guilty of "narcissist leadership" (Herr 2009: 202-10). Putting them altogether, though, creates a "superorganism"—an organic collectivity—that "feeds all five social appetites" and thrives in the market environment (Herr 2009: 231). Remember, this is a message honed by years of Herr's professional advice to practicing managers. Herr, along with Lawrence and Nohria, captures the central meaning of **Natural Corporate Management**: *a process and an approach that shapes the corporation's evolutionary behavioral legacies to achieve the firm's economizing–ecologizing goals.*

We are left, then, with a tantalizing possibility and an awesome question: Is the modern business corporation just an evolved behavioral extension—an avatar—of the *Homo sapiens* brain? Perhaps it is time now for you to accept my invitation to return to this chapter's opening comparison of American football and the human brain, substituting corporate traits for football tactics, and converting football-ese into business terminology. Is a football coach the same as a corporate CEO? Are assistant coaches like executive VPs? Do quarterbacks make offensive strategy work just as strategy jocks do in corporations? Are loyal ticket-buying fans the equivalent of corporate stakeholders? Are winning a football game and recording a business profit equivalent survival goals? You get the idea, so go back to this chapter's beginning and check it out. And while you're there, note how the brain's traits match up well with either sports teams or the modern business corporation. You may be intrigued by what you find.

The Evolutionary Cascade flows onward

Recall now what has been called in prior chapters an **Evolutionary Cascade** of cumulative natural forces beginning with the Big Bang and moving onward through time until it reaches the modern business corporation. The influence of each phase of the cascade is found in all successive phases, producing a sequential buildup of natural forces bearing down on the business firm and its managers, while influencing their decisions, policies, strategies, and goals.

The *Homo* brain clearly establishes its membership in this **Evolutionary Cascade**:

- The brain is one of nature's most efficient energy transductors, capturing free energy and driving that energy toward entropy at a remarkable speed, through multiple neural channels and diverse behavioral pathways. This cognitive center itself consumes around 20 per cent of all the energy needed to sustain the human phenotype's body, structure, and activities

- The brain is one of the most massive, condensed, concentrated, multicellular organs ever evolved, capable of directing its human carriers into adaptive ecosystem relationships that support the brain's life and its carriers' lives

- The brain, evolving and expanding over millions of years, has enabled a long line of *Homo* species to meet the three basic tests of Darwin's natural selection: to sustain their lives, reproduce their kind, and secure adaptive niches

- It would be difficult to find a better example of the evolutionary power of the selfish gene than the presence and neural functions of the human brain. All of its intricate, interrelated parts—neurons, axons, synapses, dendrites, receptors, neurotransmitters, hormones, neural modules (skill sets and emotional appetites), and incredibly complex circuitry—are manifestations of a human phenotype, a human genotype, and a human cognotype, all of them shaped by a relentless genetic drive for survival

- *Homo sapiens* stands as the sole surviving species of the *Homo* genus, principally because of a brain of large size, complex neural circuitry, specialized neural modules shaped by evolutionary experiences, cortical functions coordinated by a prefrontal cortex, and a capacity for organic symbolic expression—all of these traits contributing to evolutionary survival of the species

As the **Evolutionary Cascade** moves on, we turn in the next chapter to yet another feature, perhaps the most revolutionary of all the human brain's evolutionary functions. This new stimulative element is a brain that leads human behavior beyond simple, immediate, tangible sensing or sense-making into innovative, imaginative, symbolic behavioral and cognitive realms unknown or only weakly developed earlier. *Homo*, the tool maker, hunter-gatherer, long-distance traveler, invader of unknown lands, controller of fire, builder of shelters, breeder of offspring now moves at an ever-increasing pace toward becoming *Homo*, the innovative symbol user. The **Evolutionary Cascade** seems to have taken a step beyond phenotype and genotype by generating an expansive, creative cognotype capable of behavioral feats previously unknown. Just how this newly evolved *Homo* "symbotype" works its wonders is the subject of the next chapter.

The Big B's pivotal points

- The human brain is a massively condensed, complexly interconnected set of organic cells called neurons which generate and modulate bodily movements and cognitive expressions. Electrical impulses within neurons send activating messages through axon–synapse–dendrite connections, thus enabling responses to environmental/ecosystem events

- The human brain evolved over a 2.5-million-year period, expanding in size and specialized functions. The cortical layer known as the neocortex is the most recently evolved and highly specialized neural structure, while more ancient primitive layers continue to express behavioral impulses and potentialities

- The human brain's neocortex prefrontal lobe is the location of a neural coordinating center that regulates and moderates conflicting neural signals received as the human phenotype interacts with both internal (organic) and external (ecosystem) environments

- An organic cognotype is the sum total of all adaptive, survival-oriented behavioral traits and functions generated by the brain's neural messages, including the cognitive functions of perceiving, knowing, and understanding an organism's ecosystem context

- The managerial function of the business corporation is to coordinate its productive economizing operations with opportunities and limitations existing within the firm's ecosystem surroundings. In doing so, a managerial cadre draws principally on the neural circuits, modules, and networks within their own (and other workplace members') brains

- Management scholars have identified behavioral drives, motivations, skill sets, neural modules, and emotional impulses generated by the human brain, which shape a corporation's organizational design, its leadership function, and its economizing effectiveness within ecosystem environments. **Natural Corporate Management** is the use of this knowledge to achieve survival-based economizing–ecologizing results for the firm

- The brain, having felt the cumulative influence of the **Evolutionary Cascade**'s preceding phases, now stands ready to pass its own evolutionary heritage along to play a role in the next phase: the **Big S ≈ Symbol**

The Big B's research base

Cory, G.A., Jr. (1999) *The Reciprocal Modular Brain in Economics and Politics* (New York: Kluwer Academic/Plenum Publishers).

Cummins, D. (2005) "Dominance, Status, and Social Hierarchies," in D. Buss (ed.), *The Handbook of Evolutionary Psychology* (Hoboken, NJ: John Wiley & Sons): 676-97.

Falk, D., and K.R. Gibson (2001) *Evolutionary Anatomy of the Primate Cerebral Cortex* (Cambridge, UK: Cambridge University Press).

Frederick, W.C. (1995) *Values, Nature, and Culture in the American Corporation* (New York: Oxford University Press).

Glimcher, P.W., C.F. Camerer, E. Fehr and R.A. Poldrack (2009) *Neuroeconomics: Decision Making and the Brain* (Amsterdam: Elsevier).

Goldberg, E. (2009) *The New Executive Brain: Frontal Lobes in a Complex World* (Oxford, UK: Oxford University Press).

Herr, P. (2009) *Primal Management: Unraveling the Secrets of Human Nature to Drive High Performance* (New York: American Management Association).

Hill, D. (2008) *Emotionomics: Leveraging Emotions for Business Success* (Philadelphia, PA: Kogan Page, rev. edn).

Korzeniewski, B. (2011) *How the Brain Generates the Mind: From Neurons to Self-Consciousness* (Amherst, NY: Humanity Books).

Lawrence, P. (2010) *Driven to Lead: Good, Bad, and Misguided Leadership* (San Francisco: Jossey-Bass).

Lawrence, P., and N. Nohria (2002) *Driven: How Human Nature Shapes Our Choices* (San Francisco: Jossey-Bass).

Plutchik, R. (2001) "The Nature of Emotions," *American Scientist* 89 (July–August 2001): 344-50.

Purves, D., G.J. Augustine, D. Fitzpatrick, L.C. Katz, A.-S. LaManta, J.O. McNamara and S.M. Williams (2001) *Neuroscience* (Sunderland, MA: Sinauer Associates, 2nd edn).

Vermeij, G.J. (2004) *Nature: An Economic History* (Princeton, NJ: Princeton University Press).

7

The **Big S** ≈ **Symbol**

The first appearance of [*Homo symbolicus*] would correspond to
the first hominids who habitually used symbolic communication.
Terrence W. Deacon

Language is not a cultural artefact . . . it is a distinct piece of the
biological makeup of our brains.
Steven Pinker

Human culture—or more accurately, *Homo sapiens* culture—is an inheritance from the organic past with a continuing generative, creative core that extends that older inheritance into the future. Every step of the way—past, present, and future—is marked by each phase of that overarching **Evolutionary Cascade** of natural forces. Primordial energy in its modern forms drives human cultural behavior toward entropic destinations, while cellular-ecosystem life pushes back toward a longer-term sustainable existence. Darwinian natural selection weeds out the less adaptable features of *Homo* behavior, while the human genome guides cultural evolution in survival directions. The evolutionarily unprecedented *Homo* brain emerges from ages-long struggles and journeys into far-flung lands, seeking sustenance, sex/reproduction, and security for today's *Homo sapiens* carriers of a cultural way of life.

The central theme of **Natural Corporate Management** is that the actions and decisions taken by executive managers of the modern corporation are a manifestation of such natural evolutionary processes. Corporate operations reflect a dynamic interplay of business firm and ecosystem, which is an interlinked process of economizing and ecologizing. Most corporate managers are quite unaware of how caught up they are in this all-embracing natural network. Or just how their ongoing decisions set the fateful journey of their company, not just in this year's quarterly computations of profit-and-loss but in the longer-run chances of the firm's successful adaptation to a constantly evolving natural landscape.

Were those managers to realize that they hold in their very hands and minds perhaps the key components of those natural evolutionary processes, they would likely be startled—perhaps even dismayed—by the power and influence they possess and potentially exert on planetary life, their own and their firms' included. This chapter explores the central meaning and evolutionary source of that unique behavioral trait—the symbol and its place in human culture—which centrally affects the corporation's function within global ecosystems.

Symbols as cognition

In common usage, symbols stand for something. A national flag—the U.S. Stars and Stripes, for example—is a symbol of the nation and what it stands for and how it is distinguished from other nations whose flags carry their own distinctive symbolic meaning for their citizens. Symbols capture an idea or a quality that is somehow broader than the physical symbol itself. They have a meaning that goes beyond the immediate situation. In the business world, symbols, or "logos" as they are called, are used extensively to advertise and market products: a Coke bottle; Heinz 57 Varieties; Apple's one-bite apple; McDonald's golden arches, your car's distinctive hood ornament or trunk sticker signaling Mercedes, Lexus, Ford, or Toyota. So too do our clothes symbolize who we are: male or female, young or old, rich or poor, fashionably stylish or stodgy, with-it or out-of-it, serious or funny, formal or informal, group affiliation, sports team, fan loyalty, etc. There are symbols in mathematics, art, music, religious worship, government, politics, and education; in fact, it is difficult to identify any realm of human behavior where symbols are not present. Symbols appear to be a universal and essential part of everyday human life.

In each case, there is a physical manifestation or form that "represents" or stands for what we observe or sense or do. It's not quite a simple physical linkage between form and meaning but rather constitutes a mediating abstract bridge of sorts that marries the two. So when one says (the Pledge of Allegiance) or observes (an artistic painting) or performs (sings a hymn) the physical action, its symbolic meaning becomes clear. That cognitively generated meaning, conveyed by its physical form, is what we recognize as a symbol. Form and functional meaning blend to create the symbol.

Any word taken from any of the world's 7,000 languages "means" something to its speaker or listener, or writer or reader. There is a connection between the utterance and what that sound or sign conveys or means to the sender and others participating in this vocal exchange. The *meaning* so communicated constitutes a language symbol. Music, another human universal trait, is a vast storehouse of symbolic meanings, whether for jazz fans, religious devotees, opera audiences, or a solitary person whistling at night while passing a cemetery (Sloboda 1985/1999). The varying musical sounds carry a symbolic meaning: fun, devotion, thrill, courage. One more example, closer to this book's central theme of **Natural Corporate Management**, is money. Money, regardless of the name given it by different nations and tribal groups—dollar, euro, dinar, franc, pound, yuan, rupee, gold, silver, shells, stone wheels, *et al.*—"stands" for, or as we say, symbolizes tangible forms of economic wealth or riches. And as everyone knows for better or worse, the pragmatic *meaning*—the symbolic "value"—of money can and does change almost continuously while its physical (and now electronic) form remains constant. The main conclusion to take away from these illustrations is that *all symbols are meanings, usually represented by a variety of physical or abstract forms that stand for or represent the symbol's underlying meaning.*

The organic infrastructure of symbols

All symbols are supported by, and take their meaning from, an under-lying infrastructure composed of organism–ecosystem interactions. That should not be surprising inasmuch as symbols are yet another outcome of an evolutionary process that spawned all forms of organic life, includ-ing the *Homo* brain which is the symbol's organic-cognitive home. These organism–ecosystem linkages give life to a wide range of symbols and, taken together, constitute the operational, organic-ecosystem base on which the entire array of symbolic phenomena rests.

The basic idea is this: human *meaning* is a function of everyday life, of organisms (humans and others) interacting with ecosystem processes: searching for food, reproducing offspring, seeking secure niches, avoid-ing predators, hunting prey, gathering fruits and nuts, digging edible roots, sheltering from climate extremes, fleeing geologic and hydrologic upheavals. Human adaptation and survival depend on knowing, iden-tifying, remembering, and successfully interacting with a wide range of ecosystem elements that make life possible and sustainable over time. Having and keeping an image—a picture, if you will—of those key life components is where symbolism originates. That image is generated by and stored within nothing other than the *Homo* brain. The image's cog-nitive meaning resides there, no place else. The resultant symbols are then cognitively attached to their physical ecosystem counterparts, at the ready, so to speak, to meet diverse life challenges and opportunities. Here within this primal, basal brain–ecosystem linkage is found the birthplace, the very cradle of human symbol use.

Perception—that is, sensing something (food or an enemy)—leads to conception, an abstract idea, whereby a pictorial image of the entity "out there" is generated within the brain. Organism and ecosystem are imme-diately connected with one another. The abstract image is pasted onto the ecosystem's physiognomy: a symbol is born, a meaning emerges, a basis for acting is created, adaptation is attainable, life can (or may) go on. From such basic organic *Homo* traits has arisen a magnificent pleth-ora of pictorial images, including photography, films, television, internet photo transmissions, and numerous other digital imaging devices, which we now call "art" and which others say are evidence of an "art instinct" (Dutton 2009). Imaged symbols, one and all, bubbling up from a natural understory of organism–ecosystem linkages.

Another organic source of symbol generation is found in the rhythmic and cyclic nature of *Homo* life. As mathematician Ian Stewart says, "Nature is nothing if not rhythmic, and its rhythms are many and varied" (Stewart 1995: 93). Nothing could be more basic to continued organic existence than the life-supportive rhythms that drive the human body: heartbeats and pulse; breathing; ovulation; appetite; digestion; elimination; varying gaits and strides that carry one in search of food, prey, shelter, and mates; the irregular rhythmic patterns of storms, rainfall, river flow, and winds that have much to do with survival of individuals, family units, clans, villages, and tribes. Some of these organic rhythms are so "natural" as to be below conscious awareness, certainly true of heartbeat, breathing, and normal functioning of various internal organs. But in all cases, there is an underlying, indeed essential, rhythmic beat sustaining *Homo* life. As the popular phrase puts it, "the beat goes on"—and on and on as long as life continues.

The rhythms heard within music, dance, religious and secular rituals, even the military drumbeat of marching troops, reenact a primitive origin deeply rooted in nature, an undulating ebb and flow through time. Their symbolic meanings mirror their organic-bodily rhythmic origins (Stacey 2010: 146). Body, brain, and ecosystem find common cause once again.

So, too, do natural cycles—another rhythmic beat of sorts—give rise to other symbolic meanings. Our concept of time—one of the most basic of all human symbols—becomes a direct product of the diurnal character of an earthly planet rotating around a solar center: night and day emerge as identifiable traits marked with well-known labels, affecting human consciousness in discrete ways well understood by all who fly on airlines through and across these natural time cycles. The same is true of lunar cycles that define "months," Earth's cycles around the sun that define "days" and "years," and Earth's tilted rotational cycles marking "seasons" of spring, summer, fall, winter, plus solar sunspot cycles capable of generating the brilliant colored displays of the northern *aurora borealis* and southern *aurora australis*, as well as interfering with Earth-based satellite and other electronic communications (de Bourgoing 2001; Tracy 2012: A3; Roenneberg 2012).[1] Equally basic is the idea of a past, present, and

1 An Associated Press news story (Jordans 2012) reports a controversy over use of the "leap second" to adjust the world's clocks to the Earth's uneven rhythmic wobbles as it rotates on its axis. Doing so puts "Earth time" out of sync

future dimension of life, with the passage of years classified, even personified in one's life as "young" and "old," therefore serving as a meaningful symbol.

Symbols are brain/neural/cognitive phenomena. They originate there, are generated there, and are assigned meaning there. In a literal sense, any symbol is a cognitive avatar—an abstract idea, concept, or bit of knowledge—derived from an underlying neuro-organic process or activity. Organically, it occurs as a neurological electric impulse originating within a complex axon–dendrite–synapse network (as explained in the Big B chapter) which is stimulated by the reciprocal contact of brain and ecosystem. The adaptive or maladaptive operational result or consequence for the brain and its phenotypic/genotypic/cognotypic carrier becomes its symbolic meaning. That meaning is then projected outward from the brain to an object or activity in the ecosystem and is then recognized as and called a "symbol." It is quite common, but erroneous, to confuse a symbol's brain-generated meaning with its external physical avatar. A symbol has a two-layered character, one within and another outside the brain. The symbol's neurally generated meaning is internal; its avatar or physical representative is external. As they say, it takes two to tango.

Nature, through the megaphone of the *Homo* brain, thus speaks with a loud, persistent voice, creating and transmitting diverse symbolic meanings outward to all who are capable of receiving and translating them into daily life.

Human language: The proto-symbol

Scientific research and opinion are divided about when, where, and why human language evolved, but few doubt its central importance as the key feature of human symbolic behavior. Language—and its physical

---

with a more accurate "atomic time," thereby negatively affecting air traffic control systems, financial markets, cell phone networks, rocket launches, and planetary time-zone differences. Despite the controversy over which timekeeper system is used, both of them measure time with natural yardsticks: global rotation cycles or atomic pulsing. In the end, timekeepers added a leap second to the world's clocks in mid-2012.

manifestations, speech and writing—permitted and produced a veritable explosion of human symbolic meanings, spewed out of the *Homo* brain in unending flows, creating a cognitive and behavioral dimension unknown and unattainable by other earthly creatures.

Just *when* this novel form of communication first appeared is not securely known. Steven Pinker, author of *The Language Instinct*, speculates that "the first traces of language" could have been "as early as *Australopithecus afarensis* [better known popularly as Lucy] at 4 million years old . . . or perhaps even earlier, 5 to 7 million years ago" or it may have appeared with *Homo habilis* or the more recent *Homo erectus* (the one who strode out of Africa) 1.5 million to 500,000 years ago. If it was "modern *Homo sapiens* . . . 200,000 years ago . . . it is hard to believe that they lacked language" (Pinker 1994: 352-53).

If symbolic language was to appear, it had to follow a reshaping of the human phenotype: a larynx capable of producing speech-like sounds; an expanded brain containing specialized areas for language production and comprehension; a synchronization of throat, mouth, face, tongue, and breathing; an evolved genetic capability to articulate intelligible sounds; and mirror neurons that enable imitation of rudimentary sounds and gestures. Some researchers propose that primate animal calls signaling alarm and fear of predators, or dominance roars and submissive screams, were precursors of human speech (Holden 2004: 1,316-19). Terrence Deacon (1998: 213) identifies as language anticipations various human "homologues" of calls and gestures produced by our closest primate relatives, such as laughter, sobs, smiles, grimaces, and postures. Others point to the guttural sounds, clicks, and whistles that show up in some of today's languages as further anticipations of full-blown language usage (Pennisi 2004: 1,319-20). Pinker concludes: "Though we know few details about how the language instinct evolved, there is no reason to doubt that the principal explanation is the same as for any other complex instinct or organ, Darwin's theory of natural selection . . . The language instinct . . . bears the unmistakable stamp of nature's designer, natural selection" (Pinker 1994: 333, 362). That conclusion would reflect the same kind of organism–ecosystem evolutionary rhythms and cycles that produced music, dance, time, ritual, and other symbol-based meanings and behaviors.

Acquiring language ability would have been an immense step carrying the *Homo* genus well beyond a simple, direct one-to-one link with underlying organic functions. So says language maven Terrence Deacon: "With the final achievement of fully articulate speech, possibly as recently as the appearance of anatomically modern *Homo sapiens* just 100,000 to 200,000 years ago, many early adaptations that once were essential to successful vocal communication would have lost their urgency. Vestiges of these once-critical supports likely now constitute the many near-universal gestural and prosodic [rhythm, volume, tonality] companions to normal conversation" (Deacon 1997: 364). As an example, observe the way you gesture, smile, and frown when using your cell phone, even though the person you are talking to may be thousands of miles away and unable to see you. Your listener can't see and doesn't need your gestures to understand what you are saying because, as Deacon says, such movements "have lost their urgency." You (and everyone else) keep on doing it because it is an evolutionary leftover from earlier times before spoken language had appeared. This 2-million-year transition from grunts and gestures to today's complex syntactical and grammatical patterns of speech and writing is surely one of evolution's most remarkable products, enabling an ever-more secure adaptation and survival of *Homo sapiens* via symbolic communication.

In today's modern world, an even more remarkable—and far more extensive global-wide—symbolic communication has appeared: social media, texting, tweeting, e-mail, Google, Facebook friending, YouTube videos, blogs, LinkedIn, and others to come. Unrivaled fortunes are often the prizes won by such high-spirited, innovative entrepreneurs; Facebook, with 800 million visitors, boasted a market value of $104 billion as it entered the financial marketplace—an amount far exceeding the value of more traditional corporations such as UPS, Kraft Foods, General Motors, and Visa (Raice *et al.* 2012: A1, B1). More about this new electronic-based language system later in this chapter.

Symbols and sociality

So, what critical element carried humankind over the organic threshold into the wonderland of symbolic expression, including not just spoken and written language but the entire array of symbol usage? Could it have been a natural selection pressure as simple as rubbing shoulders with others, or in scientific lingo, human sociality? Here we consider the group-living dimension of symbol usage.

Bear in mind an important difference between human "sociality" and human "culture." They are not the same. When people live and interact in close proximity to one another, they are formed into various social living patterns, such as family, friends, neighborhoods, school or college companions, club members, sports associations, etc.—that is, they repeatedly interact with social others on a regular basis. These and other living patterns are what is meant by "sociality"—a *sociological* relationship between people. Human "culture," on the other hand, is a much broader and more inclusive relationship that involves more than just living with others, more than "sociality" alone. Beliefs, values, institutions, technology, economies, political systems, governmental structures, and much more establish a *culturological* relationship between people. You could say that human sociality and human culture interact reciprocally and recursively, rather like a two-way street with influence moving both ways. As we shall see, human sociality is evolutionarily precedent to human culture, although the two share some common traits and linkages. Expressed in formulaic language, Sociality ≠ Culture. The role played by symbols in both human sociality and human culture is a matter of central significance, as explained further along in this chapter.

The most rudimentary, and evolutionarily earliest, form of human sociality is male–female reproductive pair-bonding (of course, that involves rubbing more than just shoulders), which then typically multiplies the social dimension by the addition of offspring. The nuclear family thereby becomes what might be called the basic unit of human sociality. This lineage—a genetic one—traces far back into primate evolution some 16 million years ago (Shultz *et al.* 2011). From that initial evolutionary base, sociality is extended to increasingly larger and more complex networks: near-kin groups, bands, clans, tribes, alliances, and ever more widely dispersed groupings with recognizable common links and interests (Chapais 2008). What Bernard Chapais calls "the atom of kinship" is not a cultural construct but is composed of three basic bonds that have deep evolutionary roots: a kinship bond, a sexual bond, and a parental bond. This basic kinship structure is "an integral part of *human* nature . . . the outcome of a combined set of features that themselves have biological underpinnings" (Chapais 2008: 306-307). As these human interactions became more numerous, complicated, frequent, and occurring over a wider geographic area and in longer time periods, the demands on individual members of these overlapping social groups advanced, often at exponential rates. One must know kin from non-kin, weigh clan loyalty against little-known non-clan members, recognize and embrace tribal markers, observe and interact face-to-face with strangers whether in peaceful trade, negotiated disputes, or inter-family or inter-tribal conflict. Over long periods of evolutionary time, human sociality has constantly increased—and still does today—in group size, scope, and complexity.

The number, degree, range, and depth of these interactions with social others places a greatly enhanced demand on the *Homo* brain. Impressions, actions of others (positive and negative), remembered experiences, harbored suspicions, expectations of future encounters, protection of close kin, guarding against potential predators, communicating with group members—all of these experienced and anticipatory social linkages activate a broadened range of adaptive impulses generated within the human brain.

An intriguing evolutionary question regarding symbols and sociality then arises: Does human sociality—all of that greatly enhanced social interchange among humans—become so prominent that it begins to exert natural selection pressure capable of modifying the size, scope, and functions of the *Homo* brain? And since the human brain is the ancestral home and current residence of the symbol, would it follow that symbols, or at least some of them, owe their existence to the demands of human sociality? That would seem to reverse the classical Darwinian evolutionary logic because, as explained in earlier chapters (The Big L $\approx$ Life, The Big G $\approx$ Gene, The Big B $\approx$ Brain), all natural human traits are the outcome of long-term, gradual evolutionary changes in phenotype (organic body), genotype (DNA), and cognotype (brain). In other words, sociality would be the end product, not the initiator or generator, of the brain's symbolic functions; neural symbols generated in the brain would have preceded and led the way to human sociality. Reversing the Darwinian formula in this way seems equivalent to putting the evolutionary cart before the horse. The human-sociality cart would be pulling (reshaping) the draft horse, the human symbolic brain.

If true, this outcome leads to an even scarier and more profound question: Are humans therefore in charge of evolution? Has a collective human sociality, when combined with the awesome behavioral potentials of human symbolic usage, become the central driver of human evolution?

Bear in mind here that we are talking about human *sociality*, not human *culture*. Are we now driving ourselves rather than relying on a Darwinian chauffeur? Do we then need a course in driver training?

A raft of science researchers seem to believe so. One is Robin Dunbar, best known for demonstrating a close tie between the size of the human cortex (where symbol activity occurs) and the maximum number of people (the sociality index) who can interact meaningfully in groups (Dunbar 1992, 1993). The average close-up sociality number is around 150, whether in hunter-gatherer clans, regional tribal-like groups, or even in modern industrial societies where it betokens the number of individuals that one knows well.[2] In such intimate circles of daily, weekly, and monthly contacts, something approaching a "social brain" seems to be at work—a brain that may have reached a limit of meaningful direct person-to-person, group-to-group communication with others (Dunbar and Shultz 2007). But the link between brain and group size suggests more than mere coincidence, as if one influences the other or, more likely, a reciprocal force involving both is at work.

Dunbar's subsequent research reveals that the demands of human sociality may have been responsible for the evolution of a kind of reserve neural capacity located in—of all places—the prefrontal neocortex, where (if you will recall from the previous chapter) one finds the brain's executive-coordinator center. This "spare computing capacity . . . can be devoted to other cognitive processes" such as "the ability to mind read or imagine how another individual sees the world" (Dunbar 2006: 171, 172). Reading another's mind or imagining another person's worldview requires one to have a symbolic capability, i.e., to project an internally generated symbolic understanding outward toward some external object or activity or sound—pasting a symbolic label on it. Such labels are a powerful reinforcement of sociality. For example, "Mechanisms such as dialects . . . and social badges (the design of clothing, hair styles, knowledge of particular rituals or origin stories) play a vital role in welding social groups together . . . [via] transmitted cultural icons . . ." Furthermore, "Making the wrong kind of [symbolic] style statement may be, literally, the kiss of death in traditional societies" (Dunbar 2006: 178-79, 176). And this is not to speak about the many conflictual societal norms and the symbolic

---

2 Facebook "friends" greatly expand the face-to-face sociality index into the thousands.

signals they send in today's "modern" world. Could Dunbar's research that links *sociality* and symbols with spare brain capacity be revealing the evolutionary seeds of human *culture*? In other words, does culture grow out of sociality?

Sociality's influential power, reinforced by the use of symbols, is revealed by two other students of human evolution: "One of the most striking features of human sociality is the symbolic marking of group boundaries. Some symbolic markers are . . . distinctive styles of dress or speech, while others are complex ritual systems accompanied by elaborately rationalized ideologies. It is a commonplace that social relations are regulated by norms embedded in a group's sanctified belief system" (Richerson and Boyd 2005: 211). Here, then, is another hint of a close relationship of sociality and culture, with culture seeming to win out.

Michael Tomasello, another well-known research scholar, also finds a causative link between human sociality and a cognitive activity he calls "sociogenesis." It is sociogenesis that does "much of the actual work in creating symbolic representations that give human cognition much of its awesome power." In plainer terms, cognitive symbols have their genesis in, and from, human social groupings. For example, social behaviors such as "intentional communication, social dominance, social exchange, and cognitive exploration" generate their symbolic counterparts: "language [for communication], government [for social dominance], money [for social exchange], and science [for cognitive exploration]." Thus, Tomasello also concludes that "linguistic symbols and cultural institutions are socially constituted" and that "human forms of social-interactive processes . . . must have played a crucial role in their creation and historical evolution . . . [T]hese processes, *and not any biological event directly* . . . have created uniquely human material and symbolic artifacts" (Tomasello 2006: 214, 215, emphasis added). So, once again, we are told that human symbolic cognition owes much to human sociality but, in this case, little or nothing to biological processes.

Terrence Deacon, author of *The Symbolic Species*, appears to agree that symbol use was the key to further human evolution: "The construction of novel symbolic relationships fills everyday cognition. A considerable amount of everyday problem solving involves symbolic analysis or efforts to figure out some obscure symbolic association . . . [These] computational demands of symbolization . . . initiated and drove the prolonged evolution of . . . our language 'instinct' " (Deacon 1997: 266, 340)—and by implication, other aspects of symbolic human culture.

So, it seems that rubbing shoulders paid off big in evolutionary survival terms, whether babbling with baby, gossiping with neighbors, or shouting at enemies. Symbolic speech and other symbolic pathways had arrived, seeming to sneak into the *Homo* brain by an evolutionary back door. It was *sociality*, not the brain per se, that was thought to be the principal driver of *Homo* evolution. As one famous cultural anthropologist boasted, "Man makes himself"—and, in doing so, seems to escape from Darwin's evolutionary grasp.[3] Ah, if only this boastful anthropocentric claim were true! But it isn't; it's only a half-truth, a partial picture. The brain-sociality-symbol story is a bit more complicated, as we shall see.

Tools, symbols, and sociality

Recall from earlier chapters—the Big D, the Big H, and the Big B—the evolutionary function of the earliest stone, bone, and wood tools: They greatly enhanced the tool user's adaptive success in coping with a host of ecosystem challenges and opportunities. Tools deliver a direct, intentional, instrumental, adaptive effect for the user. The linkage of tool and ecosystem is a physical one, resulting in an observable, even empirically testable result.

In spite of similarities, symbols do not operate in quite the same way as tools. Tools are physical extensions of the human body, taking tangible form, while symbols are nothing but a form of cognitive meaning, an abstract concept, housed entirely within the human brain case. It matters not the particular symbol one has in mind, whether a word, an artistic image, a song or dance beat, a sacred belief—all are generated by, and take no other form than the electric impulses coursing through that cognitive bundle of axons, dendrites, and synapses. That is the locale, the organic birthplace, of the symbol. Its meaning is conceived there, secured within a cognitive womb. Like tools, though, a symbol's intended meaning, in

---

3 V. Gordon Childe, *Man Makes Himself* (1951), first published in 1936. Neither Darwin nor natural selection appears in the book's index.

order to be communicated to others, relies on an out-of-brain physical representative to convey the symbol's message.

In comparing the two, there is a greater cognitive distance—an abstract span—between symbol and ecosystem than between tool and ecosystem. The tool's impact is more direct, more immediate, more tangible (a spear kills a prey animal); the symbol's effect is more abstract, more indirect, and allows greater room for variation and interpretation (a spoken cry of alarm about the threat of lurking enemies may be ignored or mistaken for a friendly greeting). The comparative evolutionary effects can be dramatic. Tools act directly to promote human adaptation, while symbols exhibit or permit less adaptive discipline, depending on the symbol user's subjective or idiosyncratic interpretation. After all, symbolic meaning is very much *an individual brain's* creation, based on that particular brain's perception of outside forces. Another brain's perception of the symbol's meaning may be different, permitting a variable response to environmental forces. For example, an artist's painting or sculpture may mean one thing to one observer and quite another to someone else. The same is true of religious and ideological beliefs. Given these interpretational differences, symbolic meanings—unlike tools—are capable of being quite detached from the business of adaptation and survival. They bear an imaginative, even fantasy-like quality beyond the immediately experienced dimension.

A generative, creative power resides in both tools and symbols: new tools and new symbols are continuously generated. Each feeds upon itself in a self-generating dynamic that expands, multiplies, and magnifies its potentials. Shaped by its own evolved past, each nevertheless displays a kind of undisciplined, wandering potential—new forms of technology, new symbolic meanings—that may or may not have positive adaptive consequences. Think of it as the *Homo* brain's "wild card," an almost unlimited outpouring of imaginative meanings that take the form of both symbols and new technologies.

This open-ended, undisciplined character of tools and symbols produces both sociality and personal effects. Symbols may produce personally purposive, though often imagined, adaptive *intentions* for the symbol user, which is a psychological/emotional "felt" experience not necessarily verifiable by others.[4] "Visions," "voices," "phantoms," and "out-of-

---

4 A very large army of professionals, most notably inspired by Sigmund Freud's legacy, including psychoanalysts, psychologists of diverse types, psychological

body" sensations are quite "real" to those who see, hear, or feel them, and while their symbolic origins are entirely internal and personal, that does not prevent social others from accepting them as mirroring their own feelings. Mystics of all varieties have long drawn followers who accept their visionary experiences as fact. So, any single individual builds a personal symbosystem by acquiring and learning a range of personally and socially meaningful symbols, which may have adaptive, or maladaptive, consequences. This personal (because internally generated) symbosystem—a neuro-cognitive output of the brain—tends to become the *perceived* center of that person's supportive life system, whether it is adaptive or not. Such mystical, other-worldly fantasies are entirely comprehensible and believable for the individual who neurally creates them, and they can even be a basis for social solidarity or tribal loyalty when shared widely with like believers. In contrast, tools and technology generally are more proximate, direct, and demonstrably capable of revealing their effects on behavior and belief than is true of symbols.

It is likely that tools and symbols are differentiated by a cognitive filter or membrane, with adaptive tool-use being restrained or channeled by the presence of less-than-adaptive symbols. This may be particularly true when strong emotions and prior behavioral/group commitments play a major role, one capable of overcoming tool-based adaptive impulses. In the broader process of economic, political, and social change, diverse human groups tend to accept adaptive tools rather easily—cars, television, cell phones—but may resist the less familiar symbols of out-group cognotypes which display contrasting doctrinal beliefs, rituals, art and music traditions, and political systems.

Therefore, the relationship between tools, symbols, and human sociality may turn out to be a tad more complicated and less straightforward than previously depicted by researchers. First of all, tools emerged as the *Homo* (or pre-*Homo*) brain expanded in size and specialized functions, thus enabling adaptive responses to ecosystem challenges for those tool users. Second, another kind of cognitive output, the internalized symbol, was also generated, this time with self-perceived effects *thought to be adaptive* by the carrier and like-minded individuals, though often lacking a secure empirical grounding. In other words, symbols had yet

---

counselors for families, children, addicts, *et al.*, devotes its talents to coping with such symbol-generated problems, both real and imagined.

to make their case for being adaptively helpful. Third, though variably adaptive, both tools and symbols enhanced, encouraged, and supported human sociality through shared experiences. Rather than a sociality-shapes-brain scenario—as proposed by some researchers—aren't we then seeing a reciprocal, recursive process at work where brain, tool, symbol, and human sociality simultaneously reinforce one another, *neither one evolutionarily or functionally precedent to the others*? Each component being thoroughly natural in origin and function, their combined selection pressure, as always, favors the more adaptive trait, which resides *collectively* in brain, tool, symbol, and sociality. All four components enable adaptation within diverse ecosystem processes. As such, they are a clear case of Darwinian natural selection. Humans do not "make themselves," as claimed by a bevy of anthropologists, but are the naturological outcome of cumulative evolutionary processes. Just how this whole controversy played out involves the core meaning of "human nature," the question of whether it stems from culture or from nature itself.

The Darwin wars: Nature versus nurture

In publishing his ideas about natural selection, Darwin joined a veritable who's who of major scientific luminaries. They included Copernicus in 1543: Earth is a solar planet → Galileo in 1632: Confirmed Copernican theory → Newton in 1665–66: Laws of gravity and motion → Darwin in 1859: Natural selection → Einstein in 1916–18: General and special theory of relativity → Watson–Crick–Wilkins–Franklin in 1953: Gene/DNA. Each of these ideas shook the very foundations of Western thought. Each one revolutionized the way the world had previously been perceived. Each one transformed the literal meaning of being "human." The reverberations from these explosive ideas still echo in the modern world, much as the Big Bang's remnants continue to be registered in the leftover radiation shadows of that primordial event. Copernicus and Galileo were condemned and shunned, Newton was knighted, Einstein lauded, Crick–Watson–Wilkins praised, and Rosalind Franklin ignored. As told in the Big D chapter, Darwin faced unbounded hostility in some quarters while considered a genius by others.

Animating opposition to Darwin's explanation of human evolution was the emerging scholarly field of cultural or social anthropology. And for good reason, for it was an approach based on equally reliable scientific grounds, pursued not just within the ivory tower but through the rigors of actual on-the-spot field studies employing first-hand observations carefully recorded and preserved through verifiable ethnological techniques. Moreover, anthropology's upsurge coincided in time with Darwin's own field studies during and after his five-year *Beagle* voyage and the subsequent publication of *The Origin of Species*—a simultaneity occurring at the midpoint of the 19th century. Darwin emphasized nature, anthropologists culture or, the more popular term, nurture. Battle lines were drawn, trenches dug deep, heavy armaments rolled into place, and the bombardments began. The warfare is still raging, which might well be dubbed the 150-Year Nature–Nurture War.[5]

The issue was, and is today, about the nature of human nature: learned or inherited? The human mind: a blank slate to be filled in, or preloaded and ready to go? An open-ended, acquired trait or a closed-off, predetermined pathway? The orders went forth: Soldiers, fire at will! And fire they did, salvoes launched by eminent anthropologists, either from their university desks or directly from the field (Harris 1993). Counterattacking for the "naturist" view were sociobiologists, selfish-gene advocates, evolutionary psychologists, language-origin mavens, more recently reinforced by neurosociologists, biopsychologists, neuroeconomists, and other pro-Darwinians. Along the way, other innocent bystanders were drawn into the fray: capitalist free-market advocates, creation mythologists, gender defenders (of both sexes), and parental-care theorists. It was a colossal struggle to define the core of human nature, kicked off mainly by Darwin's simple notion of natural selection.

The spirit and intensity of this bitter, titanic contest have been captured in this passage:

> The atmosphere of mistrust that had long clouded relations between the two wings of anthropology—the biological and the social—became even more deeply entrenched during the three decades from 1965 to 1994 as a result of

---

5 For an entertaining account, see Andrew Brown's *The Darwin Wars* (1999). For a more comprehensive explanation, see Ruse 2009.

the gene-centred developments that took place in evolutionary biology ... [S]ocial anthropologists and indeed
most social scientists saw the new Darwinism not as science but as right-wing ideology ... [T]he new gene-centred
view of natural selection was denounced as a derivative
of Western capitalist economics, inevitably tainted with
political evils inherited lock, stock and barrel from "free
market" economic theory. Compounding this was the
widespread view that the new Darwinism was intent on
building a human origins myth which would legitimize
the prevailing world order as unchangeably rooted in
"human nature." [D]uring the 1970s and 1980s, not only
Darwinism but Western science itself became viewed as
little more than an ideological construct designed to serve
the dominant political powers (Knight *et al.* 1999: 4-5).[6]

The extremism shown by both social science and natural science camps
reveals the high stakes of pondering the source of human nature.

More recently, we are assured by one well-known scholar that there is
"a new mode of evolution"—one that "can *detach itself* to some degree
from its genetic basis, from chemistry, genes, and DNA. This is *cultural evolution, which involves learning...*" Moreover, we are told this
"makes us truly special ... and devastatingly successful" (Nowak 2011:
275, emphasis added). There you have an up-to-date version of nurture's
alleged power: human culture can escape the pull of nature, and humans
are "truly special" creatures (perhaps unapelike?) perched "successfully"
at the pinnacle of all creaturehood. It is nothing less than nurture triumphant. Back down, Charles Darwin!

The major thrust of today's Nurturists has been to argue that *learned
culture itself*—its diverse forms, institutions, behavioral patterns, and
traditions, along with its methods of transmission from generation to
generation—is capable of exerting a natural selection pressure on genes
and other organic features. That would mean behavior that is acquired

---

6 As an early convert to nurturism—and as a then newly graduated student
   of cultural anthropology—I recall telling the students in my first university
   classes that there was no such thing as "human *nature*." The idea was dis-
   missed with a rather "bah, humbug!" enthusiasm. Learned culture was (then)
   the whole story.

in the short term through cultural learning could then become part of a person's long-term genetic makeup, which of course reverses or contradicts the classic Darwinian idea of natural selection. Thus *culture*, not *sociality or group living*, would be the evolutionary driver. This view has been promoted most notably by Peter J. Richerson (an environmentalist) and Robert Boyd (an anthropologist) (Weingart *et al.* 1997; Richerson and Boyd 2005; Boyd and Richerson 2005). Rather than seeing a split between nature and nurture, they favor a jointure of the two, with culture playing a predominant role. A more cautious and perhaps more secure theoretical interpretation of culture's place in evolution—with notably greater attention to symbolic phenomena—comes from a group of anthropologists led by Robin Dunbar and associates (Dunbar *et al.* 1999). Symbols, they argue, are indispensable core elements of human culture derived directly from organic evolution (and not the other way around), while human sociality (group living) is another naturally evolved feature upon which culture may then be built (Dunbar *et al.* 1999: Parts I and II).

While it is perhaps overly optimistic to expect a peace treaty to be drawn up any time soon between the two warring camps—the Naturists and the Nurturists—their struggles might be at least muted and softened somewhat by taking advantage of what is now known about—what else?—symbols. Can symbols offer a way out, not by taking sides, but by rechanneling the quest for human nature? It's worth a try.

Reconciling nature and nurture

A clue comes from Matt Ridley, a seasoned observer of scientific developments and their meaning in everyday life, in his book *Nature via Nurture: Genes, Experience, and What Makes Us Human*. Ridley says, "Nature does not prevail over nurture; they do not compete; they are not rivals; it is not nature versus nurture at all . . . instinct is not the opposite of learning . . . genes are not just units of heredity . . . They are themselves exquisite mechanisms for translating experience into action . . . My argument in a nutshell is this: the more we lift the lid on the genome, the more vulnerable to experience genes appear to be" (Ridley 2003: 4, 93, 275). While that may sound like tipping the scales in favor of nurture, i.e., learned experience, it only links the two together: genes drive and channel human experiential activities, while human activities (whether inherited or learned) may influence genetic *expression*, though not the genome's basic *structure*. If anything, the scales seem to favor a natural explanation for the linkage, inasmuch as both genes and learned experience occur only via organic-based neurological processes, as will be further described in a moment.

Ridley's idea that nature and nurture are fused through a neuro-organic bridge finds support in another quarter. "One genuine solution to the nature–nurture debate requires abandoning the idea that nature and nurture are equal partners. They are not. *Nurture is a product of nature.* Nurture—learning in all its various forms—doesn't happen by magic. It doesn't occur simply by exposing an organism to the environment. It occurs when evolved learning adaptations are exposed to the environment . . . Learning is grounded in specialized adaptations that evolved just like all other adaptations" (Hagen 2005: 159, emphasis added). In other words, cultural "learning"—a neuro-cognitive activity of the brain—is just as "natural" as any other adaptive human practice.

Such "evolved learning adaptations" are an outgrowth of organism–ecosystem conditions; more specifically, they evolved via neuro-organic activity within the human brain. Here, too, we have a functional association of nature and nurture, with nurture—or what might better be called "*natural* learning"—understood as an emergent quality of underlying organic processes that confer adaptive advantages. That is a powerful combination, as proponents on both sides of the debate might well agree. Both learning and heredity—a fusion of neuro-organic elements—are actively, and even cooperatively, involved in promoting positive adaptations. But—and here is the critical point—*both learning and heredity are forms of nature.*

Better than a fixation on learning (nurture) or a fixation on genes (nature) is fusing the two to form a broader meaning of the forces that shape human behavior. Human "culture" includes the entire corpus of neuro-organically evolved symbols, tools, and sociality living patterns. Acquiring or learning behavioral or cognitive traits—normally attributed to "culture"—turns out to be nothing but the outcome of a "natural" neuro-cognitive activity of the *Homo* brain linking organism and ecosystem. Some of these links "work," i.e., are adaptive, while others don't, i.e., are maladaptive. To put the matter as plainly as possible, *symbols, tools, and sociality are major components of human "culture."* They are natural phenomena that form the organic basis of both learning (short-term acquiring) and heredity (long-term inheritance). Rather than being organically separate, the three evolved components are organically joined.

Genes alone are not the whole story because all genomes, including human genomes, interact adaptively with diverse ecosystems, thus shaping themselves and their human carriers in accordance with the naturological diversity of those ecosystem elements. Jared Diamond's monumental work *Guns, Germs, and Steel* (1998) painstakingly documents the many ways that "differences among peoples' environments [and not simply] biological differences among peoples themselves" were responsible for the diversity of the world's societies (Diamond 1998: 25). For this reason, any given collectivity of symbols and tools varies from another, displaying varying degrees of sociality and adaptability. Another way of saying the same thing is that diverse ecosystems generate diverse "cultures," i.e., diverse sets of symbols, tools, and sociality designs.

Perhaps an apt label for the combined adaptive effects of tools, symbols, human sociality, and ecosystem dynamics is **neuro-organic culture**. It tells much about human nature.

Neuro-organic culture

Neuro-organic culture is an extension, an elaboration, of the traditional concept of learned human culture as the basis of human nature. The "neuro-organic" part of the term simply refers to the brain's complex networks of cells, axons, dendrites, and synapses (described in the previous chapter). The "culture" part of the term is the behavioral and organizational outputs generated by that neural network, which is another way of saying that what we call "culture" is created by or generated within the *Homo* brain. The ability to be aware of one's surroundings, to know something or someone, to perceive an event, or to conceive an idea—all of these are forms of cognition, of knowing, *and of learning*, which links organic cognition, as a causative factor, directly with learned culture. Learning and knowing, cognition and culture are fused together, forming what the previous chapter identified as a "cognotype" or an organism whose actions are driven principally by a complex brain (Klein 2009). This means that neuro-organic culture is the cognitive equivalent of human culture. These two basic entities—the *Homo* brain and human culture—generate what we normally call human nature.

The *naturological* approach adopted here is at variance—though not fundamentally—with more familiar explanations of how we humans came to be who we are, especially the idea that peoples' behaviors are the outcome of acquired or learned cultural beliefs, habits, attitudes, and values. In that formulation, human nature is said to be the equivalent of what a person learns in one's native culture. And because cultures vary across the globe, human nature itself is therefore diverse, in spite of some shared common or universal behaviors. There is much to be said for this *culturological* point of view, based as it is on more than 150 years of dedicated research by cultural anthropologists, sociologists, psychologists, and other social scientists.

The natural evolutionary approach, rather than detracting from the idea of a learned human nature, adds a certain richness and depth to our understanding of human behavior, based on the research of yet another group of scientists, this time from the natural sciences. The social-science and natural-science explanations can be reconciled without denying the validity of either side's central proposition. This perspective permits one to understand and accept the proposition that learned cultural forms of behavior are the acting out of evolutionary functions centered in the human brain.[7]

Overall, the behavioral reach and survival implications of human neuro-organic culture are far greater than the evolutionarily earlier organic-genetic culture possessed by phenotypes of all varieties, species, and genera. The principal source of this larger arc of influence is found within the *Homo sapiens* brain that has generated multiple, and highly diverse, ways of tool-use (modern technology), symbolic meanings (language, art, music, belief systems), and sociality patterns (family, neighborhood, race, gender, tribe, nation, and now electronic Facebook friends). Finding ways to navigate these diverse, and frequently incompatible, organic pathways is high on the agenda of today's corporate managers.

---

7 A similar consilient view of nature and nurture is expressed in William H. Durham's *Coevolution: Genes, Culture, and Human Diversity* (1991).

Neuro-organic culture and NCM

The significance of neuro-organic culture for the modern corporation and its managers—and therefore for **Natural Corporate Management**—is indeed great, because all major components of neuro-organic culture are replicated on a reduced scale in the diverse corporate cultures found in business firms everywhere. If neuro-organic culture is human nature writ large, corporate culture is human nature written in a smaller but no less powerful script. The same natural processes are at home, whether in society at large or in the narrower scope of corporate activity. Managers, beware! Your managerial challenges reflect a cumulative, and still evolving, legacy of human nature. Neuro-organic culture—tools, symbols, and sociality—is only one of the cumulative phases that carry forward the evolution of energy, cellular ecosystem life, Darwinian natural selection, genetic drive, and *Homo* brain-based adaptive (and maladaptive) behavioral impulses. Your firm stands to inherit that evolutionary legacy. That's your central managerial challenge.

It is a daunting task, to say the least. Just how it is to be accomplished, if at all, takes us into this book's remaining chapters that deal with organizational patterns and dynamics, the firm's place in a market economy, the corporation's adaptive potentials, and the normative significance for business and society of the **Evolutionary Cascade**'s cumulative, ongoing phases.

The Big S's pivotal points

- Symbols are a form of meaning or knowing generated in the *Homo* brain as a result of contact between brain and ecosystem. Symbolic meaning becomes behaviorally operational through attachment to a physical avatar or representative, e.g., a spoken sound, an image, a rhythmic dance. All symbols and their physical avatars are natural in origin and function, exerting variable adaptive effects on their human users

- Some forms of human symbolic behavior—music, dance, ritual, seasonal markers, passage of time—reflect underlying rhythms and cycles found within nature, such as heartbeats, cellular-organic functions, planetary rotations, and other paced movements

- Symbolic language evolved concurrently with ancient tool use beginning some 2 to 2.5 million years ago but becoming fully developed with the appearance of early *Homo* species, possibly *H. erectus, H. neanderthalensis,* and *H. sapiens.* Language's natural emergence as yet another form of human cognition signaled a new evolutionary phase of successful survival and adaptation of the *Homo* genus

- Human sociality—group living—is so dependent on an extensive use of symbols to communicate human meaning to group members that it is believed by some experts to exert a natural selection pressure that enhances the *Homo* brain's functions by increasing its size, complexity, and adaptive effects

- An alternative scientific view is that human sociality is only one part of a complex network of tool, symbol, sociality, and ecosystem surroundings, neither one selectively precedent to the others. The adaptive effects on humans and their ecosystems vary with the relative strength of the four components, including the geophysical setting of any given society

- Human sociality and human culture are distinctive, though interrelated, kinds of human collective behavior. Sociality—group living—is evolutionarily precedent to human culture, the latter consisting of an elaboration of tools and symbolic beliefs and practices

- Tools and all modern forms of technology are physico-organic extensions of natural bodily functions that enable an ever-more effective adaptation of their human users to evolving ecosystems. Tools and technology are forms of nature itself, not artificially imposed on nature but full participants in natural evolution

- Tools and symbols differ in their evolutionary effects, with tools having a direct, instrumental function to perform while symbols' ecosystem connections can be more abstract and generalized. Symbols allow their users to perceive adaptive results, even when they are absent

- The natural evolutionary origins of symbolic human culture have been obscured by a long-running controversy about the basic determinants of human nature. Social anthropologists favor the role of nurture, while natural scientists propose nature-based explanations. An alternative view is that nature (heredity) and nurture (learning) are overlapping cognitive processes generated by the *Homo* brain, both of them displaying evolutionary adaptive potentials

- Symbols and tools are major components of human neuro-organic culture. They are natural phenomena forming the organic basis of both learning (short-term acquiring) and heredity (long-term genetic inheritance). Rather than being separate, the two are organically joined

- The long-running controversy that pits group selection (based on learned culture) against individual selection (based on inherited organic traits) is perhaps reconcilable by recognizing that neither selection factor is functionally or evolutionarily precedent to the other while both can be understood as recursive, reciprocal, and mutually self-reinforcing

- Corporate cultures are scaled-down units of a society's neuro-organic culture, and this subjects corporate managers to the natural dynamics, opportunities, and limitations of tools, symbols, sociality, and ecosystem processes, as they work to achieve advantage for their companies

The Big S's research base

Boyd, R., and P.J. Richerson (2005) *The Origin and Evolution of Cultures* (New York: Oxford University Press).

Brown, A. (1999) *The Darwin Wars: The Scientific Battle for the Soul of Man* (London: Simon & Schuster).

Chapais, B. (2008) *Primeval Kinship: How Pair-Bonding Gave Birth to Human Society* (Cambridge, MA: Harvard University Press).

Childe, V.G. (1951) *Man Makes Himself* (New York: New American Library).

Deacon, T.W. (1997) *The Symbolic Species: The Co-evolution of Language and the Brain* (New York: W.W. Norton).

Deacon, T.W. (1998) "Language Evolution and Neuromechanisms," in W. Bechtel and G. Graham (eds.), *A Companion to Cognitive Science* (Malden, MA: Blackwell): 212-25.

de Bourgoing, J. (2001) *The Calendar: History, Lore, and Legend* (New York: Harry N. Abrams).

Diamond, J. (1998) *Guns, Germs, and Steel: The Fate of Human Societies* (New York: W.W. Norton).

Dunbar, R.I.M. (1992) "Neocortex Size as a Constraint on Group Size in Primates," *Journal of Human Evolution* 22: 469-93.

Dunbar, R.I.M. (1993) "Coevolution of Neocortex Size, Group Size and Language in Humans," *Behavioral and Brain Sciences* 16: 681-735.

Dunbar, R.I.M. (2006) "Brains, Cognition, and the Evolution of Culture," in S. Levinson and P. Jaisson (eds.), *Evolution and Culture* (Cambridge, MA: MIT Press): 169-79.

Dunbar, R.I.M., and S. Shultz (2007) "Evolution in the Social Brain," *Science* 317 (September 7, 2007): 1,344-47.

Dunbar, R., C. Knight and C. Power (eds.) (1999) *The Evolution of Culture: An Interdisciplinary View* (New Brunswick, NJ: Rutgers University Press).

Durham, W.H. (1991) *Coevolution: Genes, Culture, and Human Diversity* (Stanford: CA. Stanford University Press).

Dutton, D. (2009) *The Art Instinct: Beauty, Pleasure, and Human Evolution* (New York: Bloomsbury Press).

Dyson, G. (1997) *Darwin among the Machines* (London: Penguin Books).

Ebstein, R., S. Shamay-Tsoory and S. Hong Chew (eds.) (2011) *From DNA to Social Cognition* (Hoboken, NJ: John Wiley & Sons).

Gaidos, S. (2012) "Furry Friends Forever," *Science News* 181.7 (April 2012): 18-21.

Hagen, E.H. (2005) "Controversial Issues in Evolutionary Psychology," in D.M. Buss (ed.), *The Handbook of Evolutionary Psychology* (Hoboken, NJ: John Wiley & Sons): 145-73.

Harris, M. (1993) *Culture, People, Nature: An Introduction to General Anthropology* (New York: HarperCollins).

Holden, C. (2004) "The Origin of Speech," *Science* 303 (February 27, 2004): 1,316-19.

Jordans, F. (2012) "Countries Considering a Timeout on Leap Second," *Pittsburgh Post-Gazette*, January 19, 2012: A-3.

Klein, R.G. (2009) *The Human Career: Human Biological and Cultural Origins* (Chicago: University of Chicago Press, 3rd edn).

Knight, C., R. Dunbar and C. Power (1999) "An Evolutionary Approach to Human Culture," in R. Dunbar, C. Knight and C. Power (eds.), *The Evolution of Culture: An Interdisciplinary View* (New Brunswick, NJ: Rutgers University Press).

Nowak, M.A., with R. Highfield (2011) *SuperCooperators: Altruism, Evolution, and Why We Need Each Other* (New York: Free Press).

Pennisi, E. (2004) "The First Language?" *Science* 303 (February 27, 2004): 1,319-20.

Pinker, S. (1994) *The Language Instinct: The New Science of Language and Mind* (London: Penguin Books).

Pinker, S. (2002) *The Blank Slate: The Modern Denial of Human Nature* (London: Viking Penguin Books).

Raice, S., A. Das and J. Letzing (2012) "Facebook Prices IPO at Record Value," *Wall Street Journal*, May 18, 2012.

Richerson, P.J., and R. Boyd (2005) *Not by Genes Alone* (Chicago: University of Chicago Press).

Ridley, M. (2003) *Nature Via Nurture: Genes, Experience, and What Makes Us Human* (New York: HarperCollins).

Roenneberg, T. (2012) *Internal Time: Chronotypes, Social Jet Lag, and Why You Are So Tired* (Cambridge, MA: Harvard University Press).

Ruse, M. (2009) *The Evolution Wars: A Guide to the Debates* (Millerton, NY: Greyhouse Publishing, 2nd edn).

Shultz, S., C. Opie and Q.D. Atkinson (2011) "Stepwise Evolution of Stable Sociality in Primates," *Nature* 479: 219-22.

Sloboda, J.A. (1985) *The Musical Mind: The Cognitive Psychology of Music* (New York: Oxford University Press, reprinted 1999).

Stacey, R.D. (2010) *Complexity and Organizational Reality* (New York: Routledge, 2nd edn).

Stewart, I. (1995) *Nature's Numbers: The Unreal Reality of Mathematics* (New York: Basic Books).

Tomasello, M. (2006) "Uniquely Human Cognition is a Product of Human Culture," in S.C. Levinson and P. Jaisson (eds.), *Evolution and Culture* (Cambridge, MA: MIT Press): 203-17.

Tracy, R. (2012) "Here Comes the Sunstorm," *Wall Street Journal*, May 15, 2012: A3.

Weingart, P., S.D. Mitchell, P.J. Richerson and S. Maasen (1997) *Human by Nature: Between Biology and the Social Sciences* (Mahwah, NJ: Lawrence Erlbaum Associates).

8

The **Big O ≈ Organization**

The rigorous application of Darwinian logic to business is
long overdue . . . [and] the application of these ideas to the
organizational sciences is a story of very limited engagement.
Nigel Nicholson and Rod White

Life . . . is poised between order and chaos . . . life
exists at the edge of chaos.
Stuart Kauffman

A modern symphony orchestra—its culture, organization, and membership—is a virtual mirror image of the modern corporation. Recall from the
Big S ≈ Symbol chapter that the core components of human culture are
tools, symbols, and sociality, which together make up neuro-organic culture. All three are front-and-center in the symphony orchestra: the musicians' instruments (tools), the musical sounds they create (symbols), and
the group of musicians themselves (sociality) who collectively perform
concerts (a salable product) for admiring audiences (and an occasional
cranky critic).

There is even a hint that the parallel extends to the long-term evolution of both organizations, possibly illustrating a Darwinian kind of natural selection of top-flight musicians, plus both competitive and collaborative genetic drivers of musical excellence, and most certainly musical brains adept at rendering instrumental, interpretive, and symbolic sounds in socially acceptable (and therefore adaptive) ways. Symphony orchestras and their smaller and earlier predecessor musical groups appeared far earlier than the modern business corporation and its forerunners—and perhaps set in motion organizational patterns that persist to this day, including the way both are organized and directed.

Today's symphony orchestra is organized as a pyramidal, bureaucratic, command-and-control structure: the music director (usually a male with *charisma*) is installed at the top of the pyramid, with the descending levels occupied by a concertmaster (also frequently male), principal players, and then rank-and-file musicians at the bottom of the pyramid. Reinforcing this pyramidal arrangement is a governing board of trustees, an administrative head (president or CEO), and supporting technical/service departments.

Alongside the musical pyramid one finds another contrasting organizational design based on teamwork and coordination. This includes the instrumental (tool-based) musical skills and talents of the players, the musical sounds they create from the composers' (symbolic) script, the interpretation of the musical score by the music director, and the harmonious teamwork and coordination of the orchestra's diverse sectional players. Blending the two organizational patterns—pyramid and teamwork—by coordinating the orchestral tools, symbols, and sociality components is the secret of an inspiring concert and an ongoing orchestral life. The same pattern is found within other kinds of organizations whether pursuing profits or promoting nonprofit causes. One might even see these organizational commonalities as an instance of Darwinian survival and adaptation—neuro-organic culture in action—as well as carrying a possible lesson for today's business corporation.

However well an orchestra is organized to produce great music, orchestral "train wrecks" are not unknown, arising from a complex mix of sources. They include untuned instruments, internal sectional fighting, weak musical direction, inadequate practice by musicians, limited rehearsal time, boring programs, lack of supportive funds, stressful tour engagements, poor acoustical halls—all of these unpredictable and unmanageable factors can threaten the most dedicated efforts to keep the organization afloat. So, welcome to the complexities of life on an evolving musical tundra and savanna! Corporations, even well-run ones, often encounter the same kind of chaotic complexities in the economic marketplace, as we shall see later in this chapter.

As all of the preceding chapters have shown, evolution is no picnic but is an ongoing process of adjusting organic entities to their ecological surroundings. As this chapter will try to show, the challenge for any large-scale organization, whether symphony orchestra or business corporation, lies in its organizational essence or "the way it does business." The key organizational elements to be explored in this chapter are **organizational hierarchy**, **technological organization**, and **complexity dynamics**. Each one manifests an ancient and continuing evolutionary heritage.

Organizational hierarchy

"Hierarchy" normally refers to an organization's levels of authority, command, control, prestige, income, and decision-making power. These elements are distributed inversely to the ranks of people in the organization, producing a pyramidal shape that concentrates authority in a small group at the upper levels while allocating descending amounts of authority to the larger numbers who occupy the pyramid's lower steps. This organizational pattern is found widely throughout human cultures, including business, government, education, military units, religion, social class, sports teams, and often in smaller entities such as social clubs, nonprofit institutions, social aid groups, and countless others. Monarchs, dictators, emperors, presidents, prime ministers, priests, school principals, mayors, generals, chief executive officers, imams, rabbis, governors, board chairs and directors, music directors, head coaches—all of these stand at their respective pyramid's very top, wielding authority and power in top-down, command-and-control fashion, while reaping the social and economic benefits and elitist perquisites of top dog, or top ape, status.

"Throughout history, organization has been associated with processes of social domination where individuals or groups find ways of imposing their will on others. This becomes clearly evident when we trace the lineage of the modern organization from its roots in ancient society, through the growth and development of military enterprise and empire, to its role in the modern world . . . [The Egyptian pyramid] is a metaphor of exploitation, symbolizing how the lives and hard labor of thousands of people were used to serve and glorify a privileged elite" (Morgan 1997: 303). Power aggrandizement, as practiced by Egyptian pharaohs—and now corporate CEOs—is one of hierarchy's most notable features.

The etymological origins of the English word "hierarchy" in early and medieval Europe make clear its religious (Christian) associations, by invoking angelic hosts and ranked orders, heavenly beings, priestly ecclesiastical authority and dominance, plus an all-powerful god entity ruling over all from the top of a heavenly pyramid of sorts (*New Shorter Oxford English Dictionary*, 1993). Similar mythologies and related religious creation stories dot the human landscape throughout history and across the globe's continents, socially justifying the hierarchical allocation of command-and-control authority and power to those occupying the upper ranks of a society's class and status system.

However impressive, supportive, and justificatory its current religious credentials may be, hierarchy displays an even more ancient evolutionary heritage that continues to cast its shadow on modern life, including the business corporation. The evolutionary parallels are too obvious to ignore or deny, and they trace directly to modern *Homo sapiens*' kinship with predecessor species and genera, most specifically the closely related chimpanzees, where the genetic overlap and duplication with humans is almost (but not quite) total.

Primatologist Frans de Waal tells how hierarchy plays a central role among our closest evolutionary kin: ". . . it was quite clear who was at the top of the hierarchy. [The one with] unparalleled physical strength . . . walked in an exaggeratedly slow and heavy manner . . . characteristic of the alpha male. The fact of being in a position of power makes a male physically impressive, hence the assumption that he occupies the position that fits his appearance." Lower-ranked chimps display ". . . a special form of behavior . . . the *submissive greeting* [when] the subordinate assumes a position whereby he looks up at the individual he is greeting . . . [and makes] deep bows . . . 'greeters' bring objects with them . . . kiss his feet, neck, or chest. The one almost grovels in the dust, the other regally receives the 'greeting' " (de Waal 1998: 78).

Two other students of chimpanzee life reinforce de Waal's research-based views of hierarchy's importance: ". . . a male chimpanzee in his prime organizes his whole life around issues of rank. His attempts to achieve and then maintain alpha status are cunning, persistent, energetic, and time-consuming . . . all these behaviors come . . . from a set of emotions that . . . are labeled 'pride' or, more negatively, 'arrogance' . . . The male chimpanzee behaves as if he is quite driven to reach the top of the community heap. What most male chimpanzees strive for is being on top, the one position where they will never have to grovel . . . [T]he immediate reason he vies for status . . . is simply to dominate his peers . . . Winning has become an end in itself" (Wrangham and Peterson 1996: 191, 199). The authors then add, "It looks the same with men."

The evolutionary reason for such behavior is clear, as told by evolutionary psychologist Denise Cummins: "The key to understanding the impact of status lies in appreciating its relation to *survival and reproductive success* both during our evolutionary past and in our present lives. Status (or rank) is most frequently defined *as priority of access to resources in competitive situations* . . . higher status individuals [are] less likely to die of predation or starvation and more likely to leave living offspring" (Cummins 2005: 678). In other words, high status, power, and dominance confer two of the Darwinian survival advantages on their possessors and wielders: sustenance and sex, with the third, security, an implied if somewhat shaky benefit.

Picking up on Wrangham and Peterson's comment that this kind of chimpanzee alpha male behavior "looks a lot like men," we move now a bit further along on the **Evolutionary Cascade** to confront the modern corporation and its corps of top-level executives and managers. Truth to tell, the business corporation is an institutionalized form of hierarchical power, managed, directed, and led overwhelmingly by males who act "a lot like" alpha male chimpanzees. The transition occurred slowly over many thousands of years as trade and commerce, and eventually the corporation, emerged from the shadows of chimpanzee politics and power.

"The first types of formal organization probably arose in hierarchical societies where one social group imposed itself on another, often through conquest. Such societies became further stratified as certain individuals placed themselves in the service of the ruling class as priests, scribes, *bookkeepers, traders, and merchants* . . . We find the same system reproduced in modern organization in terms of the distinctions between *owners, managers, and workers*. Thousands of years intervene between the emergence of the first formal organizations and *the corporations that we see around us today*" (Morgan 1997: 308-309; emphasis added). The evolutionary roots of business hierarchy could not be made more obvious.

Contemporary theorists of organizational behavior observed in the modern business corporation are quick to acknowledge and even endorse the hierarchical pattern of rank-order status found there. Standard textbooks describe these hierarchical levels as conferring "legitimate power" on managers who occupy the upper ranks, thereby rationalizing their subsequent wielding of such power for attaining corporate goals (Daft 2007: 490). But it goes even further, as noted by a scholarly doyen of corporate power: ". . . there is power associated with formal position. The chairman, president, the supervisor—all have power as a consequence of their formal position in the organizational hierarchy . . . The acceptance of hierarchy, of the chain of command, is so automatic that it makes news when it is violated . . . Authority is also obeyed because it is almost inconceivable not to. The power of leaders and bosses becomes institutionalized and is thus not questioned or even thought about" (Pfeffer 1992: 130, 133).[1]

Although institutional hierarchy is thus widely accepted, another scholar, Martin Mulder, points out that, "At the same time, however . . . there is a taboo surrounding the word 'power': 'When we talk of power, we are talking about someone else . . .' When referring to ourselves we prefer to speak of 'carrying responsibility,' 'being in a position of authority,' or 'helping others by taking decisions out of their hands' (quoted in de Waal 1998: 187). That evasiveness regarding hierarchy's naked power is reinforced by today's organization theorists who write virtual "manuals for managers" on how to acquire and hold power. Organizational power is accepted as fully legitimate; the point of instruction is how to get power and wield it. As such, the authors pamper and protect the corporate establishment and overlook power's biological evolutionary sources and its broader societal significance. Gareth Morgan puts the matter plainly: "much of traditional organization theory . . . has for the most part ignored values or ideological premises . . . [I]n improving the rationality and

---

1 Pfeffer's point is reinforced by a *Wall Street Journal* news report entitled "Who's the Boss? There Isn't One" about a small handful of "bossless" companies where employees self-manage the firm's operations. Even in those companies "a small cadre of top brass handles company-wide issues and external communications" and some of them appoint a Chief Executive Officer (Silverman 2012). Hierarchy remains dominant in most business corporations.

efficiency of an organization [through domination] one may be providing the basis for action that is profoundly irrational for many other groups of people . . . [D]*omination may be intrinsic to the way we organize* and not just an unintended side effect" (Morgan 1997: 341, emphasis added). *Sic transit* management education and corporate consultancy advice, both of them overlooking, or lacking knowledge of, the evolutionary origins and broader effects of hierarchical power.

Alpha males are so rife in corporate life that corporate consultants now identify an "alpha male syndrome"—a disease-like behavioral trait that goes with the executive territory and well beyond (Ludeman and Erlandson 2006: 8). We are told that "Alphas are found at every level of the organizational chart . . . they look for ways to increase their power and influence, dominating meetings, taking the lead on projects, and otherwise making their presence felt" (Ludeman and Erlandson 2006: 3)—all of which makes one recall those swaggering, hair-bristling, heavyweight alpha chimpanzees. The parallel with chimpanzee alphas is undeniable: For humans, "Alpha males' intimidating style makes other people defensive, and alphas respond to that defensiveness with disdain" (Ludeman and Erlandson 2006: 17). For chimps, "once he has been accepted as the alpha . . . his tendency for violence falls dramatically [and] they can become benign leaders" (Wrangham and Peterson 1996: 191). The negative behavioral markers of the "Alpha commander," as identified by manager-executives themselves, are Bulldozer, Chest Pounder, General, My Way or the Highway, Rant 'n' Rave, Tyrant, Warrior, and Wheeler Dealer. Less power-oriented types display other qualities, such as the Alpha visionary, the Alpha strategist, and the Alpha executor, which are variants of the basic organizational disorder called the Alpha Male Syndrome (Ludeman and Erlandson 2006: 59).

Alpha females also appear on the corporate scene, though far less frequently and manifesting lower levels of testosterone-induced behavior. ". . . alpha females get angry, but they're seldom as belligerent as alpha males. They like to win, and they set aggressive goals for themselves and their teams, but they're not as intimidating or as authoritarian as their male counterparts. And while they can be fiercely competitive, they're less likely than alpha males to use ruthless tactics or to see peers and colleagues as rivals who have to be destroyed" (Ludeman and Erlandson 2006: 4). However, that didn't stop HP's CEO Carly Fiorina and HP's Board Chair Patricia Dunn from allegedly authorizing illegal spying on board members to discover who might be leaking company secrets. Looking out for No. 1 is all too common in corporate life (Bussey 2011). We are seeing here the long-term evolutionary outcome of Darwin's sexual selection process that differentiates males and females by size, physical strength, and domineering–submissive behavioral traits, plus the evolutionary-induced trend that grants precedence to males in group life, reinforced by a symbolic/cultural system that typically rations or blocks women's access to power positions and superior status ranks.[2]

The general lesson is clear: the organizational architecture of the modern corporation is a direct evolutionary descendent of more ancient forms of organizing and regulating human group behavior in which alpha males typically dominate and rule over others of lower rank and social standing. The resultant organizational hierarchy grants goal-seeking and decision-making powers to those—male or female—who occupy the topmost ranks of the corporate pyramid.

Technological organization

An orchestral maestro does indeed occupy the topmost level of *musical* authority, while the orchestra's board chair and administrative head typically wield *financial* and *strategic* authority: an organizational triumvirate of hierarchical power and influence. The orchestra's musicians and its administrative staff members understand and generally accept this kind of top-down command-and-control organizational system, albeit with occasional grumbling about how lopsided and unfair it can seem.

However, hierarchy is not the entire organizational story because the maestro as musical director exerts another, uniquely different kind of authority based not on the position held in the pyramid of power but rather on an acquired expert knowledge of the orchestra's musical agenda and how it can best be realized through the coordinated, cooperative

---

2 "Catalyst president and CEO, Ilene Lang, has said, 'Wall Street culture is characterized by . . . masculine, macho kinds of behaviour . . . people who swagger . . . it is behavior that's admired in men but despised in women' and exists wherever traditionally macho behavior is what it takes to be successful" (Torregrosa 2012).

actions of the musicians themselves. This kind of leadership ability—based on technical skill and musical knowledge, not power per se—is the key to an orchestra's successful performance and therefore its continued existence. An orchestra's *musical* organization emerges then as a function of the musical instruments themselves, the musicians' technical skills, and the music director's interpretational and coordinative talent. Organization in this case is a combined outcome of tool, skill, and directorial talent, having little or nothing to do with hierarchical power as such.

There is a parallel with the modern business corporation. Its life depends primarily on a kind of leadership that is capable of coordinating and organizing the diverse actions of the company's workforce with the various technologies needed to achieve the goals set, the strategies to be used, and the corporation's intended economic function. Here, too, one finds the basic organizational components: tool, skill, and coordination of the whole. Technology, as we shall see, is inherently organizational in character and function. And it has been made that way by nature.

Organic technology

As told in the Big L ≈ Life chapter, all forms of organic life manifest built-in survival techniques: a drive to adapt and survive in their respective ecosystems. This would be true of even the very tiniest bacterial or pre-bacterial life forms continuing through the largest megafauna creatures. Through evolutionary (and largely genetic) behavioral traits, each life form is able to interact with its environment, tapping into energy sources that support and extend its life. It may seem unusual or even mistaken to label these gene-based traits as a form of "technology," because tools and technology are commonly believed to be unique, human-created, extra-organic, even non-organic manufactured "artificial" items. But that puts the evolutionary cart before the horse because bacteria and other cellular life forms were here long before humans emerged. *Their* adaptive organic techniques laid down the evolutionary foundations for *ours*, call them what you will, but the adaptive results are the same. Moreover, recall from earlier chapters that many pre-human creatures—ants, termites, bees, apes, chimpanzees, birds, and others—have been master builders of homes and makers of tools of varying shape and usefulness in their struggle for survival. To reject the technology appellation for those earlier adaptive efforts and behaviors is to suggest that *Homo* technology is a unique form of organic adaptation, not seen previously in the evolutionary record, which of course is patent anthropocentric nonsense. Genetic, organic "tools" enabling diverse organic life forms to adapt and survive are common throughout the animal kingdom.

"All life forms possess this kind of genetic technology. Without it, they would perish, either instantly or slowly. *It is life's most basic tool* ... Genetic tools are not 'manufactured,' nor are they deliberately or with forethought designed, made, or constructed. They are simply part of natural biotic phenomena ... self-contained within any given life unit ... inherited genetically from many preceding generations" (Frederick 1995: 174, 175). Technology, whether human or otherwise, is "all natural," a product of natural selection, greatly accelerated in the *Homo* case by an increasingly complex brain.

In this way, the long-term evolution of tools was creating the basis for a distinct kind of organizational behavior. Peter Reynolds identifies the behavioral source of such technical organization, calling it "heterotechnic cooperation," which means that different craft skills (think of orchestra musicians playing a variety of instruments) are "complementary" to one another. "... human technology is not just 'tool use,' and not just 'cooperative' tool use, but tool use combined with a social organization for heterotechnic cooperation. This heterotechnic aspect of human tool use, characterized by complementary technical roles among the participants, is manifested in all human societies by *a distinct form of social organization* ... the face-to-face task group ... [I]n all societies work is typically performed by face-to-face task groups of people cooperating to accomplish a common goal. [This kind of complementary cooperation] ... requires the *integration* of individual minds into *a larger, cooperative framework"* (Reynolds 1993: 412, emphasis added).[3]

The conclusion is inescapable: tool use by cooperating individuals is the basis of a distinctive kind of human organization that evolved in parallel fashion with the tools themselves. Reynolds even identifies "the likely evolutionary precursor for a human type of technical and economic

---

3 "Face-to-face" relationships are rapidly acquiring a new electronic meaning and form in the age of social media such as the popular Facebook phenomenon. "Face-to-face" is now often "virtual," not proximate. But these new technological forms only emphasize technology's ability to relate and organize people to each other in wider and wider social networks.

organization [as] grooming in nonhuman primates" (e.g., chimpanzees and bonobos), because it involves "face-to-face groups with exchange dynamics and reciprocal complementary roles" (Reynolds 1993: 423). There you have it defined as plainly as possible: the *evolutionary, organic, technological basis* of cooperative human organization—nothing other than human sociality itself.

Technology's reach and its organizational roots within nature are vastly greater than Reynolds envisions. Listen to another well-known student of technology, Brian Arthur, who speaks of its self-generative, self-organizing power: "the collective of technology is *self-producing* . . . it produces new technology from itself [and] technology creates itself out of itself." By being both self-organizing and taking in and giving out energy to maintain itself, "it is organic" in the sense that "technologies are acquiring properties we associate with living organisms [and] they more and more resemble living organisms." By reproducing, growing, responding and adapting to its environment, *"technology is indeed a living organism"* (Arthur 2009: 170, 189, 205, 208, emphasis added).

Science writer-thinker Kevin Kelly, another authoritative voice, agrees: "Large systems of technology often behave like a very primitive organism. Networks, especially electronic networks, exhibit near-biological behavior . . . In its origins and fundamentals, *a tool is as natural as our life* . . . We are now symbiotic with technology" (Kelly 2010: 9, 22, 37, emphasis added). Kelly intends no metaphor here but proposes a literal identity of tool and human organism, which would be another form of gene-based technology.

The coordinative tendencies of advanced technological systems induce cooperation among all who work with tools for the simple reason that the work cannot go forward on any other basis. Tool users (in factories or orchestras) must be related to one another and must be organized along technical lines if they wish to enjoy the fruits of technology's productive potential. The organizational design springs from the technology itself and from what the tools and their users are capable of doing. Behavior follows the pathways laid down by tools. Form follows function. When people use tools, they acknowledge the organizational logic implicit in technology. There is no other way to reap technology's many benefits (Frederick 1995: 190-93).

From the very earliest use of tools some 2+ million years ago by *Homo*'s earliest ancestors, the several Australopithecines of the African jungles, up to today's dazzling displays of technological marvels, humans have organized themselves both organically and technically.

Beyond technology's inherently collaborative nature, it is also worth noting that modern technology is no respecter of established structures, procedures, routines, and habits, either personal or social. As new forms and techniques are constantly generated, old ones tend to die out, although Kevin Kelly (2010) makes the interesting point that nearly all older technologies continue in use somewhere in the world, no doubt reflecting varying levels of technological advance, as well as sentimental attachment to symbolically embedded cultural customs (classic cars, dial telephones, typewriters).

Complexity dynamics and organization

Whether for a corporation or a symphony orchestra, it may seem a simple matter to identify and hire a skilled workforce of tool-users or accomplished musicians, arrange them in coordinated patterns to do their work or play music, and guide their activities to produce products and services or to thrill an audience of musical fans. All it takes, one could easily assume, is a top boss or maestro with the power to give necessary directions to workers or musicians—an organizational hierarchy—plus a dedicated talent for inducing technical cooperation from tool-users and instrument-players—a techno-logic of coordination. That is indeed the aspiration and goal of business leaders and musical maestros, as well as the underlying assumption of business schools and musical academies that prepare future business managers and tomorrow's orchestral members. Ah, if only it were so simple! But it isn't, as is increasingly recognized by those who study the complexities of organizational life. It is quite possible that the secrets of corporate (and orchestral) organization and performance are found, at least partially (if at all), in the dynamics of complex systems.

Complexity theory is . . . well, complex. However, the whole story needn't be told here in order to clarify the evolutionary dynamics of such complex organizations as corporations and orchestras. A few key concepts will suffice: self-organization, linear–nonlinear relationships, complex adaptive system, and chaos, which we examine next. Taken together, they can be a manager's or a maestro's greatest organizational nightmare or most satisfying triumph.[4]

Self-organization

Organization appears to be a built-in feature of the Universe, which means that separate, disparate, independent entities become related or attached to one another in functional ways, thereby enabling or enhancing their respective or combined evolutionary pathways. This was certainly true of Earth's earliest life forms, as prokaryote cells lacking nuclei merged with other organic components to become nucleated eukaryote cells, providing the basic cellular structure of today's organic world. An even more primal organizing tendency appeared as energy, matter, radiation, and gravity formed stars, galaxies, and other kinds of cosmic order following the Big Bang.

"Self"-organization simply means that formerly independent entities form new combinations: stars gather to become galaxies, cells gather together to form organs, organs combine to form organisms, organisms combine to form ecosystems. Complexity theorists often say that such combinations occur "spontaneously" by which they mean without any obvious outside control or controlling agency, thus justifying the idea of "self" (or undirected) organization. But "spontaneous" does not equate with "any old way" because evolution of all kinds of organizational arrangement consists of physical processes, chemical compounds, and biological entities that interact in accordance with their respective built-in characteristics or, as commonly said, according to "the laws of nature." A new function or phenomenon of some kind occurs when these elements combine in various patterns: a star is formed, an organism emerges, symbolic language is generated, a new competitor with a superior product suddenly appears. This continuous dynamic process is capable of producing an endless variety of organizational forms and structures. Corporate managers and orchestral music directors would be well advised to be on the lookout for such self-organizational tendencies that may appear

---

4 For an overview of complexity theory, see Mitchell 2009. For an even simpler version, see Frederick 1998. For more comprehensive sources, see references at the end of this chapter.

unexpectedly, for better or worse, in the workplace or during orchestral rehearsals. More about this indeterminacy a bit further along.

Linear–nonlinear relationships

A "linear" relationship, as the name implies, is a direct, straight-line, no-question-about-it, easy-to-understand phenomenon. As in a jigsaw puzzle, the separate pieces fit together logically to make a picture or pattern, and when the last piece is put in place, the puzzle is solved. In the corporate workshop, the tools of production behave likewise: they fit together in techno-logical ways to make an intended product. It is suggestive of linearity that a factory's production system is referred to as a "production line" that is easy to understand and work if all pieces are put in their proper places and perform as intended. Hear that, musicians? Follow the maestro's suggestions and interpretations, and all will be well.

"Nonlinear" is another matter altogether. Here, everything is rather uncertain. A nonlinear system seems to obey its own commands; it may change without warning, oscillate wildly or irregularly from one state to another, engage in random movements, and is not always subject to centralized control or any reliable control at all. Predictability is out the window because no one knows just where the system is headed. If this begins to sound like today's financial markets after a global breakdown, don't be too surprised. Market systems of all kinds are often nonlinear, unpredictable, unstable, now up, now down, always oscillating around an unknowable and unreachable center—the despair of government policymakers and corporate strategic planners alike. Some examples: Newly appointed Google CEO Larry Page was quickly buffeted by a host of problems including an antitrust probe by government officials, a criminal investigation into accepting ads from online pharmacies, and lack of clarity about investment plans (Efrati 2011: B1, B5). And AOL's uncoordinated culture clashes documented by the *Wall Street Journal* offer another example: The company acquired "over a half dozen companies in an effort to shake off its reputation as an Internet has-been. It hasn't worked" (Vascellaro and Steel 2011: B1, B4). Yet another well-publicized case: Yahoo fired CEO Carol Bartz after losing competitive ground to Google and Facebook, reporting flat earnings and a wavering stock price, a failed partnership with Microsoft, and becoming a possible takeover target (*Wall Street Journal* 2011). Life at the top of the corporate pyramid can be a nonlinear nightmare, though not necessarily due just to an executive's "personal" failure. Rather, the devil is in the company's complex interactions with a nonlinear, unpredictable, uncontrolled market environment. Of course, the CEO may be fired anyway, as a scapegoat of complexity's complexity.

Complex adaptive system

Another of complexity theory's key ideas is called a complex adaptive system (CAS). A CAS is much like the modern business corporation, being composed of a group of interacting participants, usually called "agents," whose collective actions enable the entire system to adapt to its environment (or not). Long before the corporation arrived on the scene, CASs were common in organic life, constituting the basic elements of life. An ecosystem is itself a very complex adaptive system. Each unit of life, from cells to genes and beyond, is a type of CAS, a collectivity of organic agents interacting in adaptive ways.

The CAS label does not endow the formal, legalistic structure of the corporation per se with an organic substance or identity because, as noted in an earlier chapter, "The Big D ≈ Darwin," organic life exists only in the *individual* participating agents whose *collective* cooperative actions produce adaptive behavior for *the whole*. This collectivity of human organic agents—trained to use both physical and conceptual tools, and disciplined in the application of symbolic language (as information)—seeks strategic pathways of survival and adaptation. As complexity theorist Stuart Kauffman says, "the modern corporation is a collectively self-sustaining structure of roles and obligations that 'lives' in an economic world . . . in ways at least loosely analogous to those of [the bacterium] *E. coli*" (Kauffman 1995: 300). By performing their designated functional jobs within the CAS, each of the individual participant-agents—executives, managers, employees—thereby secures for *itself* two of the Darwinian adaptive/survival basics: sustenance (via income) and a secure niche (via job security), with some even managing the third component, sex mates (via on-the-job mutual consent, dominance, or concealed exploitation). Simultaneously, the collective CAS, by marshalling its human, financial, technological, and symbolic capital, seeks its own adaptive means of survival on an ever-evolving fitness landscape (equivalent to an ecosystem). A complex adaptive system is held together, that is, is "organized," via the coordinated organic functioning of its separate components. In this sense, it is nature's most basic type of organization, manifested in multiple and diverse forms from the Big Bang to the present.

Chaos

Chaos is . . . well, chaotic. In common usage, something that is chaotic is without order or stable form, involving motions and activities that tend to oscillate in unpredictable and indeterminate ways. In short, chaos is a dynamic mess, with little meaning other than confusion and incomprehension by observers and participants. In the hands of complexity theorists, though, chaos describes a condition of *dis*-organization but not *non*-organization, of disorder but not complete lack of order. Sorting out this puzzle helps explain some of the negative vulnerabilities, as well as the upside potentialities, inherent in modern corporate organizational systems.

Corporate chaos arises principally, not from lack of executive rationality, nor from the irrationalities of cultural traditions, nor even from the imperfections of predictive techniques, but rather from the firm's well-intended efforts to perform its normal tasks and functions. You might say, "How can this be?" Is it then just a lack of foresight? Apparently not; after all, CEOs are not dummies. So, what's the problem? Or better still, where's the problem?

Here are the fundamentals in brief. As a complex adaptive system, a corporation's principal efforts are to try to survive by adapting to its chosen fitness landscapes, or in economic terminology, its markets. It does so by *economizing*, which is another way of describing the adaptive results produced by the CAS's collective assemblage of people, resources, technology, and financial capital. Driven fast and furiously enough in its profit-seeking economizing drive, a corporate CAS almost inevitably finds itself subject to the nonlinear, self-organizing, chaotic uncertainties and complexities inherent in human (neuro-organic) culture. Its power hierarchy strains to retain a favored competitive position via a strategy of constant growth, expansion, and innovation. The firm's dynamic technology drives the company onward and outward in a constant search for new products and markets. Complexity theorists are fond of referring to "the edge of chaos," where maximum corporate economizing is achieved but where one misstep might drive the firm over the edge into the total chaos of massive losses, downsizing, bankruptcy, and loss of identity through failure or takeover. Order becomes disorder; organization becomes disorganization; successful adaptation becomes its opposite, an entropic death. A corporate CAS perishes, scattering its individual agents—people, jobs, resources—across the market landscape where they might then seek an alternative security niche with yet another CAS. You needn't be a Nobel laureate in economics to see the equivalence of "the edge of chaos" and fiercely competitive economic markets. Although the language is different, CAS survival is the goal in both cases, whether avoiding catastrophic market defeat or plunging into chaotic failure.[5]

Are corporations too complex to manage?

It's a fair question, given the nonlinear, self-organizing, chaotic dynamics confronting the managers of corporate-type complex adaptive systems. A long-established academic tradition of management scholarship, plus a virtual army of corporate consultants, not to speak of university-level business schools that prepare future managers, would suggest or imply that the job is doable.

Complexity theorist Ralph Stacey, a leading voice, begs to differ: "there is a major contradiction between the organizational reality of uncertainty and the beliefs . . . about the capacity of executives to know what is going on and be in control." The traditional body of management theory—he calls it the "dominant discourse"—assumes that: "small groups of powerful executives are able to *choose* the 'direction' their organization will move in, realize a 'vision' for it, create the conditions in which its members will be innovative and entrepreneurial, and select the 'structures' and 'conditions' which will enable them to be in control and so ensure success . . ."

In this dominant discourse, "uncertainty plays a very minor role and leaders know what is going on." Although "leader-managers participate in dominating ways to feed their fantasies of omnipotence . . . any claim to mastery by leader-managers must be a fantasy." Lacking control as they face the uncertainties of a nonlinear, potentially chaotic market

---

5 The following chapter introduces a new concept, "economaxing," that can cause a corporation to topple over "the edge of chaos". Stay tuned.

environment, about the most they can do, according to Stacey, is to "participate in the on-going conversation of organizational life . . . in a way that deepens and widens communication [which is] a matter of great importance." However, "this does not reduce leader-managers to ornamental bystanders; it just suggests a more realistic understanding of what they can do and what they actually do" (Stacey: 2010: 1, 12, 157-58). Hear that message, all corporate CEOs who believe in the power of visionary planning and carefully crafted strategy? The complexities of nonlinear, self-organizing complex adaptive systems operative in the marketplace doom your company to lesser ends than you seek. Chaos seems to trump rational management.[6]

Really? Is it that bad? Are some of today's corporations not only "too big to fail" but also "too complex to manage"? Two strategy scholars, writing in one of the management establishment's most respected journals, *Harvard Business Review*, believe there is hope remaining, in spite of complexity's challenges. Acknowledging that prediction often fails, that simple actions produce unintended consequences, that human beings' cognitive limits deny unerring managerial vision, and that rare events can be more significant than average ones, they say nevertheless that "managers can navigate these difficulties by making fundamental changes" as they approach key tasks. And then they simply repeat what has long served as traditional advice to managerial cadres everywhere, which sounds ever so much like Stacey's "dominant discourse" by relying on "better forecasting, mitigating risks, making tradeoffs, and ensuring diversity of thought" (Sargut and McGrath 2011: 68-76). That doesn't seem to get us, or business managers, very far.

It is possible that **Natural Corporate Management** offers a way out of this seemingly unresolvable puzzle of managerial competency versus chaotic complexity.

---

6 The same doubts might be raised about the presumed mastery of orchestral maestros whose musical interpretations and directorial talents are thought to be the key to an orchestra's success. Sometimes, yes; other times, no.

Organization, complexity, and Natural Corporate Management: An evolutionary equation

The evolutionary legacy of the modern corporation comprises each of the successive, cumulative phases of what earlier chapters have called an **Evolutionary Cascade**—a continuum of physical energetics, cellular-organic entities, natural selection, genetic drivers, tool users, neuro-symbolic culture, and now, in this chapter, organizational patterns of three kinds: hierarchical, technological, and self-organizing complex adaptive systems. This evolutionary genealogy, both ancient and contemporary, has generated the modern business corporation by attaching to it the respective behavioral traits of each evolutionary phase.

The three characteristic organizational patterns based on hierarchy, technology, and complexity share an evolutionary function of overriding significance: enabling a corporation to attain its maximum adaptive potential. That may seem strange or contradictory if in doing so it risks self-destruction by tumbling over the edge of chaos into entropic oblivion. Ah, but that's where management talent comes in, not necessarily (or even usually) to prevent or avoid organizational disaster nor to "control" events but rather to seek order within chaotic disorder, so as to secure the corporate collectivity as a functioning entity. Truth to tell, all three forms of organization have helped drive the well-managed corporation straight toward the *edge* of chaos but not beyond. How can that be? And how does it differ from Stacey's "dominant discourse" posing as management wisdom?

It does indeed seem counterintuitive that evolution—a life-giving, life-supporting, life-expanding process—would have led the corporation to confront such a potentially disastrous, life-denying possibility. Natural selection is about life-survival and adaptation. Ecosystems house and shelter and nourish multiple forms of interconnected cellular life. Selfish genes seek immortality by building survival-prone bodies. Successive lines of pre-*Homo* and *Homo* primates outperformed and outlived their ancestral forebears. Expanding and ever-more-complex primate brains produced tool-using aids for enhanced survival. That same *Homo* brain generated diverse symbol systems with remarkable powers of human survival en masse; witness today's 7 billion world population.

Although it is true that meteorological (weather), geological (earthquake, volcanic), and astronomical (solar flare, sunspot cycle) forces, as well as biologically sourced processes (invasion, predator–prey dynamics)—all of these singly or combined—can disrupt ecosystem life harmonies; and although rogue genes, immune system dysfunctions, and invasive disease organisms can put life at risk; and although older pre-mammalian neural algorithms may override the more adaptively inclined, life-supportive neural impulses; and although a distressing number and diversity of symbolic meanings—familial, tribal, clan, and societal loyalty—generate uncounted slaughters, assassinations, mass murders, and warfare: In spite of all these life-negating processes that seem to be built-in features of Earthly life itself, in some way, life not only continues, but thrives.

How then is one to explain what seems most unlikely? What is it about the corporate collectivity and its organizational patterns—hierarchical, technological, and complexly adaptive—that carries it toward a positive outcome, toward an affirmative (though perilous) existence at the very edge of chaos and ruin? Is there an answer lurking somewhere within the **Evolutionary Cascade** itself? Possibly so.

The energy equation

The secret is in plain sight, hidden from view by its very obviousness. It's a bit like those neurological lab experiments that trick observers by asking them to keep close track of the numbers of specific events displayed on a video screen while a man dressed as a very large gorilla wanders through the scene. Nearly all of the experiment's participants are so focused on the task at hand that they are completely unaware of the gorilla's presence, never even seeing it. In the present case of corporate organization, the unseen "gorilla" is so commonplace and normal that we tend to miss or even dismiss its presence or importance, though it is the key to the organizational/complexity puzzle.

The most basic organizing component in the Universe is energy. Energy is the primordial parent of all subsequent forms of organization (and disorganization), whether physical, chemical, or biological. It has been so since the Big Bang, which organized basic matter, the periodic elements, stars and galaxies, generated gravitational glue to hold them together and dark matter/energy to scatter them from each other. This story of primal energy was told in the Big E ≈ Energy chapter, while succeeding chapters revealed the appearance and emergence of (organized) cellular life within (organized) ecosystems, plus the diverse (organized) forms taken by organic phenotypes, genotypes, cognotypes, and symbotypes, including the (organized) collectivity of organic agents we call the modern corporation.

*The underlying rule present in each phase of the **Evolutionary Cascade** is a constant, unwavering quest for energy.* The rule applies equally to all types of organization, whether physical, chemical, or biological, complex or simple, adaptive or not. Organic life's most basic organized form, the cell, captures and uses solar energy via its mitochondrial "batteries," just as today's solar panels and wind farms harness energy for human usage. *Organization's principal evolutionary function is to enhance and enable the capture and use of energy, to process it efficiently, and to drive that energy at maximum speed toward entropic equilibrium.* Understandably focused as we are on the biological sphere, since we are biological organisms symbiotically interacting with life-supportive organic ecosystems, most of us tend to overlook the energy "gorilla" in our midst.

All three forms of corporate organization—hierarchy, technology, and self-organizing complex adaptive systems—are proven masters at capturing and maximizing energy flow. Each is an energy-transduction mechanism that captures free energy from its environment, organizes and processes it, and reduces its initial high gradient to lower levels by driving the firm's economic production.

Consider *self-organizing complex adaptive systems*: Listen to E.W. Buck Lawrimore, an experienced consultant to corporations, governments, and nonprofit organizations, who introduces his concept of "ordergy":

> In brief, everything that exists is composed of order and energy. All forms of energy, matter, living beings, systems . . . and the entire universe, are composed of ordered energy. Energy is the very stuff of life . . . Just as individual people are living energy systems, so also are organizations and communities . . . [I]ncreasing and sustaining the order of a dynamic system requires a higher flow of energy. Complexity . . . unleashes human energy and creativity. Organizations which are "on the edge of chaos" are . . . much more likely to survive and thrive in the fast-changing 21st century (Lawrimore 2005: 130).

The key to adaptation is an organization's success in capturing and directing energy flows to support its existence.

Consider *organizational hierarchy*: "hierarchical organizations are ... powerful machineries for energy dispersal [and] hierarchically integrated systems have emerged and evolved increasingly more effective in leveling differences and gradients in energy densities" (Annila and Kuismanen 2009: 228). Like it or not, hierarchical power does drive corporations to high performance levels by forcefully concentrating energy resources on organizational tasks. The subsequent entropic price may be high for competitors and ecosystems, while beneficial for the corporation.

Consider *technology's organizational role*:

> Technology's dominance ultimately stems ... from its origin in the same self-organization that brought galaxies, planets, life, and minds into existence. Over aeons of cosmic time [the] expanding differential (between expanding emptiness and the remnant hotness of the big bang) powered evolution, life, intelligence, and eventually the acceleration of technology. Energy, like water under gravity, will seep to the lowest, coolest level and not rest until all differential has been eliminated ... While the rest of the material cosmos slips down to the frozen basement, only a remarkable few will catch a wave of energy to rise up and dance (Kelly 2010: 61, 63, 69).

The leading corporate "energy dancers" of today are those firms whose *maître de ballet*—a kind of energy gorilla—has marshaled an impressive array of coordinated technology to sustain the corporate collectivity's life and existence, even as ever-larger waves of energy are thereby accelerated toward an entropic oblivion for others less technologically adept. At once, energy triumphant, and energy destructive.

In mathematically metaphorical terms, the evolutionary energy equation would propose that corporate organization is a function of energy flows generated by three kinds of energy transduction mechanisms—hierarchy, technology, and complex self-organization—each one capable of enhancing the corporation's continued existence or driving it into chaotic destruction.

Solving the equation requires corporate managers (and orchestral maestros) to understand and accept the fundamentals of **Natural Corporate**

Management: Your work, your plans, your decisions, your visions, your successes, your failures—all are an outcome of the **Evolutionary Cascade**'s natural forces. The sooner you grasp this reality, the more likely you are to guide your corporation (or your orchestra) into achievable, survivable, and fruitful pathways.

As you take this naturological pathway, heed the words of two pioneering pathfinders: "[M]anagers with the understanding that human behavior is shaped by evolutionary influences can achieve desired organizational outcomes by cultivating a context consistent with the natural inclinations that influence human social action" (Pierce and White 1999: 851). London Business School's Nigel Nicholson had argued even earlier that "culture is the adapted product of individual psychological architecture" and that "organizational forms relate to our ancestral paradigms" (Nicholson 1997: 183). Nicholson expanded and reinforced these Darwin-like reminders in a famous *Harvard Business Review* article, "How Hardwired Is Human Behavior" (1998), and his book *Executive Instinct* (2000). The practical lesson for corporate managers is crystal clear: Heed the natural sources and consequences of evolved organizational patterns.

To aid managers in absorbing this evolutionary lesson, the following chapter depicts the economic landscape where a corporation's basic naturological functions—economizing and ecologizing—can make all the difference in achieving a company's adaptive success.

The Big O's pivotal points

- Three different organizational patterns characterize the operations and management of the modern business corporation: organizational hierarchy, technological organization, and complex self-organization. All three are the outcome of long-term evolutionary processes

- Organizational hierarchy organizes a corporation's workforce as a pyramid of power, influence, authority, and income, dominated by top-level executives who originate, direct, and review corporate policy, goals, strategy, and decision-making. Hierarchy's evolutionary heritage is found in the alpha-male behavioral patterns of chimpanzees and other primate species preceding *Homo sapiens*

- Technological organization occurs when a corporation's tool complex is coordinated with the skills of the workforce in pursuit of the firm's economic goals and functions. Technology's evolutionary heritage is found in the close functional association of organic-genetic technology with human tool-using efforts to survive and adapt to ecosystem environments

- Complexity-based organization of the corporation occurs through the interactions of self-organizing processes, nonlinear dynamics, complex adaptive system behavior, and chaotic order

- Corporate management is vastly complicated by the chaotic potentialities of highly competitive markets, where executive direction encounters unpredictable, uncontrollable, nonlinear, contradictory events that threaten the firm's adaptability and survival

- All forms of organic order—physical, chemical, bio-organic, and their modern derivatives (hierarchy, technology, complexity)—are derived from the basic energy process that organized the primordial components generated by the Big Bang. Every subsequent type of organization enables the capture and processing of energy which is then driven toward a state of maximum entropy

- Corporate survivability on complex fitness landscapes depends on executive management's grasp and acceptance of the presence and function of all phases of the **Evolutionary Cascade**. Doing so is the operational meaning of **Natural Corporate Management**

The Big O's research base

Annila, A., and E. Kuismanen (2009) "Natural Hierarchy Emerges from Energy Dispersal," *BioSystems* 95: 227-33.

Arthur, W.B. (2009) *The Nature of Technology: What It Is and How It Evolves* (New York: Free Press).

Brown, L. (ed.) (1993) *The New Shorter Oxford English Dictionary on Historical Principles* (Oxford, UK: Clarendon Press).

Bussey, J. (2011) "Chutzpah in the C-suite: Watching out for No. 1," *Wall Street Journal*, December 23, 2011: B1-B2.

Cummins, D. (2005) "Dominance, Status, and Social Hierarchies," in D. Buss (ed.), *The Handbook of Evolutionary Psychology* (Hoboken, NJ: John Wiley & Sons): 676-97.

Daft, R.L. (2007) *Organization Theory and Design* (Mason, OH: Thomson South-Western, 9th edn).

de Waal, F. (1998) *Chimpanzee Politics: Power and Sex among Apes* (Baltimore, MD: Johns Hopkins University Press, rev. edn).

Efrati, A. (2011) "For Google CEO Larry Page, A Difficult Premiere Role," *Wall Street Journal*, August 30, 2011: B1, B5.

Frederick, W.C. (1995) *Values, Nature, and Culture in the American Corporation* (New York: Oxford University Press).

Frederick, W.C. (1998) "Creatures, Corporations, Communities, Chaos, Complexity," *Business & Society* 37.4 (December 1998): 358-89.

Gibson, K.R., and T. Ingold (1993) *Tools, Language and Cognition in Human Evolution* (Cambridge, UK: Cambridge University Press).

Goldstein, J. (1994) *The Unshackled Organization: Facing the Challenge of Unpredictability through Spontaneous Reorganization* (Portland, OR: Productivity Press).

Holland, J. (1995) *Hidden Order: How Adaptation Builds Complexity* (New York: Addison-Wesley).

Kauffman, S. (1993) *The Origins of Order: Self-organization and Selection in Evolution* (New York: Oxford University Press).

Kauffman, S. (1995) *At Home in the Universe: The Search for Laws of Self-organization and Complexity* (New York: Oxford University Press).

Kelly, K. (2010) *What Technology Wants* (New York: Viking).

Lawrimore, B. (2005) "From Excellence to Emergence: The Evolution of Management Thinking and the Influence of Complexity," in K.A. Richardson (ed.), *Managing Organizational Complexity: Philosophy, Theory, and Application* (Greenwich, CN: Information Age): 115-32.

Lissack, M.R. (ed.) (2002) *The Interaction of Complexity and Management* (Westport, CN: Quorum Books).

Ludeman, K., and E. Erlandson (2006) *Alpha Male Syndrome* (Boston, MA: Harvard Business School Press).

Mitchell, M. (2009) *Complexity: A Guided Tour* (New York: Oxford University Press).

Morgan, G. (1997) *Images of Organization* (Thousand Oaks, CA: Sage, 2nd edn).

Morin, E. (2008) *On Complexity* (Cresskill, NJ: Hampton Press).

Nicholson, N. (1997) "Evolutionary Psychology and Organizational Behavior," in C.L. Cooper and S.E. Jackson (eds.), *Creating Tomorrow's Organizations* (New York: John Wiley & Sons).

Nicholson, N. (1998) "How Hardwired is Human Behavior?" *Harvard Business Review*, July–August 1998: 135-42.

Nicholson, N. (2000) *Executive Instinct: Managing the Human Animal in the Information Age* (New York: Crown Publishers).

Nicholson, N., and R. White (2006) "Darwinism: A New Paradigm for Organizational Behavior?" *Journal of Organizational Behavior* 27: 111-19.

Pfeffer, J. (1992) *Managing with Power: Politics and Influence in Organizations* (Boston, MA: Harvard Business School Press).

Pierce, B.D., and R. White (1999) "The Evolution of Social Structure: Why Biology Matters," *Academy of Management Review* 24.4: 843-53.

Reynolds, P.C. (1993) "The Complementation Theory of Language and Tool Use," in K.R. Gibson and T. Ingold (eds.), *Tools, Language and Cognition in Human Evolution* (Cambridge, UK: Cambridge University Press): 407-28.

Sargut, G., and R. Gunther McGrath (2011) "Learning to Live with Complexity," *Harvard Business Review* 89 (September–October 2011): 68-76.

Silverman, R.E. (2012) "Who's the Boss? There Isn't One," *Wall Street Journal*, June 20, 2012: B1, B8.

Sole, R., and B. Goodwin (2000) *Signs of Life: How Complexity Pervades Biology* (New York: Basic Books).

Stacey, R.D. (2010) *Complexity and Organizational Reality* (New York: Routledge, 2nd edn).

Torregrosa, L.L. (2012) "On Wall St., Gender Bias Runs Deep," *New York Times*, July 24, 2012.

Vascellaro, J.E., and E. Steel (2011) "Culture Clashes Tear at AOL," *Wall Street Journal*, September 10–11, 2011: B1, B4.

Wall Street Journal, September 7, 2011

Wrangham, R., and D. Peterson (1996) *Demonic Males: Apes and the Origins of Human Violence* (Boston, MA: Houghton Mifflin).

9

The **Big M ≈ Market**

Economic systems are founded on life. To understand economics
is to understand life and its context.
Geerat J. Vermeij

There is no known human tribe that does not trade.
Matt Ridley

Markets are where, and how, most of the world's peoples obtain the essentials and luxuries (if any) of life. Whether it's Walmart for consumables, the New York/London/Tokyo Stock Exchanges for investments, or your favorite Internet online shopping site, the market serves a basic economic purpose. The more numerous and diverse the markets are—the wider choices they offer and the greater ease of accessing them—the greater is the likelihood you will experience a successful market adventure. Competition among sellers curbs over-pricing to buyers, while competition among buyers provides a measure of assurance and confidence for sellers. The downside risks are well known: monopoly control of supply (for example, consumer goods, skilled labor, or capital); resource shortages both natural and artificial; speculative instabilities over time; systemic fluctuations either upward (inflation) or downward (deflation, recession, depression); exploitation of buyers, sellers, and supply-chain workers; lack of quality information about products, services, and resources; and concealed, misleading sales and marketing strategies—all such risks justify a cautious *caveat emptor* (buyer beware) attitude by all who rely on markets for their livelihood. Even with these well-known limitations, market systems—usually called market economies—have become global in scope, a seemingly supreme instrumental way of organizing resource acquisition, production, distribution, consumption, and capital investment—all of the economic essentials of life itself.

But wait a minute. If the market supplies life's essentials, that seems to suggest a Darwinian origin of some kind, with the market's expanding global reach a marker of natural selection at work, pushing out less successful ways of organizing economic life. Shades of Social (or Economic) Darwinism! Could it be true? Say it ain't so, Joe. Well, relax, Joe, it's only partially true, but the full answer is somewhat more complex, which will take a bit more explanation. In the meantime, Joe, just bear in mind that up to this point, we've been talking about the market's *instrumental function*, its ability to organize, deliver, and motivate a society's core economic activities.

But that's only half the story because the market plays a far larger and much more ancient role in human society and ecosystem life than mere instrumental performance. As we shall see, that other role (but not Social/Economic Darwinism) reveals the evolutionary heritage of the market. For today's business corporations, markets constitute the principal playing field for their economic operations. What effect does the market have on corporate life and on corporate managers? Is it the economic savior advocated by its supporters? Or the demon envisioned by its detractors? What *is* the market's evolutionary heritage and its adaptive function? These are the questions and issues explored in this chapter. You may be surprised by the answers.

The market's evolutionary heritage

As a prime economic, life-supporting mechanism, the market is the inheritor of all those adaptive evolutionary forces comprising the cumulative

Evolutionary Cascade. In brief review, that would include the following phases.

- The energy that drives and sustains market activities is a manifestation of the primal cosmic energy that began at the Universe's origin. Markets capture and process free energy, driving it toward an entropic condition. As such, they are energy transduction mechanisms

- All forms of organic life, including modern humans (*Homo sapiens*), are the adaptive outcome of Darwinian natural selection. Markets help sustain human life

- *Homo sapiens* culture is an organic/genetic/neurological expression of naturally evolving forces. Markets are a central economic component of that cultural complex

- The major components of *Homo sapiens* neuro-organic culture are tools, symbols, and sociality patterns. Each displays positive, negative, and passive adaptive consequences for *Homo sapiens*. Markets consist of tools, symbols, and sociality in action

- The acquisition of *Homo sapiens* culture by individuals and sociality groups is made possible through neurological sensing of ecosystem adaptive opportunities and maladaptive threats. "Nature" and "nurture" share a common source of neuro-organic origin and function. Markets combine and integrate innate and learned economic behaviors

- The diverse behavioral and institutional patterns of *Homo sapiens* culture are a consequence of interactions between ecosystem processes and astrophysical, meteorological, and geological activities occurring over extended time periods. Markets may disrupt or support ecosystems

- Differing forms of human sociality—kin selection, inclusive fitness, and reciprocal altruism—are genetically induced behavioral traits of *Homo sapiens* that display positive adaptive consequences. Markets may strengthen or weaken such genetically evolved behaviors

- Market activities—the back-and-forth flow of goods, services, resources, and capital—are organized hierarchically, technologically, and nonlinearly in ways that simultaneously support *Homo sapiens* life and maximize the flow of life-sustaining energy toward an entropic destination

For all these reasons—and more to come—the market is not quite the simple Economics 101 model of instrumental trading transactions. It carries into modern times much of the inherited baggage endowed to it by the **Evolutionary Cascade**, including an astounding array of non-instrumental, symbolic, social, ceremonial, and non-adaptive practices and customs.

Market reciprocity:
Social, psychological, and economic

The central lesson here is clear: *all* markets are permeated—some might even say "compromised" or "contaminated"—by sociality considerations. This is true of markets for consumer goods and services, production technology, labor, capital, supply-chain support services, natural resources, and information. Put another way, a market's *instrumental economic function* is always accompanied—and sometimes even overridden—by *a symbolic sociality function*. These intertwined functions can best be understood as a form of social reciprocity.

Social reciprocity

Karl Polanyi, sociologist and economic historian, took a step beyond the genetic kinship bonds of family and clan life—kin selection, inclusive fitness, and reciprocal altruism—by referring to a broader and more socially inclusive kind of reciprocal behavior he labeled "social reciprocity," which was widely present in small-scale early societies (hunter-gatherer-herder) as well as in macro-scale ancient empires and kingdoms (Babylonia, Egypt, Inca, China, India, and others) (Polanyi 1944: Chapter 4 plus Notes to Chapter 4). In such systems, reciprocating movements or "exchanges" of valued items occur along familial, clan, village, tribal, and political lines and relationships. The activity is social, not economic, by stabilizing traditional sociality ties, as well as validating the social status of the participants. Personal or group gain is not the point of such reciprocal exchanges and is carefully avoided. The participants' "gain," if any, is emotional and psychological by having conformed to social expectations.

A good example of social reciprocity among tribes is the Trobriand Islands *kula* exchange system, still in existence in the early 20th century. Note that both market functions—instrumental trade and symbolic sociality exchange—take place in the *kula* (see box overleaf).

Notice how the trade of needed, useful products was shaped and channeled by the ritualistic, ceremonial exchange of non-utilitarian *kula* items. Symbolic, sociality practices dominated utilitarian exchanges.

In more complex macro-scale societies—kingdoms, states, nations, empires—a *kula*-like social reciprocity practice emerged which was called a *reciprocity-redistribution* system. It channeled all kinds of items, utilitarian and ritualistic, from the bottom of the social pyramid—peasants—upward to the top ranks—chiefs, kings, emperors, dictators—as tribute payments. Exchange valuables, following their acceptance as tribute by the top ranks, were then redistributed downward in amounts suitable to the recipient's social status. As Polanyi notes, "Reciprocity, which plays a dominant part in most tribal communities, survives as an important although subordinate, trait in the redistributive archaic empires where foreign trade was still largely organized on the principle of reciprocity. Kin, state, magic, and religion are the outstanding noneconomic spheres to which the economic process is found attached in early society" (Polanyi 1977: 42, 57). In other words, markets were facilitating and reinforcing a tribute-like system of social exchange as well as a flow of useful goods to and fro among the social classes.

So quite clearly, long-established traditional sociality patterns based on kinship/village/clan/tribal relationships were the foundation of all exchange activities in early and ancient societies. Now recall from Chapter 7, "The Big S ≈ Symbol," that sociality is one of the core components of today's *Homo sapiens* neuro-organic culture. That leads to an intriguing question: Could the longevity of exchange behavior, and its close linkage to evolved sociality patterns, mean that social exchanges (of all kinds) are yet another outcome of Darwinian evolution? If so, that would mean that today's economic markets exhibit *kula*-like traits. Some leading research scholars who study neuro-psychological behavior believe so, as we shall now see.

The Trobriand *kula*

The Trobriand Islands are in the Western Pacific Ocean just east of New Guinea, stretching 320 miles west-to-east and 240 miles north-to-south. The ceremonial *kula* "market" involves the exchange of two ritualistic items: shell arm-bands and shell necklaces. Neither has any utilitarian or even decorative use since they are rarely worn. Their entire purpose is to be given and received as gifts. Elaborate public ceremonies are staged when the gifts are given and received. Large-scale sailing expeditions between the islands are undertaken by entire villages for the purpose of matching up *kula* exchange partners. Around the ring of islands, the necklaces move in a clockwise direction while the armbands circulate counter-clockwise. Some of the *kula* items develop reputations as especially valuable and are highly desired. Entire villages celebrate their arrival, though these gifts will be passed along the chain to others. ". . . *tribal life is permeated by a constant give and take* . . . [and] there is not even a trace of gain, since there is no enhancement of mutual utility through the exchange . . . giving for the sake of giving is one of the most important features . . . every social obligation or duty, though it may not be evaded, has to be re-paid by a ceremonial gift. The function of these ceremonial re-payments is . . . to thicken the social ties from which arise the obligations."

However, utilitarian economic trade also occurs. "The ceremonial exchange of the two articles is the main, the fundamental aspect of the Kula . . . side by side with the ritual exchange of arm-shells and necklaces, the natives carry on ordinary trade, bartering from one island to another a great number of utilities, often unprocurable in the district to which they are imported, and indispensable there. The Kula is thus an extremely big and complex institution, both in its geographical extent, and in the manifoldness of its component pursuits" (Malinowski 1953: 81-83, 1967: 211-12).

Psychological reciprocity

The presence of evolutionarily embedded exchange behavior in modern humans is strongly suggested by the research of evolutionary psychologists and behavioral economists. The pioneering research of Leda Cosmides in the early 1980s, subsequently joined by anthropologist John Tooby, led the search for a brain-centered source of reciprocal exchange behavior. Behavioral economist Ernst Fehr and colleagues reached somewhat similar conclusions, though by different research methods, during the 1990s.

You might well ask how is it possible for researchers living in today's world, far removed chronologically and behaviorally from the 2-million-year-plus beginning of the *Homo* genus, to know with certainty the origin of *any* human behavioral trait that left no physical fossils to be discovered. The answer lies in the best traditions of modern scientific inquiry: the use of an inferential, pragmatic logic that links present-day behavior with what is known about the organic processes (primarily centered in the brain) that direct human behavioral activity. If, for example, behavior A is observed to be present consistently in the majority of humans living in different and contrasting cultures, and if that behavior stems from known neurological processes, then behavior A can be hypothesized as an innate (genetically inherited) tendency expressed by the modern brain. Moreover, if the behavior is shown to prolong the lives of those who practice it, then it would display an adaptive survival function, which is a marker of Darwinian natural selection. Both evolutionary psychologists and behavioral economists adopt such an approach, although interestingly they differ in the ultimate source of evolved exchange behavior, as we shall see.

Cosmides goes right to the evolutionary point: "Engaging in social exchange is an extremely complex computational feat . . . [and] we have Darwinian algorithms [brain processes] that are up to the task." She centers this task in the human brain, saying that "the innate information-processing mechanisms that comprise the human mind are *adaptations*: mechanisms designed to solve the specific biological problems posed by the physical, ecological and social environments encountered by our ancestors during the course of human evolution" (Cosmides 1989: 188). One of those problems was the social exchange of valued items, as Polanyi demonstrated, which were a universal feature of early tribal-size societies and were built upon a foundation of social cooperation and conditional helping of others. It then follows that "Successfully conducting social exchange was such an important and recurrent feature of hominid evolution that a reliable, efficient cognitive capacity specialized for reasoning about social exchange would quickly be selected for" (Cosmides 1989: 260).

This capacity to engage intelligently in social exchange had been evolving "among our ancestors for millions and possibly tens of millions of years," perhaps antedating the emergence of *Homo* and possibly present in primitive form among chimpanzees and monkeys prior to the emergence of the pre-*Homo* Australopithecines. Thus, "natural selection could well have engineered complex cognitive mechanisms specialized for engaging in [social exchange]" (Cosmides and Tooby 2005: 587, 589).

Subsequently, an ability to reason about the pluses and minuses of engaging in social exchange emerged in the lives of small hunter-gatherer groups who depended on such cooperative exchanges: for example, sharing the bounty of successful hunts, fish catches, and fruits and roots of various plants. Dividing up the spoils might be tricky—not too much for Uncle Bill nor too little to Baby Millie—equal shares being the best rule, a kind of social reciprocity prevailing in close-knit family and clan circles. Repeating this kind of sharing for long, long periods of time from generation to generation over millions of years, especially if it consistently supported the sustenance patterns of hunter-gatherer groups, produced a big evolutionary *voilà*! Those selfish genes that promoted such survival behavior would generate a reasoning skill to guide social exchanges. "The human brain contains a neuro-cognitive adaptation designed for reasoning about social exchange [and] this neuro-cognitive specialization for social exchange reliably develops across striking variations in cultural experience. It is one component of a complex and universal human nature" (Cosmides and Tooby 2005: 623).

The resulting mental mechanism, called a neural algorithm, allows exchange partners to know if an exchange is fair to both sides and whether the principle of reciprocity (or fairness) is being observed. Put more bluntly, did someone cheat by taking advantage of an exchange partner, taking more than a fair share or not returning a fair amount? "A *cheater* is an individual who fails to reciprocate—who accepts the benefit specified by a social contract without satisfying the requirement that provision of that benefit was made contingent on" (Cosmides and Tooby 2005: 591).

Using a well-known empirical reasoning test—the Wason selection task—Cosmides and Tooby demonstrated the presence of a cheater-detection algorithm in today's human populations living in advanced modern cultures, as well as among more marginal hunter-gatherer societies that have survived into modern times. Some observers have called this possibility of cheating a kind of "moral hazard" present in all market exchanges.

Cosmides and Tooby's research does indeed seem consistent with the notion that an innate exchange module is present in the contemporary *Homo* brain, put there by groups of people repeatedly facing the challenges of conducting reciprocal, cooperative, helpful exchanges. They do note that this "social contract specialization has properties that are better adapted to the small-group living conditions of ancestral hunter-gatherers than to modern industrial societies." In other words, the greater complexity, size, and anonymity of modern society, when compared with simpler societies, may weaken the behavioral influence of the cheater-detection module (Cosmides and Tooby 2005: 623).

Behavioral economists, another group of researchers, testify to the active presence of reciprocity in both ancient and modern populations. Their key concept is labeled "strong reciprocity" to distinguish it from other, broader meanings of reciprocal behavior. "Strong reciprocity means that people willingly repay gifts and punish the violation of cooperation and fairness norms even in anonymous [one-time] encounters with genetically unrelated strangers" (Fehr and Henrich 2003: 55). In other words, this brand of strong reciprocity promotes cooperative behavior going well beyond the inner circles of closely related family and clan members, even if the exchange occurs only once and the exchange partners never see one another again. Punishing cheaters is obviously a strongly felt psychological urge.

By using several different types of game theory, behavioral economists demonstrate the lasting presence of strong reciprocity in modern society.[1] Not only that, but they also show that such cooperative propensities are found in over a dozen surviving small-scale societies that were typical in much earlier times (Henrich *et al.* 2001, 2005). This finding sounds a bit familiar, rather like the Cosmides and Tooby results reached by using a

---

1 Game theory is a research method that tests the tendency of the experimental subjects to cooperate with each other for gain or to punish non-cooperators at a cost to themselves.

different method. And both of these research groups maintain that reciprocal behavior is not just adaptive for humanity but also testifies to its evolutionary origin.

However, that's where the agreement ends. In explaining how strong reciprocity could survive in human evolution, the behavioral economists begin by rejecting key Darwinian explanations of cooperative behavior and turn to various forms of learned human culture, such as "social structures," "social norms," "conformist transmission," "social learning," "cultural group selection," even identifying culture as "our second system of inheritance" (which evokes the quaint, now-outmoded notion of Lamarckian evolution). One wonders also about speculative, unsubstantiated claims that "in pre-modern societies . . . cheating incentives are even more prevalent" than in contemporary social groups, or that "in more than 90 percent of human history no cooperative infrastructure [of laws, impartial courts, and police] . . . existed" (Fehr *et al.* 2002: 1). These views evoke—needlessly—the differences between nurturists and naturists discussed previously in Chapters 5 and 7.

This apparent split between evolutionary psychologists and behavioral economists over evolution's role in sustaining adaptive reciprocal behavior might be reconciled by relying on the concept of neuro-organic culture described in the Big S ≈ Symbol chapter. Recall that human neuro-organic culture's main components are tools, symbols, and sociality, each playing a vital role in sustaining human life, and each the outcome of long-term Darwinian evolution. Socially reciprocal behaviors—the detection of cheaters and their costly punishment by strong cooperators—are simple examples of neuro-organic culture at work. The source of cooperative, reciprocating behavior is within the evolved *Homo* brain—the "neuro" part of human culture—which is reinforced by adaptive tools/technology and diverse symbolic/sociality meanings, some adaptive, others maladaptive. Cosmides and Tooby are correct to claim that neural algorithms specialized for social exchange and cheater-detection support social reciprocity. Ernst Fehr and colleagues are correct to claim that evolved sociality patterns help explain the presence of strong reciprocity. There needn't be a tussle about the causative drivers of reciprocal human behavior because neuro-organic human culture houses both neural algorithms and adaptive sociality behaviors, each displaying positive, adaptive evolutionary effects. Perhaps both camps overstep the evidentiary authority of their respective methods, though neither seriously compromises the adaptive functions of Darwinian natural selection. In the end, psychological reciprocity remains an embedded behavioral propensity in modern society—and therefore, in modern markets.[2]

Economic reciprocity

Today's instrumental, pragmatic, economic markets—local, national, global, electronic—seem to be a far cry from the reciprocal exchanges of our ancient ancestors when social and psychological motives were dominant. However, one should not be overly hasty in dismissing the non-economic aspects of modern markets, for ancestral remnants continue to haunt and condition the movement of goods and services from provider

---

2 A long, lively controversy about the evolutionary process most responsible for the presence of cooperative human behavior separates the two camps of evolutionary psychologists and behavioral economists. The former group proposes that a gene-based process of Darwinian natural selection, operating upon individuals within the nuclear family, among close kin, and in clan/village/tribal society, generated a neural algorithm specialized for confronting and resolving issues of cooperation suitable for the very earliest phases of *Homo* life. The behavioral economist camp believes that social cooperation is a function of learned cultural forms, behaviors, and traditions, though influenced somewhat by gene-culture interactions. The basic controversy is another version of the nature–nurture argument (examined in Chapters 5 and 7): whether, and in what sequential order, natural selection exerts its influence on individuals or on groups. A thorough, balanced discussion of these issues may be found in Leigh 2010. Worth noting is the behavioral economists' strong interest in countering the self-centered, rationalist picture of economic decision-making projected in standard economic theory (Fehr and Falk 2002), and the evolutionary psychologists' search for a theory of individual behavior unencumbered by anthropocentric culture-based explanations of modern human behavior. In either case, one should bear in mind a central principle of Darwinian natural selection: genes that influence human behavior reside in a distinctive individual phenotype (a single organism), not collectively or uniformly in an entire social group; the resultant behavioral effect is felt diversely and variably within large populations over very long time periods, not necessarily or uniformly in specific cultural institutions in short historical eras such as the present. "Social gene" in that sense is an oxymoron, a self-contradictory phrase. For a more theoretically consistent concept of "social gene" and its influence on individual and collective behavior, see Cassill 2004 and Cassill and Watkins 2010.

to user even today. Our evolutionary past is an ever-present player in the market game. Social and psychological reciprocity exist side by side with economic reciprocity. As anthropologists Paul Bohannan and George Dalton point out in their study of 20th-century ancestral-like African markets, "the analyst cannot ignore the social setting which provides the impetus for transactions of resources, goods, and services" (Bohannan and Dalton 1965).

"Blended-exchange" is a good descriptor of the market's dual functions: material goods and services move in parallel with ceremonial valuables, as in the Trobriand *kula* exchange. An extended reciprocity-redistribution process emerged later that moved exchange valuables along lines laid down by the relative power implicit in kinship relationships and other sociality markers of the trading partners. Where males dominated the nuclear family, the extended family, and the patriarchal village/clan/tribe, the exchanges brought a greater flow of valuables (including material goods) to upper-level status positions than to those of lesser status and power. Proportional redistribution from top to bottom of the status pyramid secured all ranks in their traditional positions. The long-term behavioral and societal result was the solidification and validation of the established power displayed by the earliest sociality patterns. As discussed in the preceding chapter, "The Big O ≈ Organization," hierarchical, pyramidal organization is one of the primary ways of integrating economic and social life.

As early human populations grew in size, were separated from one another, and developed varied ways of surviving on diverse landscapes, blended-exchange was slowly and unevenly supplemented by "trade-and-exchange" markets where the exchange of instrumental, useful economic items was dominant. The invasion of hunter-gatherer and herder societies by European colonialists accelerated this transition, often with devastating consequences for the simpler economies (Bohannan and Dalton 1965: 24-32; Dalton 1967). Trade-and-exchange markets—which were absent entirely in some marketless groups, or peripheral and marginal in others, but were of central importance in a growing number of other societies—soon became the trademark of modern economic life.

The major distinction between blended-exchange and trade-and-exchange is the social acceptance of one-sided or unbalanced gain by trade-and-exchange partners. The meaning of "reciprocal balance" shifts from social equivalence of exchange items toward a *perceived balance* or *equity* in the minds of the exchange partners. The transactors on both sides walk away from the trade satisfied with the outcome, each having achieved what was sought, whether "equal" or not. In trade-and-exchange markets, literal equivalence of exchanged items is no longer required, only a socially acceptable balance based on adherence to prevailing sociality traditions and authority structures described above.

Trade-and-exchange—the flow of material, instrumental, economic items—is enhanced by the use of money symbols. Money symbolizes a society's concept of the worthwhileness (or "value") of exchange items; it "stands for" or symbolically represents such worthiness (Einzig 1948; Dalton 1965; Mauss 1967). In that sense, money is a "standard of value" or a measure of a product's worth to the user; and it can at the same time serve as a "store of value" or a cache of symbols possessing such social or commercial value; your bank account is a good example. As a "standard of deferred value," money is a measure of worthiness over time, which of course can vary as the standard's value fluctuates. The most familiar money usage for most of us is a means (or a "medium of exchange") to facilitate the buying and selling of items in the marketplace. Remarkably, the money symbols themselves, once physical items (gold, silver, pigs, yams, etc.), are now largely abstract electronic symbols possessing no inherent value beyond their use as an exchange symbol.

Even more remarkable is what has happened to the formerly dominant social functions of money. They have not disappeared but remain quite active and prominent, though subtly. The *social* meaning of exchange moves into, becomes embedded in, the trade items themselves rather than standing socially and ritually separate (as in the *kula*); the social message consists of the type, number, and quality of trade items one procures through market exchange. The more the better is the idea. High social status, not to speak of organizational authority, political power, and economic wealth, are signaled by the amount and the (normally lavish) use of monetary symbols. Income differentials—the well-known pyramids of socioeconomic class structure—are perhaps the best illustration of the socially symbolic messages conveyed by money in the modern era. As in ancient societies, social reciprocity-and-redistribution live on today as money flows upward before being redirected downward in socially appropriate proportions to those on the lower levels of the pyramid.

As told in Paul Seabright's *The Company of Strangers*, the emergence of reciprocal trade-and-exchange markets carried a significance that reached far beyond the greater instrumental ease of monetary exchange. Although "reciprocity . . . has enabled hunter-gatherer bands to take the first cautious steps toward conducting exchange with strangers," and although "natural selection has favored genetic mutations that encourage helping of relatives, helping nonrelatives is valuable in evolutionary terms only when the favor is returned." The problem is that "human beings cheat in more costly and dangerous ways than any other species . . . [and] have slaughtered members of its own species more vigorously, systematically, and cruelly than any other in nature." To overcome this built-in hostility toward non-kin strangers, "It has surely been reciprocity that, prehistorically, tipped the balance between hostility to strangers and a cautious willingness to deal with them." The emergence of the reciprocal, monetarized, trade-and-exchange market led to "the discovery that a willingness to trust others could produce important benefits to both sides." Seabright is thus defining a centrally important role for economic markets that create a widespread web of social trust: "markets provide a way for strangers to exchange with one another . . . [and] modern firms provide a way for strangers to collaborate . . . on productive tasks" (Seabright 2004: 58, 48-49, 58, 164). Another expert on market evolution, Matt Ridley, agrees: "[T]rust has gradually and progressively grown, spread and deepened during human history, because of exchange. Exchange breeds trust" (Ridley 2010: 100).

Think about that the next time you hand over a large sum of money to a perfect stranger at Walmart or at the New York Stock Exchange, or when your company's China-based manufacturer, whom you'll never know well, fills your order for some new electronic gadgets. Economic reciprocity does indeed pay big dividends: trade-and-exchange transactions between strangers produce a flow of material goods and services supporting economic life. It even seems to have an eerily familiar ring, perhaps an echo of evolutionary adaptive behavior? It's a prospect worth pursuing next.

Natural market functions

Modern contemporary markets are intriguing examples of nature at work. This is true also of the networks of interconnected markets that we call "market economies," some of them global in scope and expanding rapidly. As natural phenomena, they are the outcome of evolution and another phase of the **Evolutionary Cascade's** onward flow. Markets are best understood, not as places, but as a process, an activity, a means, a way of acquiring the necessities (and for some, the luxuries) of life (Bohannan and Dalton 1965: 1-32). In yet another way, markets act as an economic infrastructure, a platform on which adaptive behavior can occur, either successfully or not. Market transactions embody all of the familiar components of human neuro-organic culture (tools, symbols, and sociality): money as a *tool* facilitating exchange; money and price ratios *symbolizing* equivalencies; and *sociality* patterns (kinship and non-kin) enabling economic exchanges between both friends and potential foes or anonymous strangers.

The result has been an enormously expanded, magnified opportunity for wide sectors of the human population to seek and attain the Darwinian trio—sustenance (a material standard of living), sex (offspring and family continuity), and security (a livable niche)—thereby improving their general living conditions and chances of continued survival. This enormous evolutionary advantage has been built on three life-sustaining *Homo* behavioral patterns made possible and supported by the market process: **economizing**, **economaxing**, and **ecologizing**. These three behaviors are the contemporary forms taken by natural evolutionary processes long in the making. Their intertwined linkages and effects tell much about the modern business corporation's role in sustaining organic life in general and, specifically, *Homo* life.

Economizing

"Economizing" is a term that has an obvious economic ring to it. In the marketplace, it refers to the prudent, careful, calculated, self-centered actions of buyers and sellers to gain the benefits and minimize the costs of their market transactions. Doing so successfully and repeatedly underpins the ongoing economic life of marketplace participants, and sustains the market process itself. When working well, the market is a neat combination, admirable for the diversity of products offered, the opportunities for gain, the potential for entrepreneurial innovation, and decentralized, unforced choices. Economizing does, though, invoke a conservative, cautious, self-protective aura and attitude among both buyers and sellers—*caveat emptor* and *caveat venditor*—as if dangers still lurk in the marketplace which are capable of overriding the sense of social trust the market otherwise inculcates among anonymous strangers. Nevertheless, economizing connotes a substantive, productive, adaptive activity, even as it projects an attitude of self-protective frugality and caution in market exchanges.

Economizing's evolutionary legacy is impressively ancient and comprehensive, constituting one of the natural pillars supporting market exchange. Each phase of the **Evolutionary Cascade**—beginning with the primal flows and exchanges of Energy that began Life, navigating through Darwin's natural selection pathways, pushed onward by the Gene's immortal drivers, rooted in *Homo*'s survival instincts, activated by the Brain's neural modules, shaped and channeled by Symbol-based sociality traditions, and reflecting Organization's three designs—contributed its own bit to building what would become in time a market exchange process that supports human economizing behavior.

A new generation of researchers—they call themselves neuroeconomists—seeks the secrets of market decision-making by probing deeply into the *Homo* brain (Glimcher *et al.* 2009). After all, the economics discipline is famous for its focus on the choices made in marketplace negotiations: are the choices rational? Irrational? Risk-aversive? Culture-bound? Self-centered? Equitable? Utility-maximizing? An additive/summative social-welfare result? Neuroscientists' research findings may well knock down the theoretical props holding up standard economic theory, but more important for present purposes is whether or how neuroeconomics clarifies the source of economizing as a market-based adaptive behavior.

Markets are notoriously risky places—many uncertainties, lethal outcomes, magnificent rewards, retaliation, punishments. How does the human brain deal with these issues? Neuroeconomists search for the underlying mental processes that govern the choices people make when negotiating in the marketplace—the way the brain regulates choice and risk taking. Recall from an earlier chapter, "The Big B ≈ Brain," the presence of specialized brain areas, or modules, that receive and respond to various signals from an individual's environment. Thus far, neuroeconomic researchers have identified neural centers that seem to be an important part of buy-and-sell market behavior, such as the logic of exchange behavior, the disposition to make both rational and irrational decisions, the utility expectations of game-theory opponents, the neural circuitry of social preferences, the brain mechanisms involved in empathy, inequity, and valuation, and a generalized model of human choice-making. In other words, they find the *Homo* brain to be the key player in solving the riddles encountered in marketplace dealings: risk, quality, fairness, pricing, equity, utility. "Over the course of the past decade [2000-09] an extraordinary amount of progress has been made in identifying the basic features of the primate mechanism for choice" (Glimcher *et al.* 2009: 520).

So, if the evolved *Homo* brain is the principal driver of marketplace choices, and if those choices enhance the survival prospects of the exchange partners, that must mean that the market mechanism is indeed a way for human economizing to occur. This is equivalent to saying that market economizing behavior begins in the brains of buyers and sellers who negotiate to enhance their material well-being. This is not simply a matter of clever, or even devious, rational choice consciously undertaken but is rather the built-in (hard-wired, genetic) expression of an evolved human brain that guides its organic carrier in adaptive economizing directions. That's a big Darwinian plus for the market and for a market economy.

But keeping track of all the exchange complexities in a highly developed market economy is not only difficult but essential if buyers and sellers are to negotiate with a feeling of confidence. They need to remember past transactions—how they fared, whether victimized by clever traders, and how much they gained or lost in trades—in short, they need a way to record and encode past trade exchanges if future transactions are to produce economizing results for themselves. Could accounting be the answer?

It would not be surprising if you've never heard of neuroaccounting because it is yet another newly emerging field of inquiry based on neuroscience research (Dickhaut *et al.* 2010). It makes accounting practice into more than the well-told story about the accounting clerk who distinguished between credit and debit entries because "debits were always entered on the side closest to the office window." Beyond mere bookkeeping, accountants now see "an association between accounting principles and the behavior of the brain during economic decision making." Those widely used accounting principles "are part of the auxiliary set of tools used by the brain to successfully consummate exchange" which of course is precisely what trade-and-exchange partners need. "Accounting records of past exchange provide a basis to identify and retain in memory more subtle forms of behavior by trading partners" such as cheating. In this way, neuroaccounting becomes a prime cheater-detection tool. As discussed earlier, the market norms of greatest importance are "fairness norms ... trust-based reputations and ... altruistic punishment," all of them promoting "reciprocity [that] enables exchange." Here then is another example of the naturological foundations of human culture: "culturally evolved accounting principles will be ultimately explained by their consilience [logical connection] with how the brain has evolved biologically to evaluate social and economic exchange" (Dickhaut *et al.* 2010: 237-38, 249, 233, 227, 221).[3]

Economaxing

"Economaxing" is economic behavior that attempts to maximize and magnify a trader's gains from market activity. Economaxing is a hyperversion of economizing. Rather than economizing's prudent, cautious, frugal marketplace approach, economaxing behavior seeks unlimited, high-intensity, maximum use of any resources attainable through market trade. While both methods produce adaptive results—the acquisition of life-supporting valuables—economaxing does so more quickly, is more narrowly focused on the economaxer's well-being, and is more effective per unit of energy expended than is true of economizing. For that reason, in a trade-and-exchange negotiation, an economaxing trade partner would normally gain more than a partner seeking only economizing goals. Economaxers often feel they are "entitled" to such super gains.

This mode of market exchange is one of the consequences of monetarized trade-and-exchange markets that allow one-sided economic gains to be made from market transactions, in contrast to the earlier blended-exchanges that combined social and economic functions in a reciprocal balance. Nevertheless, market economaxers must still come to terms with the continued presence of strong social and psychological reciprocity beliefs and practices (as described above). For that reason, any one-sided,

3 Dickhaut and his co-authors present a deeply researched, sophisticated analysis of the functional ties between specific areas of the *Homo* brain and the emergence and expression of basic accounting principles. It is a pioneering model of innovative theory and research linking cultural practices and natural process.

unbalanced economaximum market gain could prevail if it were based on or justified by some socially approved symbolic feature of human culture. What could that be?

Well, recall from the Big S ≈ Symbol chapter that the symbols comprising human neuro-organic culture can be given a meaning, and can be assigned a socially approved function, irrespective of the symbol's adaptive significance. Economaxing's one-sided behavioral gain could in that way qualify for social approval if linked to such a culturally approved symbolic system. Now recall, this time from the Big O ≈ Organization chapter, that social hierarchy is an accepted way of organizing human relations, thereby forming a pyramid-shaped socioeconomic class structure with status ranks of higher and lower order, power, and social prestige. That's all it takes to make economaxing a socially OK thing to do. In fact, it is more than OK if the economaximizer can deliver market benefits not only to the economaximizer but also to other cooperating trade partners or investors. Permitting economic gain in this way—gain that is unequally distributed according to the exchange partners' relative status rank—therefore preserves a limited measure of a symbolic social reciprocity-and-redistribution system. In effect, economaxing hitches a ride on the principle of social and economic reciprocity as it works in contradiction to the whole idea of balanced market exchange. While both economizing and economaxing are organically adaptive behaviors, economaxing is an advanced, extreme, and more effectively adaptive practice for the economaxers than is the case of market participants who engage only in economizing. That added benefit, of course, is why economaxing is so attractive to investors.

Successful market economaxers come readily to mind: software mogul Bill Gates of Microsoft fame, investor Warren Buffett at Berkshire Hathaway, Apple's Steve Jobs, or the CEOs of the *Fortune* top-ranked corporations. In distinctive ways—by shrewd investments (Buffett), early entry into evolving markets (Gates), innovative technology of wide appeal (Jobs), effective marketplace strategies (Fortune 500)—each of these economaxers has amassed outsized gains from market activity. Frequently or even typically, the spectacular gains go well beyond what might be expected from economizing's more frugal, cautious approach. Since the chief economaxer has organizational confederates, the market gains are redistributed in rough equivalency to the company's (and the society's) symbolic status system, with appropriately proportional amounts going to managers, employees, investors, bank creditors, and stockholders. In that way, economaxing achieves social acceptance, and the top econo-maxers are widely admired—and emulated where possible.

Successful economaxers occasionally overreach. After all, they typically are high-risk alpha males with competitive, even aggressive, sometimes ruthless strategies that reveal economaxing's dark underside. Examples unfortunately abound; here are two among several others that could be identified, including Enron, WorldCom, Tyco, and HealthSouth, whose top executives served jail terms for their economaxing enthusiasms (Frederick 2006: 180-98).

MF Global Holdings, Ltd was a giant commodity trader with more than 150,000 customers and assets of $41 billion. The firm's alpha-male CEO "had a four-decade career that touched the pinnacles of Wall Street and politics," and possessed "a strong appetite for risk" (*Wall Street Journal*, November 5/6, 2011: B1, November 4, 2011: C2). In trying to maximize MF Global profits, he unfortunately drove the company into bankruptcy by investing over $6 billion in high-return but high-risk (nearly worthless) government bonds of economically weak European nations. It was the eighth largest bankruptcy in U.S. history, with "50,000 accounts frozen, hurt[ing] thousands of investors and employees and [causing] unusual problems and uncertainties to the firm's customers" whose accounts worth $600 million to $1.2 billion were misappropriated, and probably lost, in a desperate last-minute rush to avoid the firm's bankruptcy (*Wall Street Journal*, November 8, 2011: C2, November 22, 2011: A1, December 31, 2011, January 1, 2012: B1, January 30, 2012: A1-A2). A subsequent news report was more optimistic about recovering customers' losses (*Wall Street Journal*, August 1, 2012: A1, A4).

Bernard Madoff Investment Securities, a firm in New York that managed funds for wealthy clients, was owned and operated by financier Bernard Madoff. For some 25 years, he attracted billions of dollars from carefully chosen clients who found the investment returns unusually high and steady over long periods, which is one of economaxing's defining features. Madoff and his satisfied clients were in the game of economaxing by seeking the highest possible profit from their investments that enabled all of them to live the life of multimillionaires for years and years. The "impossible dream" ended in 2008 when Madoff was arrested and subsequently jailed for life, after admitting that it was all "a big lie." Instead of investing new clients' funds, he used their incoming money to pay returns owed to previous investors, which is called a Ponzi scheme in financial circles. Eventually, all of the returns expected by the investors could not be paid because not enough new capital came into the firm. The victims lost $12–20 billion, and efforts were made to "claw back" the phantom profits they had gained during the years the fraud lasted. Once again, as with MF Global, economaxing backfired on its leader and participants (or victims). As one observer said of MF Global, "The failure illustrates how much financial markets are about trust and confidence. Once you lose those, you are done" (*Wall Street Journal*, November 8, 2011: C2). The same market lesson applies to Madoff. Economaxing's outsized gains, if driven to extreme levels, violate not just the market's reciprocity principle but laws and regulatory rules.[4]

Ecologizing

"Ecologizing" is the collective economic behavior of all the organisms living in an ecosystem, including their direct and indirect interactions with each other and with abiotic environmental forces. As explained in Chapter 2, "The Big L ≈ Life," there is a necessary, unavoidable link between any life form and an ecosystem, however simple and rudimentary each may be, and this has been true from the origin of Earthly life some 3.75 billion years ago. The necessitous feature of an ecosystem that makes life possible is the presence of energy in various forms—sunlight, chemicals, heat, physical matter, climate—that enabled their combination into unique relationships, some of which led to the formation and emergence of diverse organic life forms.

Ecologizing, as a form of economic behavior, enfolds and embraces both economizing and economaxing within the totality of ecosystem dynamics. In a way, ecologizing is a mélange of such actions by diverse populations in an ecosystem, some competing, others passive, still others relatively uninvolved due to the system's scale and size. All three kinds of economic

---

4 Since MF Global made profits only sporadically, and Madoff's Ponzi scheme by definition did not generate profits at all, one might well ask if these are valid examples of economaxing inasmuch as little or no market gain was "maximized" by either firm. However, economaxing as well as economizing are efforts to use marketplace resources for economic gain, one prudent (economizing), the other extreme (economaxing). There is no guarantee that either approach will succeed in achieving the gains sought.

activities have adaptive effects on their users and on connected others within the ecosystem. However, they differ in their respective functions and scales of operation. Economizing is focused on the adaptive survival and sustenance needs of individual organisms and species, as mediated by existing sociality patterns (kinship, common ancestor, population group). Economaxing's narrower function is to achieve maximum adaptive advantage for the maximizer (and associates, if any), even though the costs to other ecosystem denizens is high (and possibly maladaptive for them). Ecologizing behavior preserves, protects, and prolongs the integrity and homeostasis of an entire ecosystem and its interdependent, interwoven web of organic life.

These three economic descriptors, though displaying differential adaptive results for organic life, are simply the outcome of an evolutionary process governing the existence, character, dynamics, and continuity of Earthly life. As such, each plays a central role in all economic systems.

Human economy *IS* natural economy

Contemporary market economies owe almost everything—their existence, functions, dynamics, structure, size, decision systems, successes, failures, and productivity—to nature. And for a very good reason: Market economies *are a form of nature itself*. We are not talking metaphor here—not at all. The reality, as revealed throughout this chapter and in preceding ones, is that nature rules in every aspect of market behavior: negotiations, exchange relationships, resource acquisition, supply-chain transactions, production, marketing, consumption, and investment. All of these everyday manifestations of economic behavior are derivatives of one natural process or another, whether physical, chemical, biological, or some combination of these as found, for example, in the three components of human neuro-organic culture: tools, symbols, and sociality.

This linkage of economics and nature has been the central research theme of two remarkably accomplished, highly regarded natural scientists: ecologist Geerat J. Vermeij of the University of California-Davis and ecologist Egbert G. Leigh, Jr. of the Smithsonian Tropical Research Institute in Panama. Their books and journal articles speak with impressive authority.

In his *Nature: An Economic History* (2004), Vermeij develops a comprehensive, detailed account of the relations between natural economies and human economies, anchoring his argument in the research literature of economics and ecology. Straightforwardly, he says that: ". . . our [human] economic system is only one of the many variations on a simple common theme: an array of adaptable entities competing for resources . . . [T]here is nothing in the human sphere that has fundamentally altered the principles common to all other economies of nature" (Vermeij 2004: 44). Unsurprisingly, one can detect a decidedly Darwinian tone as these two scholars pool their research findings to expand on the basic idea: "[H]uman economies share essential features with natural ecosystems, [which] are similar because they are both adaptive systems in which cooperation and competition among individuals for locally limiting resources affect the fates of individuals and groups" (Vermeij and Leigh, Jr. 2011: 1). That's a researcher's way of describing natural selection at work in the economic sphere.

And it doesn't matter whether the economy is a coral reef, a human metropolitan cityscape, a tropical rainforest (Leigh, Jr. 2002), an Antarctic homeland for penguins, or a worldwide market for Apple iPods. Each one is "a network of life-forms that interact with one another by performing different, often complementary functions." Though highly diverse in membership, numbers, and size, these economies display such common features as "competition, cooperation, differential propagation of more competitive agents [for example, Microsoft vs. Apple; Amazon's Kindle e-reader vs. Barnes & Noble's Nook; Verizon wireless transmission vs. AT&T], production, consumption, and trade." In turn, these can generate common economic trends where physical conditions permit: "innovation, diversification, increased productivity, the emergence of competitive dominants (or centers of authority) [think Google, Walmart, Amazon], and increased geographic reach of interaction [think GPS, iPhone]" (Vermeij and Leigh, Jr. 2011: 1-2). These trends are the essence, not just of economic life on an African savanna or in a tropical rainforest but are also the natural architecture of today's globalized market economy.

Obviously, the differences among economies can be great—and of great importance—for planetary life in general. "Compared to natural economies, human economies change much more rapidly, advanced civilizations last much less long and appropriate an ever larger and less sustainable portion of our planet's resources." These differences are attributed to the presence and influence in human economies of human culture acting as an economic change-agent. Although "... *genetic adaptation* remains the predominant norm in *natural* economies, [by] contrast, adaptation in the *human* economy is by the spread of ideas, knowledge, and technology, as expressed in *symbols* ... *Cultural transmission* of adaptation has propelled humanity to its current status as the dominant economic agent on Earth" (Vermeij and Leigh, Jr. 2011: 6, emphasis added). Thus, in an all-too-familiar refrain, human culture is said to trump genes in adaptive power, even though culture "is enabled by gene-based evolution of the brain and associated sensory and motor systems" (Vermeij and Leigh, Jr. 2011: 10).

This is one of those "distinctions without a difference." The reason is found in the Big S ≈ Symbol chapter where what is normally labeled "human culture" turns out to be just another manifestation of natural processes, taking the form of tools, symbols, and sociality patterns, which are the components of human neuro-organic culture. Human symbolic culture is *literally* an expression, an elaboration, and an adaptive form of gene-based natural culture. Neither one trumps the other. They work in tandem. Human economy *is* natural economy.[5]

---

5 What may seem to be a mere technical quibble among specialists about the choice of words and phrases to describe phenomena actually may reveal (or even conceal) a more substantive issue lurking underneath the terminology. For example, even to distinguish between "human economy" and "natural economy" assumes a fundamental difference between the two attributable to the unique presence of "humans" and their "culture" in "human economy" and their absence in "natural economy," particularly if the human cultural element is believed to arise from "non-natural" or "extra-natural" sources. Social and cultural anthropologists are inclined to this view by assigning a major behavioral role to "nurture" (acquired learning) and a minor role to "nature" (biological heredity). Hence, the anthropocentric notion that humans are uniquely separated from nature is perpetuated by the choice of terms and phrases to describe their relationship, e.g., "natural economy" and "human economy," even where this seeming distinction may not be intended by all users.

Managers and markets

The Market phase of the **Evolutionary Cascade** presents corporate managers and their companies with an almost unlimited array of economic opportunities but, at the same time, with formidable challenges to their very existence. That is true of all phases of that powerful cascade of natural forces that flows on and on through cosmic time from the very beginning of the Universe and Earthly life to the present and on into the future. In that ongoing cosmic drama, the modern business corporation plays a role whose significance extends far beyond the day-to-day world of the marketplace, touching the quality—and possibly even the continuity—of life for all. Such awesome influence would seem to outrun and magnify what has been called "corporate *social* responsibility" and "corporate *ethical* responsibility" which extend corporate obligations beyond mere *economic* responsibility. The **Evolutionary Cascade** signals the arrival of a new dimension of corporate management: *corporate cosmic responsibility*. The stakes are that high. Just how it works out within the corporation—and what corporate managers can or might do about assuming this exalted mantle of responsibility—is explored in the following chapter.

The Big M's pivotal points

- Markets—ancient and modern, local and global—display all of the behavioral traits and structural features originating in the **Evolutionary Cascade**, beginning with the Big Bang's primal energy up to modern-day human culture

- Markets simultaneously perform two kinds of interrelated function: an instrumental economic function and a symbolic sociality function

- The exchange of valuables in early hunter-gatherer societies was guided by the principle of social reciprocity where exchanges were equal, gain was absent, and sociality patterns were preserved

- Cooperation and exchange of life's necessities over long periods of time spurred the evolution of the *Homo* brain's neural modules capable of detecting gain-seeking cheaters who disregarded the principle of social reciprocity

- Markets evolved away from socially reciprocal blended-exchange to trade-and-market exchange that allows one-sided economic gain by an exchange partner, while the market's sociality function is preserved in the form of socioeconomic status

- As evolutionary phenomena, modern markets perform three basic economic functions: economizing, economaxing, and ecologizing. Each activity can produce evolutionarily adaptive, maladaptive, and neutral economic results for organic life

- As evolved exchange systems, contemporary human market economies are similar in all basic respects (except scale) to the life-supporting networks found in natural ecosystems

- The cumulative evolutionary impact of the market on the modern business corporation and its managers generates a new dimension of responsibility reaching beyond social and ethical realms: corporate *cosmic* responsibility

The Big M's research base

Bohannan, P., and G. Dalton (eds.) (1965) *Markets in Africa: Eight Subsistence Economies in Transition* (Garden City, NY: Doubleday & Co., Anchor Books).

Burley, P., and J. Foster (eds.) (1994) *Economics and Thermodynamics: New Perspectives on Economic Analysis* (Boston, MA: Kluwer Academic Publishers).

Cassill, D. (2004) "The Social Gene," *Journal of Bioeconomics* 6: 1-12.

Cassill, D., and A. Watkins (2010) "The Evolution of Cooperative Hierarchies through Natural Selection Processes," *Journal of Bioeconomics* 12: 29-42.

Cosmides, L. (1989) "The Logic of Social Exchange: Has Natural Selection Shaped how Humans Reason? Studies with the Wason Selection Task," *Cognition* 31: 187-276.

Cosmides, L., and J. Tooby (2005) "Neurocognitive Adaptations Designed for Social Exchange," in D.M. Buss (ed.), *The Handbook of Evolutionary Psychology* (Hoboken, NJ: John Wiley & Sons): 584-627.

Dalton, G. (1965) "Primitive Money," *American Anthropologist* 67: 45-65.

Dalton, G. (ed.) (1967) *Tribal and Peasant Economies: Readings in Economic Anthropology* (Garden City, NY: Natural History Press).

Dickhaut, J., S. Basu, K. McCabe and G. Waymire (2010) "Neuroaccounting: Consilience between the Biologically Evolved Brain and Culturally Evolved Accounting Principles," *Accounting Horizons* 42.2: 221-55.

Einzig, P. (1948) *Primitive Money: In Its Ethnological, Historical and Economic Aspects* (London: Eyre & Spottiswoode).

Fehr, E., and A. Falk (2002) "The Psychological Foundations of Incentives," *European Economic Review* 46: 687-724.

Fehr, E., U. Fischbacher and S. Gachter (2002) "Social Reciprocity, Human Cooperation and the Enforcement of Social Norms," *Nature* 13: 1-25.

Fehr, E., and J. Henrich (2003) "Is Strong Reciprocity a Maladaptation? On the Evolutionary Foundations of Human Altruism," in P. Hammerstein (ed.), *The Genetic and Cultural Evolution of Cooperation* (Cambridge, MA: MIT Press): 55-82.

Frederick, W.C. (2006) *Corporation, Be Good! The Story of Corporate Social Responsibility* (Indianapolis, IN: Dog Ear Publishing).

Glimcher, P.W. (2011) *Foundations of Neuroeconomic Analysis* (New York: Oxford University Press).

Glimcher, P.W., C.F. Camerer, E. Fehr and R.A. Poldrack (2009) *Neuroeconomics: Decision Making and the Brain* (Amsterdam: Elsevier).

Henrich, J., R. Boyd, S. Bowles, C. Camerer, E. Fehr, H. Gintis and R. McElreath (2001) "In Search of Homo Economicus: Behavioral Experiments in 15 Small-Scale Societies," *The American Economic Review* 91.2 (May 2001): 73-78.

Henrich, J., R. Boyd, S. Bowles, C. Camerer, E. Fehr, H. Gintis, R. McElreath, M. Alvard, A. Barr, J. Ensminger, N. Smith Henrich, K. Hill, F. Gil-White, M. Gurven, F.W. Marlowe, J.Q. Patton and D. Tracer (2005) " 'Economic Man' in Cross-Cultural Perspective: Behavioral Experiments in 15 Small-Scale Societies," *Behavioral and Brain Sciences* 28: 795-855.

Jacobs, J. (2000) *The Nature of Economies* (New York: Modern Library).

Leigh, E.G., Jr. (2002) *A Magic Web: The Tropical Forest of Barro Colorado Island* (New York: Oxford University Press).

Leigh, E.G., Jr. (2010) "The Group Selection Controversy," *Journal of Evolutionary Biology* 23: 6-19.

Leigh, E.G., Jr., and G.J. Vermeij (2002) "Does Natural Selection Organize Ecosystems for the Maintenance of High Productivity and Diversity?" *Philosophical Transactions of the Royal Society, London B* 357: 709-18.

Leigh, E.G., Jr., G.J. Vermeij and M. Wikelski (2009) "What Do Human Economies, Large Islands and Forest Fragments Reveal about the Factors Limiting Ecosystem Evolution?" *Journal Compilation* 22: 1-12.

Malinowski, B. (1953) *Argonauts of the Western Pacific: An Account of Native Enterprise and Adventure in the Archipelagoes of Melanesian New Guinea* (New York: E.P. Dutton).

Malinowski, B. (1967) "Tribal Economics in the Trobriands," in G. Dalton (ed.), *Tribal and Peasant Economies: Readings in Economic Anthropology* (Garden City, NY: Natural History Press): 185-223.

Mauss, M. (1967) *The Gift: Forms and Functions of Exchange in Archaic Societies* (trans. Ian Cunnison; New York: W.W. Norton).

Ofek, H. (2001) *Second Nature: Economic Origins of Human Evolution* (Cambridge, UK: Cambridge University Press).

Polanyi, K. (1944) *The Great Transformation: The Political and Economic Origins of Our Time* (Boston, MA: Beacon Press).

Polanyi, K., and H.W. Pearson (eds.) (1977) *The Livelihood of Man* (New York: Academic Press).

Ridley, M. (2010) *The Rational Optimist: How Prosperity Evolves* (New York: Harper-Collins).

Ruth, M. (1993) *Integrating Economics, Ecology and Thermodynamics* (Dordrecht, Netherlands: Kluwer Academic Publishers).

Seabright, P. (2004) *The Company of Strangers: A Natural History of Economic Life* (Princeton, NJ: Princeton University Press).

Vermeij, G.J. (2004) *Nature: An Economic History* (Princeton, NJ: Princeton University Press).

Vermeij, G.J., and E.G. Leigh, Jr. (2011) "Natural and Human Economies Compared," *Ecosphere [ESA Journals]* 2.4 (April 2011): Art. 39.

Wall Street Journal (2011/2012) September 10-11, 2011; November 5/6, 8, 22, 2011; December 31, 2011; January 1, 20, 30, 2012; August 1, 2012: A1, A4.

Williams, R.J.P., and J.J.R. Frausto da Silva (2006) *The Chemistry of Evolution: The Development of Our Ecosystem* (Amsterdam: Elsevier).

10

The **Big C ≈ Corporation**

CORPORATE EVOLUTIONARY CASCADE

All companies exhibit the behavior and certain
characteristics of living entities.
Arie de Geus

(N)atural. A natural thing or object; a matter having its basis in
the natural world or in the usual course of nature.

(C)orporation. A body of people that has been given a legal
existence distinct from the individuals who compose it.

(M)anagement. The application of skill or care in the conduct of
an enterprise.
Oxford English Dictionary

Nature and the corporation

As this book has proposed from its beginning, the modern business corporation is a manifestation of evolving natural forces, acquiring its meaning and functions in a cumulative fashion from an onflowing **Evolutionary Cascade**. The cascade is a series of natural processes acting successively, chronologically, and influentially on one another. The collective impact on the corporation and its managers defines the functions and dynamics of corporate operations as well as the boundaries and opportunities of managerial decision-making. To emphasize the close kinship of corporation and cascade, this chapter's symbolic icon is labeled **Corporate Evolutionary Cascade**.

The idea that the corporation is none other than a natural "living entity" has been expressed by Arie de Geus, a seasoned corporate executive with Royal Dutch Shell who is noted for initiating the concept of the learning organization: "All companies exhibit the behavior and certain characteristics of living entities . . . Like all organisms, the living company exists primarily for its own survival and improvement: to fulfill its potential and to become as great as it can be." Grasping this reality "has enormous practical, day-to-day implications for managers . . . The fact that many managers ignore this imperative is one of the great tragedies of our times" (de Geus 1997: 10, 11).

This kinship of corporation and nature has thus begun to generate a new way of thinking about how corporate managers do their jobs, called in this book **Natural Corporate Management**. So, before illustrating the corporation's deep involvement in nature—and in all phases of the **Evolutionary Cascade**—a brief recap and clarification of **NCM**'s meaning and function is provided.

Natural Corporate Management: Its core meaning

Natural Corporate Management (NCM) is a new way of thinking about the actions of the modern business corporation and the behavior of its managers. Its core premise is that corporate actions and behaviors are a direct consequence of natural forces—astrophysical, biochemical, organic, and ecological—which simultaneously promote and threaten the corporation's economic stature and its continued existence. The most important management trait evoked by these natural forces is an emergent, growing awareness or consciousness by managers that nature is of central importance to the successful management of the corporation. **NCM** is not a managerial method or technique, nor is it a set of how-to-do-it instructions for managers. Neither does it replace or contradict current concepts of how management is understood by practitioners and scholars. **NCM** rather is a reinterpretation, a reformulation, a new perspective of what it means and requires to manage a business firm. Its novelty stems from insights generated by a steady and cumulative flow of new multidisciplinary research on the origins and evolution of human and organizational behavior. The resultant behavioral focus of this innovative approach is thus cumulative, historical, continuity-oriented, and—especially important for managers—appropriately practical, pragmatic, and empirically grounded. **NCM** might well be called a natural theory of the firm.

Natural Corporate Management permits and encourages a range of managerial actions to secure the corporation's future. In that sense, the concept is supportive of business, not negatively critical. Moreover, this nature-based corporate/managerial approach is thoroughly consistent with prevailing concepts of corporate social responsibility and ecosystem sustainability, to be discussed later in the chapter. However, **NCM** is neither predictive nor futuristic in outlook, focusing mainly on the present-day dimensions and consequences of managerial decision-making.

Corporate managers need, first of all, to develop a conscious awareness of the natural forces that influence corporate activities at all levels and in all operational spheres of the organization, and, second, to learn whether, how, and when to integrate this new understanding of nature into workplace behavior.

An **Evolutionary Cascade**—the cumulative, evolving natural phases described in earlier chapters—is the author and source of all the natural challenges faced by managers of the modern business corporation. As noted above, grasping that naturological reality is a first essential step if the corporation is to achieve its goals. Therefore, this chapter identifies the key natural management challenges, along with the action potentials, associated with the cascade's phases. In each phase, we shall be searching for the immediate practical impacts—behavioral and organizational—that are most relevant to corporate operations. Doing so creates a formidable agenda for responsive corporate actions.

Rafting down the Evolutionary Cascade

Corporations and their managers are in for a rough and exciting ride in maneuvering their way along the whirling, tumbling rapids of the **Evolutionary Cascade**. Bravery, skill, technical know-how, experience, anticipation, risk-taking, quick reaction, teamwork—and not just a little sheer luck—help, but there is no guarantee of a safe and secure arrival at base camp, nor even of arriving at all. There are, however, some common-sense guidelines to keep in mind; and one might (cleverly) call them the principles of **Natural Corporate Management**. Here is the way it looks as each of the cascade's huge boulders, breathtaking waterfalls, and tricky whirlpools loom ahead. Managers! Take paddle in hand! Secure your life vest! Here we go!

Phase I: ENERGY

ENERGY's essence: Stemming from the Big Bang, energy is the most basic natural component of the Universe, generating, shaping, and driving all subsequent forms of nature: physical, chemical, organic, and symbolic

The corporate challenge: To secure and effectively use a supply of energy—in all of its many forms—adequate to sustain the corporation's survival and continued existence

The behavioral/operational consequences: The modern business corporation is one of nature's most effective energy transductors, capable of capturing solar free energy and its embedded planetary derivatives (coal, oil, gas), organizing and utilizing that energy for corporate purposes, and distancing the corporation from entropic energy equilibrium, which is tantamount to corporate death or bankruptcy

The managerial opportunities: To guide the company's energy acquisitions—investment capital, human capital, social capital, market capital—to achieve both corporate efficiency and societal well-being in confronting and resolving the multiform energy demands, needs, and problems of human populations

The management choices: As true of all phases of the **Evolutionary Cascade**, corporate managers face choices of whether, how, or when to respond to the opportunities presented. They can *Ignore*, *Accept*, *Reshape*, and/or *Integrate* each phase's impact into the firm's operations. *Ignoring* energy's unavoidable opportunities and consequences is tantamount to corporate suicide. *Accepting* energy's potentials for extending the firm's existence into the far future opens up immense possibilities for both corporation and its host communities across the globe. *Reshaping* and redirecting energy flows into innovative channels of entrepreneurship is an undeniable plus for firm and firmament. *Integrating* energy into corporate goal-seeking and strategic planning initiatives is perhaps the top priority of corporate management

Phase II: LIFE

LIFE's organic essence: Life is an organic manifestation of solar energy's interactions with Earth's abiotic (non-living) environment, taking the initial form of self-sustaining cellular entities and subsequently evolving into a diversity of phenotypic forms. Life itself is a primal form of energy. All organic entities exist only within a surrounding cocoon of support drawn from ecosystem dynamics

The corporate challenge: Nature's central message to business is simple and profound: heed life, which includes the entirety of an ecosystem's life web

The behavioral/operational consequences: The generic association of energy and life pushes the corporate firm into one of nature's most difficult corners: choosing which, and how many, life forms to support through the firm's productive output

The managerial opportunities: To formulate a company's purposes, goals, and strategies in ways that simultaneously promote its own survival and the well-being of the life entities touched by its operations, e.g., adopting a "green energy" policy

The management choices: *Ignoring* the firm's close association with eco-system life is possible, though short-sighted, and threatens the continu-ity and quality of life for both corporation and ecosystem. *Accepting* the life-ecosystem linkage is the starting point for reorienting the corpora-tion from a firm-centered purpose to a more inclusive, ecosystem-wide mission. *Reshaping* corporate policy toward acceptance of ecosystem-life imperatives, while difficult, can and must proceed with caution and care to preserve the life interests of the firm and its stakeholders. *Integrat-ing* a corporation's economic motives, its productivity, and the inno-vative potentials of its workforce with the full spectrum of organic life would indeed support and sustain the lives of both firm and ecosystem inhabitants

Phase III: DARWIN

DARWIN's (natural selection's) essence: Natural selection—a concept introduced by Charles Darwin—is a process of organic change occurring over long time periods which favors the survival of life forms that are most adaptable to ecosystem environments. Natural selection of organic ecosystem life is generated by the more ancient process of thermodynamic energy evolution

The corporate challenge: To acknowledge the presence, function, and impact of natural selection pressures within the corporate workplace, and to distinguish between inherited, innate organic behavior produced by natural selection and the learned behaviors of corporate culture—plus the effect of both on the corporation's workforce

The behavioral/operational consequences: Human behavioral tendencies inherited via natural selection are operative in managers, employees, and stakeholders of all business firms, motivating them to seek and strengthen their own sustenance, security, and family/kinship bonds. Business firms, as collectivities of human organic entities (but not constituting organisms themselves) experience adaptive natural selection pressures indirectly, usually in the form of market competition with other such organic groupings. The evolutionary outcome is often similar to the results of natural selection-driven organic evolution—adaptation and survival of the firm, or its maladaptation and termination. These behavioral tendencies are not synonymous with "Social Darwinism"

The managerial opportunities: To recognize the presence of natural selection-derived behaviors within the firm and to organize, motivate, manage, and coordinate these workplace behaviors to promote the firm's goals, policies, and strategies

The management choices: Darwinian natural selection, as a behavioral influence within the firm, cannot simply be *ignored*, although alternative explanations exist and may be preferred. *Accepting* natural selection's presence provides the firm's managers with an understanding of the central behavioral motives activated among fellow managers and employees. *Reshaping*, redirecting, and channeling the course of such behaviors to support the company's goals can lead toward an *integration* of the firm and adaptively positive natural selection processes

Phase IV: GENE

GENE's essence: Genes are cellular components inherited from an organism's kinship predecessors. An organism's phenotypic traits—body type, behavior, and life functions—are determined by the collective actions of its genes (DNA)

The corporate challenge: To recognize that the behavioral traits of all members of the corporate workplace are genetically implanted and therefore resistant to change, although modifiable to a limited extent

The organizational/operational consequences: The self-centered, competitive, gene-driven behavior of corporate managers, employees, and stakeholders is matched, and sometimes countervailed, by collaborative, cooperative tendencies also rooted in the human genome

The managerial opportunities: Acknowledging genes' influence on all forms of organic life opens up new realms of product development through genetic engineering: pesticide-resistance compounds, healthcare advances, and genetically modified foods, among many others

The management choices: *Ignoring* the active presence and behavioral influence of genes deprives corporate managers of chances to improve the corporate workplace and to contribute to the company's own survival in marketplace competition. *Accepting* the gene as a behavioral influence is controversial but essential for continued economic success of the corporation. *Reshaping* genes is scientifically feasible in some cases, thereby benefiting a corporation economically but posing normative questions for some corporate stakeholders and society generally. Genetic know-how can become an *integral* part of a company's strategy for market success, provided cautionary safeguards are included.

Phase V: *HOMO*

HOMO's **essence**: Today's humans—scientifically called *Homo sapiens*—are the lineal descendents of ancient ancestral hominid primates, physically distinguished from their forebears by differing phenotypes (bodies), genotypes (genomes), and cognotypes (brains)

The corporate challenge: To recognize, organize, and direct the inborn energy and innate behavioral tendencies of the human members of the firm's workforce

The organizational/operational consequences: A corporation's economic success depends significantly on channeling key *Homo* behavioral traits—aggressiveness, competitive drive, pragmatic focus, proximate time frame, group loyalty, risk taking, and innovative search—to attain the firm's goals

The managerial opportunities: A human species that out-competed its evolutionary cousins, trekked into all of the planet's continents, boated across its oceans, developed tool uses, controlled fire, survived countless geological upheavals and climatic crises, invented agriculture, evolved languages, settled in villages, towns, cities, states, empires, and now the entire global landscape—all of this should convince even the most resistant corporate managerial mind that *Homo sapiens* is a prime resource and a type of human capital worth protecting, cultivating, and putting at the forefront of corporate operations

The management choices: *Ignoring* the inherent, innate nature of human personality as an evolved product of natural selection is hiding the managerial mind in the sands of corporate failure. *Accepting* the grounded reality of evolved human behavior is a first step toward utilizing its sometimes hidden potential as a corporate resource. *Reshaping* and *integrating* an understanding of the *Homo* behavioral complex into the daily life of a company's culture is not only possible but necessary for the firm's own survival. The corporate landscape is littered with the bodies of companies that failed to mesh these basic elements within their cultures

Phase VI: BRAIN

BRAIN's essence: The *Homo sapiens* brain is the locus and organic source of human cognition, consciousness, self-awareness, and behavior. It has

evolved and expanded in size, complexity, and cognitive functions over a 2–2.5-million-year period, consisting now of cellular regions, layers, and neural networks that interact with external environments

The corporate challenge: To be aware of the human brain's enormous actual and potential power to engage productively in the economic work of the corporation

The organizational/operational consequences: Organizing and motivating a firm's workforce to pursue organizational goals efficiently and effectively requires managers to recognize, and to respect, the complexity, diversity, and potentials of the neural mindsets found within its employees and stakeholders

The managerial opportunities: The human mind is a function of brain-based behavioral drives, motivations, skill sets, neural modules, and emotional impulses which, when released for expression in the workplace, can move a corporation toward its economic goals. Coordinating those cognitive components is the function of organizational leadership

The management choices: *Ignoring* the nature-influenced workplace mind—acting as if it didn't exist and is not worth management attention—is indeed a choice made by some corporate managers who thereby overlook, forgo, and forfeit a virtual treasure trove of creative energy that might otherwise be dedicated to corporate purposes and missions. *Accepting, reshaping,* and *integrating* these human propensities rooted in the *Homo sapiens* brain would testify to the presence, and pragmatic use by managers, of the neocortex's executive function that coordinates the many diverse neural signals arising within a firm's workplace population

Phase VII: SYMBOL

SYMBOL's essence: A symbol is a cognitive meaning generated by the brain in response to an organism's internal state (pain, hunger, anger) or

the organism's interactions with an external environment (search for food, predator threat). The symbol's meaning is projected outward from the brain and associated with an external physical object (friend or enemy) or activity (speech, music) that represents the internally generated meaning. Symbols are one of three major components of human culture, the other two being tools and sociality patterns, all three collectively known as neuro-organic culture

The corporate challenge: To identify the potentials and limitations of human neuro-organic culture for achieving corporate goals

The organizational/operational consequences: Human neuro-organic culture, consisting of symbols, tools, and sociality, is replicated on a reduced scale in a business firm and is known as corporate culture. Company operations can be powerfully influenced by the kinds of symbols (adaptive or maladaptive), tools (pragmatic, innovative), and sociality patterns (family, company, community) that are emphasized and encouraged by the firm's directors and managers

The managerial opportunities: Corporate cultures are malleable in spite of the innate and acquired tendencies built into human culture generally. Managers can map symbolic pathways for employees to follow, can reward innovative tool use, can encourage productive sociality groupings (flexible work teams), and can feed the emotional appetites of employees who contribute creatively to company goal achievement. Nature and nurture are powerful productive partners when skillfully coordinated by management

The management choices: Without doubt, many business firms do *ignore*—or worse, they actively deny—the positive policy and behavioral potentials of both human and corporate culture, to the detriment, and sometimes the economic ruin, of a company, its employees, stakeholders, and host communities. By contrast, leading corporations learned long ago that *accepting* the realities of evolved human behavior, and *reshaping* its broad outlines for corporate purposes, will pay big dividends of increased productivity and organizational harmony. While *integrating* the positives of symbolic corporate culture, managers need always to remember the potential negatives for ecosystem organic life

Phase VIII: ORGANIZATION

ORGANIZATION's essence: Natural evolution has generated three basic patterns of organization: hierarchy (power, status), coordination (tools and skills), and nonlinear complexity (chaotic order). All three are present and active in the modern business corporation

The corporate challenge: To acknowledge the negative effects of hierarchy, the productive potentials of technological coordination, and the surprise element of nonlinear behavior. Such effects—good and bad—are felt internally by the firm's managers and employees, and externally by stakeholders and market competitors. Finding a workable balance of these organizational patterns is a central challenge of corporate leadership

The organizational/operational consequences: Effective organizational leadership and executive power are often, or even usually, conflated, while technical coordination's role is diminished and often demeaned. Such attitudes are an understandable heritage of evolution's impact on a managerial mind that exaggerates its own importance as it overlooks or downplays the productive power of the firm's tools, technology, and skilled workforce. The quest for organizational efficiency rests principally on skilled tool use plus a sophisticated acceptance of the uncertainties of nonlinear surprises, rather than relying primarily on symbolic executive power

The managerial opportunities: Creating a flatter corporate profile by amending hierarchical power can release the innovative potentialities of a workforce prepared to generate new products and is an unparalleled pathway to corporate success. To do so, tool use would trump power hierarchy—a tough choice for domineering alpha-male managers. The relaxed, open, creative atmosphere of leading high-tech firms is often given credit for their resultant innovative styles and outputs

The management choices: *Ignoring* the workplace presence of nature's organizational trio and their impact on operations is a mark of extreme managerial myopia. *Accepting* and attempting to *integrate* them into the corporate body by *reshaping* their respective behavioral patterns for the firm's purposes is a worthy path for managers to follow

Phase IX: MARKET

MARKET's essence: Markets are socioeconomic transaction systems, displaying two naturally evolved functions: equitable trade of instrumentally useful economic objects (goods and services) and reciprocally balanced exchange of sociocultural symbols (social status, power)

The corporate challenge: To maximize the corporation's marketplace well-being through prudent economizing while simultaneously preserving ecosystem integrity through ecologizing practices

The organizational/operational consequences: A business firm's facility in negotiating market transactions (minimizing its costs, maximizing its benefits) is crucial to the firm's survival and its economic/financial stature, and can be supportive (or not) of the firm's stakeholders. Finding an acceptable balance among the competitive economic and social interests involved in market transactions defines the central task of corporate strategy

The managerial opportunities: Repurposing the corporation—reorienting its evolution-induced managerial drive from self-centeredness (recall the selfish gene) to a broader-based ecosystem-life approach—is a sought ideal of some corporate observers but remains an elusive goal. The clash of market instrumentalism and social reciprocity—both naturally evolved features of human society—may well present corporate managers with an irreconcilable conundrum posed by natural evolution

The management choices: *Ignoring* the prospects of firm–ecosystem contradictions recruits a sizeable number of more hopeful and determined anti-corporation protestors. *Acceptance* of the market's restrained ability to cope with an emerging crisis of long-term human survival and global inequality is emerging among a growing number of corporate leaders. *Reshaping* market incentives and *integrating* those new standards into corporate operations is presently a symbolic, not a significant nor a sufficiently practical, response to current human concern and aspiration. When such dysfunctional, visionary symbolism trumps technological instrumentality, human (and business) evolution falter. The ultimate choice is in corporate management's hands

Thus, in these many ways, the **Evolutionary Cascade**'s first nine phases generate a comprehensive agenda of corporate opportunities, policy options, and strategic choices. We need now to pose the critical question: Is corporate management up to the task?

Phase X: THE CONUNDRUMS OF CORPORATE CHOICE

Living the sometimes tumultuous life of a corporation's executive manager is no easy task. The corporate-scape is littered with an array of those who, for one reason or another, could not and did not meet the many challenges their companies encountered. But perhaps an even greater number can be found on the upward slopes and towering peaks of economic achievement, successful for themselves and their vigorously competitive enterprises. While there are Enrons galore, there may be even more Apples exultant. The reasons can be numerous: skill, ingenuity, foresight, real-world practicality, endurance, fortitude, imagination—or even luck. I once heard a former CEO known for the long successful run of his corporation say publicly that he had been the luckiest man alive by being "in the right place at the right time." Of course, he also made the "right" decisions "at the right time," as many other CEOs have done to their credit.

Both the potentials of corporate achievement and the obstacles that cause some firms to stumble and fall are the outcomes of the many natural forces that surround and give life to any business corporation. Although the modern business corporation is itself not a living organism, "it" is impelled across the eco-scape by the actions of its collective "live-in" organic inhabitants. Identifying all of the major impellers—a confluence of evolutionary processes—and judging how, and how well, they affect the firm becomes a key—perhaps *the* key—function and responsibility of corporate managerial leadership.

The core conundrums—the real puzzlers—that stand out from all the other contradictions, complexities, and confusions that nature poses to corporate leaders are four in number, each one raising the stakes to the level of cosmic corporate responsibility.

Entropy versus Life

All organic life, including the corporation's organic collectivity, confronts entropy. Since Earthly life's beginnings, no organic form has outrun or escaped entropy's fatal, final grasp. Entropy trumps life. Organisms generated and activated by inflowing solar energy are nonessential though instrumental to entropy's destination of finality. The modern business corporation has proved to be one of nature's most effective finders, accumulators, and processors of thermodynamic energy; it is an energy transduction mechanism of perhaps unsurpassed potential. In so doing, the corporation extends not just its own life but also enriches the lives of countless others by its productivity. Today's and tomorrow's energy crises testify to the corporation's central role in creating, and possibly also solving, the energy dilemma. But there is a downside. By maximizing entropic energy flows through its powerful drive to survive, the corporation at times puts at risk the lives, the quality of life, and the survival chances of its market competitors, its employees, its stakeholders, and the integrity of ecosystems around the world—all of which are thereby moved closer to a fatal entropic equilibrium. Who—which forms of organic life—shall survive and for how long? The managerial choice is stark, unyielding, inescapable.

Genotype versus Cognotype

Genes are the essence of all cellular life, forming organic phenotypes, perpetuating themselves through time, constituting the most basal form of organic energy (its mitochondrian "batteries"), and thus driving the behavior of all organic forms of life, including humans and their business corporations. The *Homo sapiens* brain—that astoundingly creative cellular mass—is an outcome of the focused activity of genes interacting with ecosystem adaptive pressures. Ironically, a relatively flexible and creative cognotype thus owes its very existence to the inflexible genotype's drive for perpetual life. Does Gene thus trump Brain by channeling cognition to promote genetic continuity rather than human adaptive purpose? Are corporate decision-makers, policymakers, and strategists unwitting pawns doing the work of their genes rather than the presumed rational work of their brains? Is corporate purpose defined and shaped by genotypes, not by cognotypes? Does managerial planning and strategizing even matter? Can we count on genotypes to do the job unassisted by cognotypes?

Symbol versus Tool

Symbols and tools—major components of human culture—share a common trait: immense generativity and creativity, constantly expanding the range and quality of symbols' meanings and tools' instrumental usages. These capabilities—something like a "wild card" of unpredictable potential—are expressions of the *Homo sapiens* brain having variable and often contradictory adaptive effects. Instrumental tool use has long supported human adaptation to varying ecosystem exigencies; tools are one of natural selection's most potent partners. Today's business corporations are the home of modern tools/technology, sheltering technical experts and pushing them to reach the outer edges of technological innovation. The resultant technological juggernaut is matched though, and perhaps even over-matched, by symbolic creativity—a deep wellspring of human belief, meaning, and purpose bubbling up from the depths of that fertile *Homo* brain. Symbolic meaning need not be entirely instrumental, as attested by human devotion to myth-making, magical incantations, other-worldly realms, out-of-body experiences, visions, mysticism, spiritualism, cult beliefs, taboos, rituals, ceremonials, extra-natural belief, and other behaviors with imputed teleological purpose and meaning. At that fateful juncture where Symbol and Tool confront one another in human (and corporate) affairs, choices are sometimes needed. Should it be the adaptive instrumental Tool? Or the adaptively lax, or even maladaptive, *Homo*-centered Symbolic meaning? The questions are real for the corporate moguls who formulate the goals, visions, purposes, and strategies of their companies. Should tools/technology be favored for their adaptive effects on the corporation, its workforce, and the communities it serves? Should broader symbolic human purpose be given equal standing? Should technology's potential for ecologically destructive behavior—direct threats to life, ecosystem, and human purpose—be limited? What shall it be—Tool or Symbol?

Market Efficiency versus Social Reciprocity

Modern markets are the natural inheritors of dual intertwined functions: the exchange of economic valuables at socially reciprocal rates. Market efficiency requires minimizing economic costs and maximizing economic benefits for the exchange partners. Social reciprocity requires a regard for the socioeconomic standing of the exchange partners. Mutual benefits are normally expected, shared costs a possibility. However, the economic function—an econotype—may be held hostage to the social function—a symbotype—thereby reducing the market's efficiency (by increasing costs or reducing benefits), while the social function may be compromised by an overzealous search for economic efficiency (by increasing and/or ignoring social costs and reducing social benefits). Market efficiency constitutes a natural selection pressure on corporate enterprise enabling the firm to adapt and survive. Social reciprocity signals the presence of a natural selection pressure on human sociality groups enabling them to adapt and survive. The resultant conundrum: Will natural selection let either of the exchange partners off the hook? Does market efficiency trump social reciprocity, or is it the other way around? While Adam Smith's free-market admirers abound, others favor social contracts (Donaldson and Dunfee 1999; Fort and Noone 1999; Fort 2001; Frederick and Wasieleski 2002). The debate goes on. What market price is just? Which exchange is the most efficient? Does nature care? Do managers care?

In the face of these four epic, indeed cosmic, puzzles, it is sobering to recall the relative recency and impermanence of *Homo* life and organic life generally. *Homo sapiens* is the "last person standing" in the long line of *Homo* predecessors. Massive extinctions in past ages—five in number—have eliminated most forms of then-existing organic life, and another extinction may be under way in today's world, possibly aided by corporate decisions, policies, and actions. On Earth, a far more ancient kind of evolution—thermodynamic energy—preceded the appearance of organic life, with power to create or destroy ecosystem life webs. Organic life itself is a cosmically recent event—a youngster of only 3.75 billion years on a globe some 5 billion years of age in a Universe that began 14–15 billion years ago.

Although they are major players in this cosmic drama, corporate leaders and executives need to remind themselves of their own companies' precarious existence. One of their number, Arie de Geus, points out that the average life span of most corporations is approximately 40 years— far less than today's human life expectancy of 67 years (de Geus 1997: 2). Matt Ridley also comments on the brevity of corporate life: "Half of the biggest companies of 1980 have now disappeared by take-over or bankruptcy; half of today's biggest companies did not even exist in 1980" (Ridley 2010: 111). This suggests that natural selection, aided perhaps by rogue executive decisions, takes its toll among even the best runners in the corporate race to adapt and survive.

As they search for answers to the cosmic puzzles, corporate managers can take either of two paths to the future. Sir Martin Rees, a leading cosmologist, opines in *Our Final Hour* that "the odds are no better than fifty–fifty that our present civilization on Earth will survive to the end of the present [21st] century," succumbing to a combination of human-induced catastrophic events (Rees 2003: 8). A more cheerful view is promoted by seasoned science thinker Matt Ridley in *The Rational Optimist*: "economic evolution will raise living standards of the twenty-first century to unimagined heights, helping even the poorest people of the world to afford to meet their desires as well as their needs" (Ridley 2010: 352). A third more cautious but hopeful possibility is envisioned by two other renowned scholars: a "SEE Change" toward a "Sustainable Enterprise Economy" that would create a "balance between the public interest and free markets" (Waddock and McIntosh 2011: 19). Whatever the longer-term outcome may be, it is a sure bet that corporations will be near the center of the eventual denouement.

Corporate prominence flows naturally from nature's **Evolutionary Cascade** that has produced the corporation in all of the following forms:

- An **entropy** maximizer

- A **life-ecosystem** inhabitant

- A survivor of **natural selection**

- A **genetic** competitor–collaborator
- A *Homo*-generated economizer
- A set of **neural** algorithms
- A socioeconomic **symbol**
- An **organizational** trio
- A **market** duality
- A **living** company
- An **organic** collectivity
- A **planetary** inhabitant
- A citizen of the **cosmos**

The ultimate conclusion: This multifaceted naturological entity we call a corporation can find its way, its purpose, its mission, and its evolutionary fate by accepting and adhering to the principles of **Natural Corporate Management**, thereby embracing the entire realm of nature, planetary life, and cosmic responsiveness.

A natural theory of the firm

As a summative statement of the central theme of **Natural Corporate Management**, a natural theory of the firm is now proposed. This theory or model of the modern business corporation encapsulates all of the major natural components described in the preceding chapters. The theory adopts the standard language used to identify and to organize the major features of a theory of the firm. These categories include a firm's **initiator/founder, authorization, goals/motives, economic functions, organization, governance, decision system, strategy**, and **purpose**. For each of these standard categories, an equivalent set of terms is substituted that identifies the major characteristics of a natural theory of the firm. In both kinds of theory—whether standard or natural—the essential meaning and function of the categorical trait is the same, although the language usage and labels differ from one to the other by reflecting the nature-based traits found in a natural theory of the firm. In one sense, these language differences tend to conceal the functional similarity or sameness of the standard and natural categories as experienced in actual business firms.

A description of each category of the natural theory of the firm follows, and an accompanying chart depicts them in outline form. The numerous legal and practical variations and subtleties that are typically present in the actual performance of any business firm are necessarily missing from this brief, condensed version.

Initiator/founder and authorization

A business firm is normally proposed by an entrepreneurial group to achieve some public purpose, and therefore its activities are authorized by a recognized public entity, usually a government agency. A formal charter is issued, which describes the specific purpose(s) of the firm, plus detailed legal rights and limits involved in the firm's operations.

Inasmuch as this book proposes that *all* business firms are manifestations of an evolving natural process that affects the general public interest, they are subject to a process of public acceptance and authorization. Long before the modern corporate form of organization appeared, business activities were subject to a variety of public approval processes, ranging from norms of market reciprocity to more explicit rules governing product quality, fair prices, and apprenticeship training. Medieval guild rules, religious edicts, town ordinances, feudal land rights, royal decrees, and nation-state laws constituted early forms of authorization and regulation of business entities.

The initiating factor in all such historical cases—as is true today—has been an entrepreneurial group that proposes to engage in commercial enterprise by producing and selling products or services to buyers. In the natural theory of the firm, this founding entrepreneurial group, plus the subsequent addition of other owners, employees, and managers, constitutes the organic collectivity that defines the firm or corporation as an economic entity.

Goals and motives

The ultimate goal of a privately owned business firm is to generate profitable returns for the owner(s) resulting from commercial activities undertaken in the market. Profit-seeking and profit-making are the firm's principal drivers and motives.

In the language of the natural theory of the firm, the firm's goal is *survival of the firm through economizing* plus *adaptation to its natural environment through ecologizing*. **Economizing** is a thoroughly natural process whereby a business firm strives to maximize its earnings by exerting prudent control over its costs while offering goods and services at prices that will be perceived by buyers as benefits worth purchasing. A firm that does so consistently will normally survive for successive quarters over extended periods. **Ecologizing** is a natural process that enables a business firm to adapt successfully to its economic, social, and ecosystem environments by interacting in positive ways with other organic entities: competitors, consumers, suppliers, local and global (sometimes called "glocal") communities, stakeholders, and governments. Balancing a firm's economizing and ecologizing activities is required if the firm is to adapt and survive over long periods. Ecologizing behavior preserves, protects, and prolongs an entire ecosystem in which the business firm operates.

Economic functions

The primary economic functions of the business firm are three: capital acquisition and accumulation, production of goods and/or services, and distribution through market transactions.

In the standard theory of the firm, **capital** takes the form of accumulated money funds; goods and services are **produced** by the skills of employees using relevant technology; and **distribution** to buyers is accomplished through coordination of supply chains and marketplace negotiations.

In the natural theory of the firm, the self-same functions are carried out, although with different and expanded descriptors of the categories. Capital takes several different forms: organic capital, mineral/chemical capital, tool/technology capital, human capital, social capital, symbolic capital (including money), and information capital. These kinds of natural capital are a form of thermodynamic energy, each one an offshoot of an underlying process of evolutionary development and each one helping the business firm to attain a maximum rate of thermodynamic energy transduction, thus avoiding a condition of entropic equilibrium which is equivalent to economic failure and bankruptcy. The accumulation of capital in the natural firm is therefore best described as a process of **energy intake** whereby the firm acquires the energy sources needed for survival and adaptation on natural economic landscapes and ecosystems.

Production of goods and services occurring in the natural firm can similarly be considered as an activity labeled **energy processing** whereby the various forms of capital are converted into items that are saleable in the marketplace. The distribution function can likewise be characterized as a process of **energy transfer** whereby goods and services are moved by marketing techniques from production sites to markets that are governed by social reciprocity-redistribution guidelines that allow a socially acceptable amount of economic gain by the natural firm. This is not to deny the presence of monopolies, corruption, bribery, and other anti-market activities that can defeat or diminish the overall economic benefits generated by the firm through such energy transfers.

Governance, organization, and decision system

For-profit business firms are governed by their owners or by the owners' representatives, typically an elected board of directors headed by a chairperson, and including a vice-chairperson and other directorial posts, plus committees responsible for overseeing various operational and policy areas. Board members are responsible for overall company policy aimed at achieving the firm's goals. The board appoints the firm's executive managers, determines their compensation, reviews their performance, and has power to dismiss them for underachievement. These board powers, responsibilities, and goals constitute the basic governance system of most large-scale corporations.

The organization of a business firm's operations is derived primarily from its governance system, which centers power and control in a relatively small number of directors and executive managers. These senior-level officers and executive managers identify and appoint a series of professional managers to oversee diverse operational divisions of the company, thereby creating a hierarchical layering of personnel to carry out the needed technical and economic tasks of the company. The resultant organizational system thus reflects both a hierarchical allocation of decision-making and policymaking power and a significant participatory role for technical professional personnel as decisions are made and policies are set and reviewed. Thus, the firm's decision system is a blend of scalar rank and technology-based professional skills.

Restated now in the language of a natural theory of the firm, this governance-organization-decision system can be understood as a type of evolutionary inheritance of behaviors passed on to the modern era from an ancient past. The modern business firm is the inheritor of three basic kinds of organizing pattern. One is top-to-bottom rankings, having the shape of a pyramid that places a few powerful executives at the pyramid's peak, while lower levels are occupied by managers and employees who generally are expected to follow orders issued by the topmost officials. This is hierarchical organization. A second kind of organizational design is made possible by marshalling the collective technological skills of the firm's workforce, with the goal of coordinating and focusing these professional talents in ways that accomplish the company's goals. This is technological organization. A third, less well-known way of organizing a business firm's economic activities relies on nonlinear, complex, or at times even chaotic systems that are constantly open to unexpected change, innovation, and new discoveries. This is complex organization.

All decisions made by the directors, executives, managers, and employees of the business firm are heavily influenced by these three inherited organizational patterns. The principal decision-makers are mainly powerful alpha males at the pyramid's top level. They tend to be dominant over all others, aggressive, and highly competitive—but also pragmatically collaborative in their dealings with employees and with competing companies or government regulators. Technological skills and talents that lead to new innovative products are respected and rewarded. Complex, ever-changing markets require rapid, sometimes radical, reorganization and redefinition of a company's goals.

In these ways, a business firm's decision system reflects an ancient behavioral heritage—but one that supports its continuing existence.

Strategy

Strategy is a business firm's way of gaining an advantage for itself over marketplace rivals, competitors, government regulators, or other power centers. The many ways of doing so, by identifying key factors both inside and outside the company, is the work of strategic thinkers.

Strategy for the natural firm involves integrating the various phases of the **Evolutionary Cascade** into the firm's operations. That means finding and utilizing essential energy sources, adjusting its economizing actions to the potentials and limits of the ecosystems in which it operates, recognizing the genetic components of human behavior, accepting the selection power of natural forces, acknowledging the inherited behavioral traits of human beings, respecting the human brain's neural modules that shape workplace behaviors, understanding the reach and range of symbolic culture, knowing the firm's organizational patterns and the market's potentials and constraints, and accepting the realms of responsibility and responsiveness that accompany a business firm's activities as it pursues an adaptive economizing-ecologizing strategy.

The strategic maneuvers of the natural business firm can succeed only if it focuses prime attention on the physical-chemical-organic-symbolic-market environment that gives the firm—and all life forms—an ability to adapt, survive, and achieve its natural potential.

Corporate purpose

The natural business firm's broader purpose or meaning contrasts strikingly with what is normally believed to be a company's economic market function. Conventionally, the business firm is seen in strictly instrumental terms—as a useful, practical way of providing goods and services to a public willing to pay for them. As such, the firm has indeed long contributed to the economic well-being of human society. Without rejecting this standard meaning of business's purpose, the natural theory of the firm proposes a more fundamental concept of corporate meaning and purpose.

The basic idea can be expressed as a formula: Corporate Purpose = (f) Cosmic Evolution, which simply means that a corporation's purpose is a function of cosmic evolution as described in the chapters of this book.

Cosmic evolution here refers to all phases of the **Evolutionary Cascade**—beginning with the Big Bang and continuing onward through time to the present and on into the future. The natural firm is one outcome of that long evolutionary pathway from past to present. The firm sustains itself and countless others through its economizing operations. It also displays a potential ability to spread its economic benefits more widely by adopting an ecologizing philosophy plus an organic strategy to move in that direction. The managers of the modern natural corporation sense, whether explicitly or intuitively, that corporate purpose is broader and deeper in scope, function, and community commitment than conventionally believed. Managers' goals, functions, organizational designs, decisions, and strategies are part of an ancient and ever-widening arc of evolutionary development—literally, an evolution of cosmic proportions—creating a cumulative, nested set of natural processes that define the overall purpose of the natural firm.

The major components of a natural theory of the firm are summarized in the accompanying box (see next page).

A NATURAL THEORY OF THE FIRM

Based on Natural Corporate Management

Initiator/Founder	An individual person or an entrepreneurial group
Authorization	Created by government authority as a legal entity to pursue a public purpose
Goals/Motives	Survival ⇒ Economizing: Profits and increase of capital value Adaptation ⇒ Ecologizing: Sustainable development of firm within ecosystem
Economic Functions	Energy intake ⇒ Capital acquisition ⇒ Physical/mineral/chemical/organic/human/social/symbolic/technological/informational Energy processing ⇒ Production of goods and services Energy transfer ⇒ Distribution of goods and services ⇒ Reciprocal market transactions
Governance	Policy and decision authority centered in board of directors, CEO, and upper-level executives
Organization/Culture	Firm as organic collectivity: Owner-shareholders, managers, employees, stakeholders Organizational design: Hierarchical/Technological/Nonlinear complexity Corporate culture: Micro-scale version of human neuro-organic culture
Decision System	Alpha-male dominance: aggressive, competitive, pragmatically collaborative Techno-scientific expertise: Innovative, entrepreneurial
Strategy	Integrating of all phases of the Evolutionary Cascade into the firm's operations to achieve economizing and ecologizing goals
Purpose	Corporate purpose = (f) Cosmic Evolution:　Energy ⇒ Life ⇒ Natural Selection ⇒ Gene ⇒ Humans ⇒ Brain ⇒ Symbol ⇒ Organization ⇒ Market ⇒ Corporation ⇒ Economic, Social, Cosmic Responsibility

The Big C's pivotal points

- The modern business corporation is a manifestation of evolving natural forces, a product of an **Evolutionary Cascade** consisting of physical, chemical, biological, and ecosystem components

- **Natural Corporate Management** is a nature-based perspective of what it means and requires to manage a business firm

- Each phase of the **Evolutionary Cascade** presents corporate managers with challenges, behavioral-operational consequences, opportunities, and choices that affect the company's present and future existence

- Four fundamental puzzles confront the managers of the modern corporation: entropy versus life; genotype versus cognotype; symbol versus tool; and market efficiency versus social reciprocity. Confronting and acting upon these problems by adopting **Natural Corporate Management** principles evokes a new concept of corporate cosmic responsibility

- A natural theory of the firm summarizes all of the major components of nature that shape, influence, and activate the management of the modern business corporation, including the firm's initiator/founder, authorization, goals and motives, economic functions, governance, organization, decision system, strategy, and purpose

The Big C's research base

de Geus, A. (1997) *The Living Company* (Boston, MA: Harvard Business School Press).

Donaldson, T., and T. Dunfee (1999) *Ties That Bind: A Social Contracts Approach to Business Ethics* (Boston, MA: Harvard Business School Press).

Fort, T.L. (2001) *Ethics and Governance: Business as Mediating Institution* (Oxford, UK: Oxford University Press).

Fort, T.L., and J.J. Noone (1999) "Banded Contracts, Mediating Institutions, and Corporate Governance: A Naturalistic Analysis of Contractual Theories of the Firm," *Law and Contemporary Problems* 62.3: 163-213.

Frederick, W.C., and D.M. Wasieleski (2002) "Evolutionary Social Contracts," *Business and Society Review* 107.3: 283-308.

Rees, M. (2003) *Our Final Hour* (New York: Basic Books).

Ridley, M. (2010) *The Rational Optimist: How Prosperity Evolves* (New York: Harper-Collins).

Waddock, S., and M. McIntosh (2011) *SEE Change: Making the Transition to a Sustainable Enterprise Economy* (Sheffield, UK: Greenleaf Publishing).

Bibliography

Allen, T., and G. Cowling (2011) *The Cell: A Very Short Introduction* (New York: Oxford University Press).

Ambrose, S.H. (2001) "Paleolithic Technology and Human Evolution," *Science* 291 (March 2, 2001): 1,748-53.

Andrews, P., and C. Stringer (1993) "The Primates' Progress," in S.J. Gould (ed.), *The Book of Life* (New York: W.W. Norton).

Anholt, R.R.H., and T.F.C. Mackay (2010) *Principles of Behavioral Genetics* (Amsterdam: Elsevier).

Annila, A. (2009) "Space, Time, and Machines," *International Journal of Theoretical and Mathematical Physics* 2.3: 16-32 (arxiv.org/abs/0910.2629 arXiv:0910.2629v1).

Annila, A., and E. Annila (2008) "Why Did Life Emerge?" *International Journal of Astrobiology* 7: 293-300.

Annila, A., and E. Kuismanen (2009) "Natural Hierarchy Emerges from Energy Dispersal," *BioSystems* 95: 227-33.

Arthur, W.B. (2009) *The Nature of Technology: What It Is and How It Evolves* (New York: Free Press).

Balter, M. (2002) "What Made Humans Modern?" *Science* 295 (February 15, 2002): 1,219-25.

Bhanoo, S.N. (2011) "Skull-Caps in British Cave Conjure an Ancient Rite," *New York Times*, February 16, 2011.

Blackmore, S. (1999) *The Meme Machine* (New York: Oxford University Press).

Bohannan, P., and G. Dalton (eds.) (1965) *Markets in Africa: Eight Subsistence Economies in Transition* (Garden City, NY: Doubleday & Co., Anchor Books).

Bower, B. (2004) "One-Celled Socialites," *Science News* 166 (November 20, 2004): 330-32.

Bower, B. (2012a) "Stone Age Fire Rises from the Ashes," *Science News* 181.9 (May 2012): 18.

Bower, B. (2012b) "Tangled Roots," *Science News* 182.4 (August 2012): 22-26.

Boyd, R., and P.J. Richerson (2005) *The Origin and Evolution of Cultures* (New York: Oxford University Press).

Bradsher, K. (2010) "China to Close 2,000 Factories," *New York Times*, reprinted in *Pittsburgh Post-Gazette*, August 10, 2010: A-4.

Brown, A. (1999) *The Darwin Wars: The Scientific Battle for the Soul of Man* (London: Simon & Schuster).

Brown, J.H. (1995) *Macroecology* (Chicago: University of Chicago Press).

Brown, L. (ed.) (1993) *The New Shorter Oxford English Dictionary on Historical Principles* (Oxford, UK: Clarendon Press).

Burley, P., and J. Foster (eds.) (1994) *Economics and Thermodynamics: New Perspectives on Economic Analysis* (Boston, MA: Kluwer Academic Publishers).

Burt, A., and R. Trivers (2006) *Genes in Conflict: The Biology of Selfish Genetic Elements* (Cambridge, MA: Harvard University Press).

Bussey, J. (2011) "Chutzpah in the C-suite: Watching out for No. 1," *Wall Street Journal*, December 23, 2011: B1-B2.

Cann, R.L. (2001) "Genetic Clues to Dispersal in Human Populations: Retracing the Past from the Present," *Science* 291 (March 2, 2001): 1,742-48.

Carroll, S.M. (2010) *From Eternity to Here: The Quest for the Ultimate Theory of Time* (New York: Dutton).

Cassill, D. (2004) "The Social Gene," *Journal of Bioeconomics* 6: 1-12.

Cassill, D., and A. Watkins (2010) "The Evolution of Cooperative Hierarchies through Natural Selection Processes," *Journal of Bioeconomics* 12: 29-42.

Chaisson, E.J. (2001) *Cosmic Evolution: The Rise of Complexity in Nature* (Cambridge, MA: Harvard University Press).

Chapais, B. (2008) *Primeval Kinship: How Pair-Bonding Gave Birth to Human Society* (Cambridge, MA: Harvard University Press).

Cheetham, N.W.H. (2011) *Introducing Biological Energetics: How Energy and Information Control the Living World* (Oxford, UK: Oxford University Press).

Childe, V.G. (1951) *Man Makes Himself* (New York: New American Library).

Cluss, P., J. Hill-Finegan and G. Peaslee (2010) "Employers vs. Partner Violence," *Pittsburgh Post-Gazette*, September 19, 2010: B-1, B-4.

Corning, P.A. (2005) *Holistic Darwinism: Synergy, Cybernetics, and the Bioeconomics of Evolution* (Chicago: University of Chicago Press).

Cory, G.A., Jr. (1999) *The Reciprocal Modular Brain in Economics and Politics* (New York: Kluwer Academic/Plenum Publishers).

Cosmides, L. (1989) "The Logic of Social Exchange: Has Natural Selection Shaped how Humans Reason? Studies with the Wason Selection Task," *Cognition* 31: 187-276.

Cosmides, L., and J. Tooby (2005) "Neurocognitive Adaptations Designed for Social Exchange," in D.M. Buss (ed.), *The Handbook of Evolutionary Psychology* (Hoboken, NJ: John Wiley & Sons): 584-627.

Cummins, D. (2005) "Dominance, Status, and Social Hierarchies," in D. Buss (ed.), *The Handbook of Evolutionary Psychology* (Hoboken, NJ: John Wiley & Sons): 676-97.

Daft, R.L. (2007) *Organization Theory and Design* (Mason, OH: Thomson South-Western, 9th edn).

Dalton, G. (1965) "Primitive Money," *American Anthropologist* 67: 45-65.

Dalton, G. (ed.) (1967) *Tribal and Peasant Economies: Readings in Economic Anthropology* (Garden City, NY: Natural History Press).

Darlington, C.D. (1959) "The Origin of Darwinism," *Scientific American*, May 1959: 60-66.

Darwin, C. (1859) *The Origin of Species: By Means of Natural Selection or The Preservation of Favored Races in the Struggle for Life* (New York: Modern Library).

Darwin, C. (1871) *The Descent of Man: And Selection in Relation to Sex* (New York: A.L. Burt Publishers).

Darwin, C. (1874) *The Descent of Man: And Selection in Relation to Sex* (New York: A.L. Burt Publishers, 2nd edn).

Dawkins, R. (1976) *The Selfish Gene* (Oxford, UK: Oxford University Press).

Dawkins, R. (1982) *The Extended Phenotype: The Long Reach of the Gene* (New York: Oxford University Press, 1999).

Dawkins, R. (2006) *The Selfish Gene* (Oxford, UK: Oxford University Press, 30th anniversary edition).

de Bourgoing, J. (2001) *The Calendar: History, Lore, and Legend* (New York: Harry N. Abrams).

de Geus, A. (1997) *The Living Company* (Boston, MA: Harvard Business School Press).

de Waal, F. (1998) *Chimpanzee Politics: Power and Sex among Apes* (Baltimore, MD: Johns Hopkins University Press, rev. edn).

Deacon, T.W. (1997) *The Symbolic Species: The Co-evolution of Language and the Brain* (New York: W.W. Norton).

Deacon, T.W. (1998) "Language Evolution and Neuromechanisms," in W. Bechtel and G. Graham (eds.), *A Companion to Cognitive Science* (Malden, MA: Blackwell): 212-25.

Deal, T.E., and A.A. Kennedy (1982) *Corporate Cultures: The Rites and Rituals of Corporate Life* (Reading, MA: Addison-Wesley).

Deamer, D. (2011) *First Life: Discovering the Connection between Stars, Cells, and How Life Began* (Berkeley, CA: University of California Press).

Diamond, J. (1998) *Guns, Germs, and Steel: The Fate of Human Societies* (New York: W.W. Norton).

Dickhaut, J., S. Basu, K. McCabe and G. Waymire (2010) "Neuroaccounting: Consilience between the Biologically Evolved Brain and Culturally Evolved Accounting Principles," *Accounting Horizons* 42.2: 221-55.

Dodds, W.K. (2009) *Laws, Theories, and Patterns in Ecology* (Berkeley, CA: University of California Press).

Donaldson, T., and T. Dunfee (1999) *Ties That Bind: A Social Contracts Approach to Business Ethics* (Boston, MA: Harvard Business School Press).

Dunbar, R., C. Knight and C. Power (eds.) (1999) *The Evolution of Culture: An Interdisciplinary View* (New Brunswick, NJ: Rutgers University Press).

Dunbar, R.I.M. (1992) "Neocortex Size as a Constraint on Group Size in Primates," *Journal of Human Evolution* 22: 469-93.

Dunbar, R.I.M. (1993) "Coevolution of Neocortex Size, Group Size and Language in Humans," *Behavioral and Brain Sciences* 16: 681-735.

Dunbar, R.I.M. (2006) "Brains, Cognition, and the Evolution of Culture," in S. Levinson and P. Jaisson (eds.), *Evolution and Culture* (Cambridge, MA: MIT Press): 169-79.

Dunbar, R.I.M., and S. Shultz (2007) "Evolution in the Social Brain," *Science* 317 (September 7, 2007): 1,344-47.

Durham, W.H. (1991) *Coevolution: Genes, Culture, and Human Diversity* (Stanford: CA. Stanford University Press).

Dutton, D. (2009) *The Art Instinct: Beauty, Pleasure, and Human Evolution* (New York: Bloomsbury Press).

Dyson, G. (1997) *Darwin among the Machines* (London: Penguin Books).

Ebstein, R., S. Shamay-Tsoory and S. Hong Chew (eds.) (2011) *From DNA to Social Cognition* (Hoboken, NJ: John Wiley & Sons).

Efrati, A. (2011) "For Google CEO Larry Page, A Difficult Premiere Role," *Wall Street Journal*, August 30, 2011: B1, B5.

Efrati, A., and J.S. Lublin (2011) "Yahoo Ousts Bartz as CEO," *Wall Street Journal*, September 7, 2012.

Eigen, M., with R. Winkler-Oswatitsch (1992) *Steps Towards Life: A Perspective on Evolution* (New York: Oxford University Press).

Einzig, P. (1948) *Primitive Money: In Its Ethnological, Historical and Economic Aspects* (London: Eyre & Spottiswoode).

Eiseley, L.C. (1959) "Alfred Russel Wallace," *Scientific American*, February 1959: 70-84.

Falk, D., and K.R. Gibson (2001) *Evolutionary Anatomy of the Primate Cerebral Cortex* (Cambridge, UK: Cambridge University Press).

Fehr, E., and A. Falk (2002) "The Psychological Foundations of Incentives," *European Economic Review* 46: 687-724.

Fehr, E., and J. Henrich (2003) "Is Strong Reciprocity a Maladaptation? On the Evolutionary Foundations of Human Altruism," in P. Hammerstein (ed.), *The Genetic and Cultural Evolution of Cooperation* (Cambridge, MA: MIT Press): 55-82.

Fehr, E., U. Fischbacher and S. Gachter (2002) "Social Reciprocity, Human Cooperation and the Enforcement of Social Norms," *Nature* 13: 1-25.

Finlayson, C. (2009) *The Humans Who Went Extinct: Why Neanderthals Died Out and We Survived* (Oxford, UK: Oxford University Press).

Fort, T.L. (2001) *Ethics and Governance: Business as Mediating Institution* (Oxford, UK: Oxford University Press).

Fort, T.L., and J.J. Noone (1999) "Banded Contracts, Mediating Institutions, and Corporate Governance: A Naturalistic Analysis of Contractual Theories of the Firm," *Law and Contemporary Problems* 62.3: 163-213.

Fox, R.F. (1988) *Energy and the Evolution of Life* (New York: W.H. Freeman).

Frederick, W.C. (1995) *Values, Nature, and Culture in the American Corporation* (New York: Oxford University Press).

Frederick, W.C. (1998) "Creatures, Corporations, Communities, Chaos, Complexity," *Business & Society* 37.4 (December 1998): 358-89.

Frederick, W.C. (2004) "The Evolutionary Firm and Its Moral (Dis)Contents," *Business, Science, and Ethics* 4 (Ruffin Series of the Society for Business Ethics): 145-76.

Frederick, W.C. (2006) *Corporation, Be Good! The Story of Corporate Social Responsibility* (Indianapolis, IN: Dog Ear Publishing).

Frederick, W.C., and D.M. Wasieleski (2002) "Evolutionary Social Contracts," *Business and Society Review* 107.3: 283-308.

Futuyma, D.J. (2005) *Evolution* (Sunderland, MA: Sinauer Associates).

Gabora, L. (2012) "An Evolutionary Framework for Culture: Selectionism versus Communal Exchange," arXiv:1206.4386v1 [q-bio.PE].

Gaidos, S. (2012) "Furry Friends Forever," *Science News* 181.7 (April 2012): 18-21.

Gibbons, A. (2006) *The First Human: The Race to Discover Our Earliest Ancestors* (New York: Doubleday).

Gibbons, A. (2010) "Close Encounters of the Prehistoric Kind," *Science* 328 (May 7, 2010): 680-84.

Gibson, K.R., and T. Ingold (1993) *Tools, Language and Cognition in Human Evolution* (Cambridge, UK: Cambridge University Press).

Glimcher, P.W. (2011) *Foundations of Neuroeconomic Analysis* (New York: Oxford University Press).

Glimcher, P.W., C.F. Camerer, E. Fehr and R.A. Poldrack (2009) *Neuroeconomics: Decision Making and the Brain* (Amsterdam: Elsevier).

Goldberg, E. (2009) *The New Executive Brain: Frontal Lobes in a Complex World* (Oxford, UK: Oxford University Press).

Goldman, D. (2012) *Our Genes, Our Choices: How Genotype and Gene Interactions Affect Behavior* (Amsterdam: Elsevier Academic Press).

Goldsmith, D. (1997) "Who Saw the Face of God?" *Scientific American*, March 1997: 126-27. A review of John C. Mather and John Boslough, *The Very First Light: The True Inside Story of the Scientific Journey Back to the Dawn of the Universe* (New York: Basic Books, 1996).

Goldstein, J. (1994) *The Unshackled Organization: Facing the Challenge of Unpredictability through Spontaneous Reorganization* (Portland, OR: Productivity Press).

Gouyon, P.-H., J.-P. Henry and J. Arnould (2002) *Gene Avatars: The Neo-Darwinian Theory of Evolution* (New York: Kluwer/Plenum Publishers, original publication: *Les avatars du gène: La théorie néodarwinienne de l'évolution*, 1997, Berlin: Editions).

Greene, B. (2005) *The Fabric of the Cosmos: Space, Time, and the Texture of Reality* (New York: Vintage Books).

Hagen, E.H. (2005) "Controversial Issues in Evolutionary Psychology," in D.M. Buss (ed.), *The Handbook of Evolutionary Psychology* (Hoboken, NJ: John Wiley & Sons): 145-73.

Hamilton, W.D. (1964) "The Genetical Evolution of Social Behavior," *Journal of Theoretical Behavior* 7: 1-52.

Hammerstein, P. (ed.) (2003) *The Genetic and Cultural Evolution of Cooperation* (Cambridge, MA: MIT Press).

Harris, M. (1993) *Culture, People, Nature: An Introduction to General Anthropology* (New York: HarperCollins).

Henrich, J., R. Boyd, S. Bowles, C. Camerer, E. Fehr, H. Gintis and R. McElreath (2001) "In Search of Homo Economicus: Behavioral Experiments in 15 Small-Scale Societies," *The American Economic Review* 91.2 (May 2001): 73-78.

Henrich, J., R. Boyd, S. Bowles, C. Camerer, E. Fehr, H. Gintis, R. McElreath, M. Alvard, A. Barr, J. Ensminger, N. Smith Henrich, K. Hill, F. Gil-White, M. Gurven, F.W. Marlowe, J.Q. Patton and D. Tracer (2005) " 'Economic Man' in Cross-Cultural Perspective: Behavioral Experiments in 15 Small-Scale Societies," *Behavioral and Brain Sciences* 28: 795-855.

Herr, P. (2009) *Primal Management: Unraveling the Secrets of Human Nature to Drive High Performance* (New York: American Management Association).

Hill, D. (2008) *Emotionomics: Leveraging Emotions for Business Success* (Philadelphia, PA: Kogan Page, rev. edn).

Hogan, C.J. (2002) "Observing the Beginning of Time," *American Scientist* 90 (September–October 2002): 420-427.

Holden, C. (2004) "The Origin of Speech," *Science* 303 (February 27, 2004): 1,316-19.

Holland, J. (1995) *Hidden Order: How Adaptation Builds Complexity* (New York: Addison-Wesley).

Jaakkola, S., S. El-Showk and A. Annila (2008) "The Driving Force behind Genomic Diversity," *Biophysical Chemistry* 134: 232-38.

Jacobs, J. (2000) *The Nature of Economies* (New York: Modern Library).

Johanson, D., and B. Edgar (1996) *From Lucy to Language* (New York: Simon & Schuster).

Jordans, F. (2012) "Countries Considering a Timeout on Leap Second," *Pittsburgh Post-Gazette*, January 19, 2012: A-3.

Jorgensen, S.E. (2002) *Integration of Ecosystem Theories: A Pattern* (Dordrecht, Netherlands: Kluwer Academic Publishers, 3rd edn).

Jorgensen, S.E., and Y.M. Sverizhev (2004) *Towards a Thermodynamic Theory for Ecological Systems* (Amsterdam: Elsevier).

Kaila, V.R.I., and A. Annila (2008) "Natural Selection for Least Action," *Proceedings of the Royal Society A* 464: 3,005-70.

Kauffman, S. (1993) *The Origins of Order: Self-organization and Selection in Evolution* (New York: Oxford University Press).

Kauffman, S. (1995) *At Home in the Universe: The Search for Laws of Self-organization and Complexity* (New York: Oxford University Press).

Kelly, K. (2010) *What Technology Wants* (New York: Viking).

Klein, R.G. (2009) *The Human Career: Human Biological and Cultural Origins* (Chicago: University of Chicago Press, 3rd edn).

Kleinsmith, L.J., and V.M. Kish (1995) *Principles of Cell and Molecular Biology* (New York: HarperCollins, 2nd edn).

Klug, W.S., and M.R. Cummings (2005) *Essentials of Genetics* (Upper Saddle River, NJ: Pearson Prentice Hall, 5th edn).

Knight, C., R. Dunbar and C. Power (1999) "An Evolutionary Approach to Human Culture," in R. Dunbar, C. Knight and C. Power (eds.), *The Evolution of Culture: An Interdisciplinary View* (New Brunswick, NJ: Rutgers University Press).

Kondratyev, K.Y., K.S. Losev, M.D. Ananicheva and I.V. Chesnokova (2004) *Stability of Life on Earth: Principal Subject of Scientific Research in the 21st Century* (Springer-Praxis Books in Environmental Science; Chichester, UK: Praxis Publishing).

Korzeniewski, B. (2011) *How the Brain Generates the Mind: From Neurons to Self-consciousness* (Amherst, NY: Humanity Books).

Lawrence, P. (2010) *Driven to Lead: Good, Bad, and Misguided Leadership* (San Francisco: Jossey-Bass).

Lawrence, P., and N. Nohria (2002) *Driven: How Human Nature Shapes Our Choices* (San Francisco: Jossey-Bass).

Lawrimore, B. (2005) "From Excellence to Emergence: The Evolution of Management Thinking and the Influence of Complexity," in K.A. Richardson (ed.), *Managing Organizational Complexity: Philosophy, Theory, and Application* (Greenwich, CN: Information Age): 115-32.

Leigh, E.G., Jr. (2002) *A Magic Web: The Tropical Forest of Barro Colorado Island* (New York: Oxford University Press).

Leigh, E.G., Jr. (2010a) "The Evolution of Mutualism," *Journal of Evolutionary Biology* 23: 2,507-28.

Leigh, E.G., Jr. (2010b) "The Group Selection Controversy," *Journal of Evolutionary Biology* 23: 6-19.

Leigh, E.G., Jr., and G.J. Vermeij (2002) "Does Natural Selection Organize Ecosystems for the Maintenance of High Productivity and Diversity?" *Philosophical Transactions of the Royal Society, London B* 357: 709-18.

Leigh, E.G., Jr., G.J. Vermeij and M. Wikelski (2009) "What Do Human Economies, Large Islands and Forest Fragments Reveal about the Factors Limiting Ecosystem Evolution?" *Journal of Evolutionary Biology* 22: 1-12.

Lewis, R. (2012) *Human Genetics: Concepts and Applications* (New York: McGraw-Hill, 10th edn).

Lima-de-Faria, A. (1988) *Evolution without Selection: Form and Function by Autoevolution* (Amsterdam: Elsevier).

Lima-de-Faria, A. (1995) *Biological Periodicity: Its Molecular Mechanism and Evolutionary Implications* (Greenwich, CN: JAI Press).

Lissack, M.R. (ed.) (2002) *The Interaction of Complexity and Management* (Westport, CN: Quorum Books).

Lorenz, K. (1967) *On Aggression* (New York: Bantam Books).

Ludeman, K., and E. Erlandson (2006) *Alpha Male Syndrome* (Boston, MA: Harvard Business School Press).

Malinowski, B. (1953) *Argonauts of the Western Pacific: An Account of Native Enterprise and Adventure in the Archipelagoes of Melanesian New Guinea* (New York: E.P. Dutton).

Malinowski, B. (1967) "Tribal Economics in the Trobriands," in G. Dalton (ed.), *Tribal and Peasant Economies: Readings in Economic Anthropology* (Garden City, NY: Natural History Press): 185-223.

Margulis, L., and D. Sagan (2002) *Acquiring Genomes: A Theory of the Origin of Species* (New York: Basic Books).

Martin, J. (2002) *Organizational Culture: Mapping the Terrain* (Thousand Oaks, CA: Sage).

Maslow, A.H. (1954) *Motivation and Personality* (New York: Harper).

Maslow, A.H., D.C. Stephens and G. Heil (1998) *Maslow on Management* (New York: John Wiley).

Mauss, M. (1967) *The Gift: Forms and Functions of Exchange in Archaic Societies* (New York: W.W. Norton, trans. Ian Cunnison).

Maynard Smith, J., and E. Szathmary (1999) *The Origins of Life: From the Birth of Life to the Origin of Language* (New York: Oxford University Press).

Mayr, E. (2000) "Darwin's Influence on Modern Thought," *Scientific American*, July 2000: 79-83.

Mitchell, M. (2009) *Complexity: A Guided Tour* (New York: Oxford University Press).

Morgan, G. (1997) *Images of Organization* (Thousand Oaks, CA: Sage, 2nd edn).

Morin, E. (2008) *On Complexity* (Cresskill, NJ: Hampton Press).

Naik, G. (2010) "Gene-Altered Fish Close to Approval," *Wall Street Journal*, September 21, 2010: A1ff.

Nicholson, N. (1997) "Evolutionary Psychology and Organizational Behavior," in C.L. Cooper and S.E. Jackson (eds.), *Creating Tomorrow's Organizations* (New York: John Wiley & Sons).

Nicholson, N. (1998) "How Hardwired is Human Behavior?" *Harvard Business Review*, July–August 1998: 135-42.

Nicholson, N. (2000) *Executive Instinct: Managing the Human Animal in the Information Age* (New York: Crown Publishers).

Nicholson, N., and R. White (2006) "Darwinism: A New Paradigm for Organizational Behavior?" *Journal of Organizational Behavior* 27: 111-19.

Nitecki, M.H., and D.V. Nitecki (eds.) (1987) *The Evolution of Human Hunting* (New York: Plenum Press).

Nowak, M.A., with R. Highfield (2011) *SuperCooperators: Altruism, Evolution, and Why We Need Each Other* (New York: Free Press).

Oakley, K.P. (1961) *Man, the Tool-Maker* (Chicago: University of Chicago Press).

Ofek, H. (2001) *Second Nature: Economic Origins of Human Evolution* (Cambridge, UK: Cambridge University Press).

Oxford Dictionary of Biology (2000) *Dictionary of Biology* (New York: Oxford University Press, 4th edn).

Parker, B. (1993) *The Vindication of the Big Bang* (New York: Plenum Press).

Pennisi, E. (2003) "Fast Friends, Sworn Enemies," *Science* 302 (October 31, 2003): 774-75.

Pennisi, E. (2004) "The First Language?" *Science* 303 (February 27, 2004): 1,319-20.

Pfeffer, J. (1992) *Managing with Power: Politics and Influence in Organizations* (Boston, MA: Harvard Business School Press).

Pierce, B.D., and R. White (1999) "The Evolution of Social Structure: Why Biology Matters," *Academy of Management Review* 24.4: 843-53.

Pietak, A.M. (2011) *Life as Energy: Opening the Mind to a New Science of Life* (Edinburgh: Floris Books).

Pinker, S. (1994) *The Language Instinct: The New Science of Language and Mind* (London: Penguin Books).

Pinker, S. (2002) *The Blank Slate: The Modern Denial of Human Nature* (London: Viking Penguin Books).

Plutchik, R. (2001) "The Nature of Emotions," *American Scientist* 89 (July–August 2001): 344-50.

Polanyi, K. (1944) *The Great Transformation: The Political and Economic Origins of Our Time* (Boston, MA: Beacon Press).

Polanyi, K., and H.W. Pearson (ed.) (1977) *The Livelihood of Man* (New York: Academic Press).

Popa, R. (2004) *Between Necessity and Probability: Searching for the Definition and Origin of Life* (Berlin: Springer).

Purves, D., G.J. Augustine, D. Fitzpatrick, L.C. Katz, A.-S. LaManta, J.O. McNamara and S.M. Williams (2001) *Neuroscience* (Sunderland, MA: Sinauer Associates, 2nd edn).

Raice, S., A. Das and J. Letzing (2012) "Facebook Prices IPO at Record Value," *Wall Street Journal*, May 18, 2012.

Raffaelli, D.G., and L.J.F. Christopher (eds.) (2010) *Ecosystem Ecology: A New Synthesis* (New York: Cambridge University Press).

Rees, M. (2003) *Our Final Hour* (New York: Basic Books).

Reynolds, P.C. (1993) "The Complementation Theory of Language and Tool Use," in K.R. Gibson and T. Ingold (eds.), *Tools, Language and Cognition in Human Evolution* (Cambridge, UK: Cambridge University Press): 407-28.

Richerson, P.J., and R. Boyd (2005) *Not by Genes Alone* (Chicago: University of Chicago Press).

Ridley, M. (1999) *Genome: The Autobiography of a Species in 23 Chapters* (New York: HarperCollins).

Ridley, M. (2003) *Nature Via Nurture: Genes, Experience, and What Makes Us Human* (New York: HarperCollins).

Ridley, M. (2010) *The Rational Optimist: How Prosperity Evolves* (New York: HarperCollins).

Rightmire, G.P. (1990) *The Evolution of* Homo Erectus: *Comparative Anatomical Studies of an Extinct Human Species* (Cambridge, UK: Cambridge University Press).

Roenneberg, T. (2012) *Internal Time: Chronotypes, Social Jet Lag, and Why You Are So Tired* (Cambridge, MA: Harvard University Press).

Ruse, M. (2009) *The Evolution Wars: A Guide to the Debates* (Millerton, NY: Greyhouse Publishing, 2nd edn).

Ruth, M. (1993) *Integrating Economics, Ecology and Thermodynamics* (Dordrecht, Netherlands: Kluwer Academic Publishers).

Sapp, J. (ed.) (2005) *Microbial Phylogeny and Evolution: Concepts and Controversies* (New York: Oxford University Press).

Sapp, J. (2009) *The New Foundations of Evolution: On the Tree of Life* (New York: Oxford University Press).

Sargut, G., and R.G. McGrath (2011) "Learning to Live with Complexity," *Harvard Business Review* 89 (September–October 2011): 68-76.

Sawyer, G.J., and V. Deak (2007) *The Last Human: A Guide to Twenty-two Species of Extinct Humans* (New Haven, CT: Yale University Press).

Schneider, E.D., and D. Sagan (2005) *Into the Cool: Energy Flows, Thermodynamics, and Life* (Chicago: University of Chicago Press).

Schrenk, F., and S. Muller with C. Hemm (2005) *The Neanderthals* (London: Routledge).

Seabright, P. (2004) *The Company of Strangers: A Natural History of Economic Life* (Princeton, NJ: Princeton University Press).

Sharma, V., and A. Annila (2007) "Natural Process—Natural Selection," *Biophysical Chemistry* 127: 123-28.

Shultz, S., C. Opie and Q.D. Atkinson (2011) "Stepwise Evolution of Stable Sociality in Primates," *Nature* 479: 219-22.

Silverman, R.E. (2012) "Who's the Boss? There Isn't One," *Wall Street Journal*, June 20, 2012: B1, B8.

Sloboda, J.A. (1985/1999) *The Musical Mind: The Cognitive Psychology of Music* (New York: Oxford University Press).

Smil, V. (2008) *Energy in Nature and Society: General Energetics of Complex Systems* (Cambridge, MA: MIT Press).

Sole, R., and B. Goodwin (2000) *Signs of Life: How Complexity Pervades Biology* (New York: Basic Books).

Stacey, R.D. (2010) *Complexity and Organizational Reality* (New York: Routledge, 2nd edn).

Stein, R. (2010) " 'Superbug' Problem Small but has Potential to Become Larger," *The Washington Post*, reprinted in *Pittsburgh Post-Gazette*, October 13, 2010: A-3.

Sterner, R.W., and J.J. Elser (2002) *Ecological Stoichiometry: The Biology of Elements from Molecules to the Biosphere* (Princeton, NJ: Princeton University Press).

Stewart, I. (1995) *Nature's Numbers: The Unreal Reality of Mathematics* (New York: Basic Books).

Stringer, C., and P. Andrews (2005) *The Complete World of Human Evolution* (London: Thames & Hudson).

Sykes, B. (2001) *The Seven Daughters of Eve: The Science that Reveals Our Genetic Ancestry* (New York: W.W. Norton).

Tattersall, I. (2000) "Once We Were Not Alone," *Scientific American* 282.1 (January 2000): 56-62.

Tattersall, I. (2007) "We Were Not Alone," in G.J. Sawyer and V. Deak (eds.), *The Last Human: A Guide to Twenty-two Species of Extinct Humans* (New Haven, CT: Yale University Press): 18-23.

Thorne, A.G., and M.H. Wolpoff (1992) "The Multiregional Evolution of Humans," *Scientific American*, April 1992: 76-83.

Tomasello, M. (2006) "Uniquely Human Cognition is a Product of Human Culture," in S.C. Levinson and P. Jaisson (eds.), *Evolution and Culture* (Cambridge, MA: MIT Press): 203-17.

Torregrosa, L.L. (2012) "On Wall St, Gender Bias Runs Deep," *New York Times*, July 24, 2012.

Tracy, R. (2012) "Here Comes the Sunstorm," *Wall Street Journal,* May 15, 2012: A3.

Trivers, R.L. (1971) "The Evolution of Reciprocal Altruism," *Quarterly Review of Biology* 46: 35-57.

Vascellaro, J.E., and E. Steel (2011) "Culture Clashes Tear at AOL," *Wall Street Journal*, September 10–11, 2011: B1, B4.

Vermeij, G.J. (2004) *Nature: An Economic History* (Princeton, NJ: Princeton University Press).

Vermeij, G.J., and E.G. Leigh, Jr. (2011) "Natural and Human Economies Compared," *Ecosphere [ESA Journals]* 2.4 (April 2011): Art. 39.

Waddock, S., and M. McIntosh (2011) *SEE Change: Making the Transition to a Sustainable Enterprise Economy* (Sheffield, UK: Greenleaf Publishing).

Wall Street Journal (2011/2012) September 10-11; November 5/6, 8, 22; December 31; January 1, 20, 30, 2012.

Wasieleski, D.M. (2008) "Reciprocal Altruism," in R.W. Kolb (ed.), *Encyclopedia of Business Ethics and Society* (Vol. 4; Thousand Oaks, CA: Sage): 1,777-79.

Weingart, P., S.D. Mitchell, P.J. Richerson and S. Maasen (1997) *Human by Nature: Between Biology and the Social Sciences* (Mahwah, NJ: Lawrence Erlbaum Associates).

White, R., and B. Decker Pierce (1999) "The Evolution of Social Structure: Why Biology Matters," *Academy of Management Review* 24.4: 843-53.

White, T. (2001) "Once Were Cannibals," *Scientific American*, August 2001: 58-65.

Wilford, J.N. (2000) "New Data Suggests Some Cannibalism by Ancient Indians," *New York Times*, September 7, 2000: A1, A20.

Williams, R.J.P., and J.J.R. Frausto da Silva (2006) *The Chemistry of Evolution: The Development of Our Ecosystem* (Amsterdam: Elsevier).

Wilson, A.C., and R.L. Cann (1992) "The Recent African Genesis of Humans," *Scientific American*, April 1992: 68-73.

Wilson, E.O. (1992) *The Diversity of Life* (London: Allen Lane).

Winslow, R., and J.D. Rockoff (2012) "Gene Map of Body's Microbes Is New Health Tool," *Wall Street Journal*, June 14, 2012: A-1, 2.

Wrangham, R. (2009) *Catching Fire: How Cooking Made Us Human* (New York: Basic Books).

Wrangham, R., and D. Peterson (1996) *Demonic Males: Apes and the Origins of Human Violence* (Boston, MA: Houghton Mifflin).

Yang, J.L. (2010) "With DNA of Chocolate Nearly Decoded, Could Sweeter Treats Be Ahead?" *Washington Post*, reprinted in *Pittsburgh Post-Gazette*, September 19, 2010: A-2.

Zimmer, C. (2012) "Tending the Body's Microbial Garden," *New York Times*, June 19, 2012.

Apologies and confessions

In writing this book, I have been aware of its limitations in providing a complete account of corporate management. Not being a business manager—not having actually faced the challenges of such a position—is the biggest shortcoming, of course. Academic scholars who draw on even the most current scientific research, as I have attempted to do, may not capture the essence of managerial activity or may misinterpret or overlook more compelling evidence. Richard Feynman, one of our most accomplished scientists, once put the matter this way: "Scientists are used to dealing with doubt and uncertainty. I believe that to solve any problem that has never been solved before, you have to leave the door to the unknown ajar. *You have to permit the possibility that you do not have it exactly right.*" Feynman's words capture the sense I want to convey about the contents of this book.

Another inspirational quotation that I have long kept pinned close to my computer—and have used as a guide—is a comment made by Pyotr Tchaikovsky, in speaking of his musical compositions: "Talking with you yesterday about the process of composition, I did not express myself clearly about that phase of work which follows the working out of the sketch. This phase is of prime importance. All that has been written in the heat of the moment must now be critically examined, corrected, augmented and especially contracted, as the form demands. Sometimes one must do oneself violence, be ruthless and brutal, i.e., completely chop up passages conceived with love and inspiration." All authors—and I hope this one—have faced this challenge with varying degrees of success.

Some readers will notice the absence of quantum theory from my discussion of corporate management. Though unquestionably related to the biological and human worlds—and therefore offering a further realm of behavioral explanation—the mysteries of quantum mechanics continue to be pursued while remaining elusive, even to the best of minds. Two recent books explore the current status of quantum theory: *Quantum Aspects of Life* by Derek Abbott, Paul C.W. Davies, and Arun K. Pati and *The Quantum Universe* by Brian Cox and Jeff Forshaw. A reviewer of the latter book had this to say: "As with many scientific discoveries, quantum physics gives us reason to doubt that we occupy a privileged place in the universe while at the same time furnishing a tribute to the power of human imagination" (Alex Stone, *Wall Street Journal*, February 25–26, 2012: C8). Quantum theory's significance for human and business behavior awaits clarification by others.

String theory is yet another scientific frontier, holding the prospect of formulating "a theory of everything" which logically should explain all aspects of human behavior, including the business realm. I hope I might be excused for not probing the possibilities of that still-developing area of scientific inquiry.

Perhaps the wisest guideline for authors and their readers is another provided by Tchaikovsky: "One must not wait about. Inspiration is a guest who does not like visiting the lazy. She comes to those who invite her." Bear that in mind as you contemplate this book's central theme. I hope you will be inspired to travel new pathways.

Acknowledgments

Books are always joint undertakings, even when only a single author is identified, so I wish to acknowledge the generous assistance I have received from others.

Through the marvels of the Internet, I discovered the imaginative, pioneering research and writing of Dr. Arto Annila, Professor of Physics and Principal Investigator of the Institute of Biotechnology at the University of Helsinki, Finland, whose intellectual reach includes degrees in technology-physics, engineering, and biochemistry. Although he was only marginally aware of my intellectual indebtedness to him as I composed this book, Arto Annila's seminal work in the field of energy evolution underlies the central theme of this book's concepts of **Natural Corporate Management** and an **Evolutionary Cascade**. While I am immensely grateful for his unparalleled, creative insights, I absolve him and his co-authors of responsibility for any of my errors or misinterpretations of their work.

The pre-publication manuscript was critiqued and vastly improved by five highly qualified academic scholars: Dr. Mildred S. Myers, Teaching Professor of Management Communication Emerita in The Tepper School of Business at Carnegie Mellon University; Dr. David M. Wasieleski, Associate Professor of Management and Chair of the Management Department at Duquesne University and Affiliated Research Professor at ICN Business School, Nancy, France; Dr. Ronald Paul Hill, who holds the Richard J. and Barbara Naclerio Chair in Business and is Professor of Marketing and Business Law at Villanova University; Dr. Deby Cassill, Associate Professor, Department of Biological Sciences at the University of South

Florida-St. Petersburg, Florida; and Dr. Nancy Kurland of Franklin & Marshall College's Department of Business, Organizations, and Society.

Practitioner viewpoints were generously offered by Larry Weidman, currently President and CEO of Bridge Semiconductor and former CEO of other computer-science firms; Paul Herr, business consultant, inventor of science-based workplace incentive systems, and author of *Primal Management: Unraveling the Secrets of Human Nature to Drive High Performance*; and Benno Bernt, Chairman, Griffin Group Partners, LP, former President and CEO of Rayovac Corporation, a former chief financial officer, and the former Director of Technology Transfer at Carnegie Mellon University.

Every academic scholar needs the help and guidance of knowledgeable professional librarians who are guardians of the world's collective knowledge as preserved in journals, books, and electronic sources. Two such professionals staff the University of Pittsburgh's Langley Library, a treasure trove of biological resources: Laurel Povazan-Scholnick and Laura Dougherty. I thank both of them for their always efficient, cheerful, and enormously helpful advice, resourcefulness, and ongoing building of a splendid library collection.

The chapter icons are the work of Deborah Cavrak, a professional designer who also has designed and now manages my website, www.williamcfrederick.com, thereby keeping me in touch with scholars around the globe. For her expertise, I am most grateful.

In writing this multidisciplinary book by exploring evolution's many surprising byways, I experienced a quite marvelous kind of support—informal, friend-based, imaginative, and inspirational—coming from two unique sources.

Professor Franco Sciannameo is Associate Dean for Interdisciplinary Initiatives, College of Fine Arts, Carnegie Mellon University, Artistic Director of ETC-ITALIA Entertainment Technology Center also at Carnegie Mellon University, an author, film musicologist, and an experienced symphonic violinist. Professor Sciannameo invited me to share my evolving multidisciplinary insights with students in one of his classes, all of whom were studying the various intersections where science and arts, humanities and arts, and computer science and arts crisscross in exciting, innovative ways. By hearing firsthand their diverse imaginative plans for the future bubbling up from those young, fertile, multidisciplinary minds—well, without question, I gained more from that classroom experience than I conveyed to the students, encouraging me to believe my book might be on the right track, after all. My thanks to this imaginative multi-artistic scholar, Franco Sciannameo.

I want to mention also a seasoned scholar and management expert for whom my admiration has known no bounds, the late Paul Lawrence, Professor of Management at the Harvard Business School for many years. His several books dispensed much knowledge and wisdom about corporate management and, in recent years, about the links between managerial actions and neuroscience research. Paul Lawrence's passing leaves a significant gap in the roster of pioneering scholars of the practitioner arts. I deeply regret that he did not live to see my great indebtedness to his ever-creative evolutionary insights.

About the author

Bill Frederick's scholarly fields of study are corporate social responsibility, business ethics, managers' values, and evolutionary interpretations of business behavior. Books reflecting these interests include *Values, Nature, and Culture in the American Corporation* and *Corporation, Be Good! The Story of Corporate Social Responsibility*, plus several editions of the textbook *Business and Society*. As a consultant to foundations and governments, he has made ethnological studies of management education in Spain, Italy, Egypt, Yugoslavia, Hungary, and Australia, and has advised business schools in Ecuador and Nigeria. He holds a PhD in economics and anthropology from the University of Texas-Austin, and is Professor Emeritus, Katz Graduate School of Business, University of Pittsburgh. More information is available at www.williamcfrederick.com.

Index of names

Index of subjects